MICHELIN GUIDE

HONG KONG MACAU 2010

RESTAURANTS & HOTELS

米芝蓮指南
香港 / 澳門 2010
餐廳及酒店

DEAR READER

We are thrilled to present our second edition of the MICHELIN Guide Hong Kong Macau 2010.

Our teams have made every effort to update the selection in order to fully reflect the richness and diversity of the Hong Kong and Macau restaurant and hotel scene.

As part of our meticulous and highly confidential evaluation process, Michelin inspectors conducted anonymous visits to Hong Kong and Macau restaurants and hotels.
The Michelin inspectors are the eyes and ears of our customers and thus their anonymity is key to ensuring they receive the same treatment as any other guest.

All the restaurants within this guide have been chosen first and foremost for the quality of their cooking. You'll find comprehensive information on over 200 dining establishments within these pages and they range from noodle shops to internationally renowned restaurants. The diverse and varied selection also bears testament to the rich and buoyant dining scene in Hong Kong and Macau, with both cities now enjoying a worldwide reputation for the quality and range of their restaurants.

You'll see that Michelin Stars are not our only awards – look out also for the Bib Gourmands. These are restaurants where the cooking is still carefully prepared but in a simpler style and, priced at under $300, they represent excellent value for money.

As well as the restaurants, our team of independent inspectors has also chosen over 50 hotels.
These carefully selected hotels represent the best that Hong Kong and Macau have to offer. All have been chosen for their individuality and personality.

On behalf of all Michelin employees, we wish you the very best in your Hong Kong and Macau hotel and dining experiences.

Bon appétit!

親愛的讀者

很高興向您宣佈:《米芝蓮指南 香港 澳門 2010》第二版隆重登場!

我們的隊伍傾盡全力,搜羅香港及澳門一系列豐富而多元化的餐廳和酒店的最新資訊。

米芝蓮評審員到訪香港及澳門的餐廳和酒店時不會透露身份,因此評選過程一絲不苟而且高度保密。他們充當顧客的耳目,保持神秘身份能確保與任何其他顧客都享受相同遇待。

本指南介紹的餐廳都以高質素的廚藝掛帥,從小小的麵家到享譽全球的餐廳,我們為您帶來超過200間食肆最全面的資料。港澳兩地的餐廳一向以優質和種類繁多而聞名,本指南內各式各樣的餐廳均經過精挑細選,能充份表現兩個城市多姿多彩的美食佳餚。

您會發現除了獲得米芝蓮星級評分的餐廳之外,我們也有評審員的推介榜。這些餐廳的食物煮法雖然簡單,但一點也不馬虎,而且價錢在$300以下,絕對是價廉物美的起值之選。

另外,我們獨立的評審員也揀選了超過50間酒店。這些酒店全都經過悉心挑選,並以其獨特的個性而取勝,是香港和澳門兩地最出色的酒店。

我們謹代表米芝蓮全體員工,祝您在香港和澳門擁有精彩、愉快的住宿和美食體驗!

祝您的飲食旅程愉快!

"This volume was created at the turn of the century and will last at least as long".

COMMITMENTS

This foreword to the very first edition of the MICHELIN Guide, written in 1900, has become famous over the years and the Guide has lived up to the prediction. It is read across the world and the key to its popularity is the consistency of its commitment to its readers, which is based on the following promises.

Anonymous inspections:
Our inspectors make regular and anonymous visits to restaurants and hotels to gauge the quality of products and services offered to an ordinary customer. They settle their own bill and may then introduce themselves and ask for more information about the establishment. Our readers' comments are also a valuable source of information, which we can then follow up with another visit of our own.

Independence:
Our choice of establishments is a completely independent one, made for the benefit of our readers alone. The decisions to be taken are discussed around the table by the inspectors and the

editor. Inclusion in the Guide is completely free of charge.

Selection and choice:

The Guide offers a selection of the best restaurants and hotels. This is only possible because all the inspectors rigorously apply the same methods.

Annual updates:

All the practical information, the classifications and awards are revised and updated every single year to give the most reliable information possible.

Consistency:

The criteria for the classifications are the same in every country covered by the Michelin Guide.

...And our aim:

to do everything possible to make travel, holidays and eating out a pleasure, as part of Michelin's ongoing commitment to improving travel and mobility.

承諾

「這冊書於世紀交替時創辦，亦將繼續傳承下去。」

這是1900年米芝蓮首冊指南的前言，多年來享負盛名，並如預期般一直傳承下去。 指南在世界各地均大受歡迎，關鍵在其秉承一貫宗旨，履行對讀者的承諾。

匿名評審：

我們的評審員以匿名方式定期到訪餐廳和酒店，以一般顧客的身份對其產品和服務質素作出評估。 評審員自行結賬後，有時可能會介紹自己，並詢問更多關於餐廳的資料。 讀者的評語和推薦也是寶貴的資訊來源，我們隨後會根據讀者的推薦親身到訪。

獨立性：

餐廳的挑選完全是基於我們獨立的決定， 純以讀者的利益為依歸。 經評審員和編輯一同討論後才作出決定， 被指南收錄的餐廳完全不會被收取任何費用。

選擇：

全賴所有評審員都使用相同的嚴謹方法， 指南才能提供一系列的最佳餐廳和酒店。

每年更新：

所有實用資訊、 分類及評級每年都會修訂和更新， 務求為讀者提供最可靠的資料。

一致性：

米芝蓮指南涉及的每個國家都用相同的分類準則。

…至於我們的目標：

盡全力令旅遊、放假及外出用膳成為一大樂事，實踐米芝蓮一貫優化旅遊和外出的承諾。

CONTENTS

目錄

THE MICHELIN GUIDE OVER THE YEARS

Today the Michelin Guide with its famous red cover is known around the world. But who really knows the story behind this "travellers' bible" that has served people in so many countries for such a long time? After winning over Europe and the United States, Bibendum – "The Michelin Man" – is now in Asia, and will continue the fantastic adventure that started in France, a long time ago...

The first steps

Everything began one fine day in 1900, when André and Édouard Michelin published a guide to be offered free of charge to motorists. It included information to help these pioneers (barely 3,500 automobiles were on the road) to travel around France: location of garages, town plans, sights to see, lodgings and restaurants, and so forth. The guide was an instant success and became the indispensable companion to all drivers and travellers.

On the strength of this success and driven on by the development of the motor car, the *Manufacture française* extended the scope of "the little book with the red cover" to other European countries, beginning in 1904. A few years later (1908) the *Guide France* was published in English.

A star is born

As of 1920, the guide was no longer free, but marketed for sale. Little by little, the practical information gave way to a wider selection of hotels and restaurants.

The mysterious, daunting "Michelin inspector" was, however, not in the picture at first. It was touring clubs and readers who contributed to the selection of establishments.

In 1926 the *Étoile de Bonne Table* – the first Michelin star – was awarded to places where "one dines well" and was later followed by two and three-star establishments (1931 for the provinces and 1933 for Paris). The focus was now on gastronomy and the quest for good restaurants became its real driving force.

GUIDE MICHELIN FRANCE 1933 *les bonnes tables...*

A European journey

The guide flourished until the outbreak of war in 1939, when all guide activity was suspended. But it was revived in 1945 and, from 1950, a new generation of guides appeared – from Spain in 1952 to Switzerland in 1994. In 1982 Michelin's European credentials were confirmed with the publication of the *Main Cities of Europe* guide.

100 years young...

2000 was a winning year for Michelin: the Guide celebrated its 100th anniversary and Bibendum was voted best corporate logo of the century!

More dynamic than ever, the "little red guide" took on new challenges and set off for the United States. The guide New York not only lived up to expectations, but also the first edition was crowned "Best Restaurant Guide in the World". Next off the presses: San Francisco in 2006, Los Angeles and Las Vegas in 2007.

The newest challenge? Discovering the best restaurants in Asia. In autumn 2007, we published Michelin Tokyo guide which had a big topic. Tokyo is well known as one of the world's great capitals of fine cuisine.

Twenty countries covered in Europe, two guides to US cities, two guides in Japan and one guide to Hong Kong and Macau: as the third millennium begins, the Michelin Guide confirms its truly international standing.

Just a gleam in the eyes of the founders more than a century ago, Bibendum is now an international star to be proud of, carrying the Michelin tradition into the 21st century.

米芝蓮指南的歷史

今時今日，米芝蓮享譽國際，它的紅色封面家傳戶曉。多年來，這本「旅遊聖經」為很多國家的人提供寶貴資訊，但又有多少人知道它背後的故事呢？

必比登「米芝蓮車胎人」(Bibendum, "The Michelin Man")，在歐洲和美國駐足後，現在終於來臨亞洲，將會延續當年在法國展開的探險旅程 …

旅程的開始

1900年晴朗的一天，André 和 Édouard Michelin 出版了一本指南，免費贈予駕車人士。當時法國只有約3,500部汽車行駛。指南涵蓋環遊法國的資訊：車房位置、城市地圖、觀光景點、住宿、餐廳等等。指南的出版取得空前成功，成為所有駕駛者和旅客的必需品。

適逢指南的空前成功和當時汽車業的迅速發展，米芝蓮公司便乘勝追擊，於1904年把這本「紅色指南」帶到其他歐洲國家。1908年，這本「法國指南」更開始以英文出版。

星的誕生

自1920年起，指南開始在市面上發售，不再是免費贈閱。除了實用資訊外，指南日漸覆蓋更多酒店及餐廳資料。

在神秘的米芝蓮評審員出現之前，餐飲推介與選擇的訊息都是來自旅遊俱樂部和讀者。

直至1926年，米芝蓮首次引入星級評分制度，得到一星 (Étoile de Bonne Table) 的餐廳為最為美味的餐廳；其後，各省份和巴黎更分別於1931年和1933年實行二星及三星評分。此後指南便集中評選美食，致力搜羅一流餐廳的資訊。

歐洲之旅

指南業務蒸蒸日上，直至1939年戰爭爆發，一切運作暫停。1945年業務回復正常，從1950年起，新一代指南陸續面世：由1952年的西班牙到1994年的瑞士指南，期間更於不同的歐洲國家出版。1982年，米芝蓮出版歐洲主要城市指南 (Main Cities of Europe guide)，確立其歐洲主導地位。

長青一百歲

2000年是米芝蓮的勝利年，不但是指南出版的百週年紀念，「米芝蓮車胎人」必比登更獲選為世紀最佳公司標誌！這本「紅色小指南」比以往更顯積極，不斷迎接新挑戰，並進軍美國市場。紐約指南不但不負眾望，更於初版被譽為「世界上最佳餐廳指南」。其後，米芝蓮在美國大展拳腳，2006年出版三藩市指南，及推出洛杉磯和拉斯維加斯2007指南，成績驕人。

米芝蓮面臨的最新挑戰是甚麼呢？就是尋找亞洲的最佳餐廳。2007年秋季，米芝蓮東京2008指南隆重面世。於世界美食之都出版飲食指南，米芝蓮東京指南成為一時佳話。

踏入二十一世紀，米芝蓮指南已涵蓋二十個歐洲國家、兩本於美國，兩本於日本，以及一本於香港澳門，其國際地位實在毋庸置疑。

一個多世紀前，始創人的一絲靈感造就了米芝蓮車胎人-必比登的誕生。今天，必比登是令人引以為榮的國際巨星，引領米芝蓮於二十一世紀與時並進。

HOW TO USE
THIS RESTAURANT GUIDE
如何使用餐廳指南

Map number / coordinates
地圖號碼 / 座標

Cuisine type
菜式種類

Name of restaurant
餐廳名稱

Stars for good food
美食星級

🏵 to 🏵🏵🏵

**Bib Gourmand
(Inspectors' favourite
for good value)
Bib Gourmand
(評審員的推介榜)**

😋

**Restaurant classification
according to comfort**
餐廳 — 以舒適程度分類

🍴	Simple shop	簡單的食店
✗	Quite comfortable	頗舒適
✗✗	Comfortable	舒適
✗✗✗	Very comfortable	十分舒適
✗✗✗✗	Top class comfort	高級舒適
✗✗✗✗✗	Luxury	豪華

Particularly pleasant if in red
紅色代表上佳

◆French contemporary/時尚法式   ◆MAP/地圖 16/D-3

L'Atelier de Joël Robuchon

🏵 🏵   ✗✗

🛋8 🚬 ⓞ🍴 ⚗

The hallmark colours of red and black are once again evident at this branch of the Robuchon Empire. The restaurant is divided into two sections: the main one, L'Atelier, offers a ringside seat at the show kitchen while Le Jardin is more discreet and comfortable. On both sides, the French contemporary cuisine focuses on top seasonal ingredients which are simply cooked to preserve their original flavours. Superb wine list

紅黑色的標記清楚顯示這是世紀大廚Robuchon集團旗下的餐廳。餐廳分成兩個主要區域：主區L'Atelier的開放式廚房提供前排座位可供觀賞，而Le Jardin則較沉穩舒適。兩區的當代法國菜，以簡約方法烹調頂級時令食材，保留原汁原味。精選出色美酒。

■ ADDRESS/地址
TEL.2166 9000
Shop 401, 4F, The Landmark, 15
Queen's Road, Central
中環皇后大道中15號置地廣場4樓401號鋪
www.robuchon.hk

■ OPENING HOURS, LAST ORDER
營業時間，最後點菜時間
Lunch/午膳 12:00-14:30 (L.O.)
Dinner/晚膳 18:30-22:30 (L.O.)

■ PRICE/價錢
Lunch/午膳 set/套餐 $390-1,850
            a la carte/點菜 $500-1,500
Dinner/晚膳 set/套餐 $560-1,850
            a la carte/點菜 $500-1,500

136

Lau Sum Kee (Fuk Wing Street)
劉森記麵家 (福榮街)

This is one noodle shop that is not afraid of the competition. In a street overflowing with noodle shops, Lau Sum Kee (and its sister shop around the corner) are packed with customers buzzing in and out. Run by the third generation of the family, the noodles are pressed by bamboo and the wontons are freshly made at the shop. Recommendations include wonton noodles, dry prawn roe mix with noodles and pork knuckles mixed with noodles.

這是間麵店可謂經得起競爭。在滿佈各家麵店的街上，劉森記麵家（及其轉角位的姐妹店）擠滿來往的食客。此麵店由家族第三代經營，在店內新鮮製造竹昇麵及雲吞。推薦菜式包括雲吞麵、蝦子麵及豬手麵。

■ ADDRESS/地址
TEL.2386 3583
82 Fuk Wing Street, Sham Shui Po, Kowloon
九龍深水埗福榮街82號

■ ANNUAL AND WEEKLY CLOSING
休息日期
Closed 3 days Lunar New Year
農曆新年休息3天

■ OPENING HOURS, LAST ORDER
營業時間，最後點菜時間
12:30-23:30 (L.O.)

■ PRICE/價錢
Lunch/午膳   a la carte/點菜 $22-40
Dinner/晚膳   a la carte/點菜 $22-40

Restaurant symbols
餐廳標誌

S	Cash only	只收現金
♿	Wheelchair access	輪椅適用
🏠	Terrace dining	陽台用餐
≼	With a view	有景觀
🔑	Valet parking	代客泊車
P	Car park	停車場
25	Private room with maximum capacity	私人房間及容納人數
	Counter	櫃檯式
ⓧ	Reservation required	需訂座
ⓧ	Not possible to make a reservation	不可訂座
🍇	Interesting wine list	供應優良的酒類

HOW TO USE
THIS HOTEL GUIDE
如何使用酒店指南

Map number / coordinates
地圖號碼 / 座標

Name of hotel
酒店名稱

Hotel classification
according to comfort
酒店 — 根據舒適程度分類

 Quite comfortable
頗舒適

 Comfortable
舒適

 Very comfortable
十分舒適

 Top class comfort
高級舒適

Luxury
豪華

Particularly pleasant if in red
紅色代表上佳

MAP/地圖 18/B-2

Conrad
港麗

With its enviable location above the Pacific Place shopping and entertainment complex, this skilfully mixes the traditional and the modern. The vast oval lobby superbly showcases Chinese vases and bronze sculptures. Bedrooms are located between the 40th and 61st floors ensuring sweeping views; the suites are particularly spacious and have elegantly marbled bathrooms. An outdoor swimming pool offers an equally dramatic panorama of the city.

268

20

RESTAURANTS/ 餐廳

Recommended/推薦			Also/其他
Golden Leaf/金葉庭	❀	XxX	Brasserie on the Eight/
Nicholini's/意寧谷		XxXX	懷歐敘
			Garden Café/咖啡園
			Lobby Lounge/樂敘廊

酒店位處集購物娛樂於一身的太古廣場之上，巧妙地混合了傳統和現代元素。龐大的橢圓形大堂展示着中式花瓶及銅像，優雅而壯麗。寢室全在40至61樓之間，坐擁遼闊美景，而套房則特別寬敞，設有雲石浴室。室外游泳池同樣讓你飽覽香港全景。

■ ADDRESS/地址
TEL.2521 3838
FAX. 2521 3888
Pacific Place, 88 Queensway,
Admiralty
金鐘金鐘道88號太古廣場
www.conradhotels.com

■ ROOMS AND SUITES/客房及套房
Rooms/客房 =467
Suites/套房 =46

■ PRICE/價錢
♦	$4,400-5,800
♦♦	$4,400-5,800
Suites/套房	$7,000-38,000
⚏	$280

Restaurant information
餐廳資料

Hotel symbols
酒店標誌

♿	Wheelchair access	輪椅適用
≼	With a view	有景觀
🅿️	Valet parking	代客泊車
P	Car park	室外停車場
🚗	Garage	室內停車場
⚬	No smoking bedrooms	非吸煙臥室
☺	Conference rooms	會議室
⚑⚑	Outdoor/Indoor Swimming pool	室外 / 室內游泳池
Spa	Spa	水療
⚐	Exercise room	健身室
⬭⬭⬭	Casino	娛樂場

HONG KONG
香港

RESTAURANTS
餐廳

STARRED RESTAURANTS

Within this selection, we have highlighted a number of restaurants for their particularly good cooking. When awarding one, two or three Michelin Stars there are a number of factors we consider: the quality and compatibility of the ingredients, the technical skill and flair that goes into their preparation, the clarity and combination of flavours, the value for money and above all, the taste. Equally important is the ability to produce excellent cooking not once but time and time again. Our inspectors make as many visits as necessary, so that you can be sure of the quality and consistency.

A two or three star restaurant has to offer something very special that separates it from the rest. Three stars – our highest award – are given to the very best.

Cuisines in any style of restaurant and of any nationality are eligible for a star. The decoration, service and comfort levels have no bearing on the award.

星級餐廳

在這系列的選擇裡，我們特意指出菜式上佳的餐廳。給予一、二或三粒米芝蓮星時，我們考慮到以下因素：材料的質素和相容性、烹調技巧和特色、氣味濃度和組合、價錢是否相宜，以及味道。同樣重要的是能夠持續提供美食。我們的評審員會因應需要而多次到訪，所以讀者可肯定食物品質和一致性。二或三星餐廳必有獨特之處，比其他餐廳更出眾。

最高評級 - 三星 - 只會給予最好的餐廳。

不論餐廳的風格如何，供應哪個國家的菜式，都可獲星級。餐廳陳設、服務及舒適程度亦不會影響評級。

Exceptional cuisine, worth a special journey.
出類拔萃的菜餚，值得專程到訪。

One always eats here extremely well, sometimes superbly. Distinctive dishes are precisely executed, using superlative ingredients.

食客可在這裡享用美味的菜餚，有時令人更讚不絕口。獨特的菜式以最高級的材料精密地烹調。

Caprice	XXXX	66	MAP/地圖 16/C-1
Lung King Heen 龍景軒	XXX	157	MAP/地圖 16/C-1

Excellent cuisine, worth a detour.
傑出美食，值得繞道前往。

Skilfully and carefully crafted dishes of outstanding quality.

有技巧地精心烹調菜餚，品質優秀。

Amber	XXX	59	MAP/地圖 16/C-3
Fook Lam Moon (Wan Chai) 福臨門 (灣仔)	XXX	98	MAP/地圖 19/B-3
L'Atelier de Joël Robuchon	XX	136	MAP/地圖 16/D-3
Ming Court 明閣	XXX	163	MAP/地圖 9/B-2
Petrus 珀翠	XXXX	182	MAP/地圖 18/A-2
Shang Palace 香宮	XXX	198	MAP/地圖 12/D-2
T'ang Court 唐閣	XXXX	218	MAP/地圖 11/B-2
Tim's Kitchen 桃花源小廚	X	232	MAP/地圖 15/B-2

A very good restaurant in its category.
同類別中出眾的餐廳。

A place offering cuisine prepared to a consistently high standard.

持續高水準菜式的地方。

Bo Innovation	XX	64	MAP/地圖 19/B-3

BIB GOURMAND

This symbol indicates our inspector's favourites for good value. Restaurants offering good quality cooking for $ 300 or less (price of a 3 course meal excluding drinks).

這標誌表示評審員認為價錢合理而美味的餐廳。300 元或以下便可享用優質美食（三道菜式的價錢，不包括飲料）。

Café Siam	✗	65	MAP/地圖 17/A-1
Che's 車氏粵菜軒	✗	71	MAP/地圖 19/B-2
Cheung Kee 祥記飯店	✗	73	MAP/地圖 19/B-2
Chilli Fagara 麻辣燙	✗	76	MAP/地圖 15/B-3
Crystal Jade La Mian Xiao Long Bao (Kowloon Bay) 翡翠拉麵小籠包（九龍灣）	✗	80	MAP/地圖 13/B-3
Crystal Jade La Mian Xiao Long Bao (TST) 翡翠拉麵小籠包（尖沙咀）	🍜	81	MAP/地圖 11/A-2
Crystal Jade La Mian Xiao Long Bao (Wan Chai) 翡翠拉麵小籠包（灣仔）	✗	82	MAP/地圖 20/C-3
Da Ping Huo 大平伙	✗	85	MAP/地圖 15/B-2
Fung Lum 楓林小館	✗✗	100	MAP/地圖 5/A-2
Golden Valley 駿景軒	✗✗	107	MAP/地圖 26/A-3
Hing Kee 避風塘興記	✗	116	MAP/地圖 11/B-1
Ho Hung Kee 何洪記	🍜	117	MAP/地圖 21/B-3
Jade Garden (Lockhart Road) 翠園（駱克道）	✗	130	MAP/地圖 21/B-2
Kin's Kitchen 留家廚房	✗	133	MAP/地圖 23/A-3
Lei Garden (Kowloon Bay) 利苑酒家（九龍灣）	✗✗	141	MAP/地圖 13/B-3
Lei Garden (Kwun Tong) 利苑酒家（觀塘）	✗✗	142	MAP/地圖 14/C-1
Le Soleil	✗✗	148	MAP/地圖 12/D-2

RESTAURANTS BY AREA
餐廳 — 以地區分類

Hong Kong Island/香港島

Admiralty/金鍾

Domani		XX	89	MAP/地圖 18/A-2
Golden Leaf 金葉庭	✿	XxX	106	MAP/地圖 18/B-2
Lippo Chiuchow 力寶軒		XX	151	MAP/地圖 18/A-2
Lobster Bar and Grill 龍蝦吧		XX	154	MAP/地圖 18/A-2
Man Ho 萬豪殿		XX	161	MAP/地圖 18/B-2
Nicholini's 意寧谷		XxX	168	MAP/地圖 18/B-2
Peking Garden (Admiralty) 北京樓 (金鍾)		XX	178	MAP/地圖 18/B-2
Petrus 珀翠	✿✿	XxXX	182	MAP/地圖 18/A-2
Roka		XX	188	MAP/地圖 18/B-2
Summer Palace 夏宮	✿	XxX	207	MAP/地圖 18/A-2
Thai Basil		X	223	MAP/地圖 18/B-2
Yè Shanghai (Admiralty) 夜上海 (金鍾)		XxX	253	MAP/地圖 18/B-2
Zen 采蝶軒		XxX	261	MAP/地圖 18/B-2

Causeway Bay/銅鑼灣

At Corner		X	62	MAP/地圖 21/B-2
Chee Kei 池記		🍜	70	MAP/地圖 21/B-3
D17		XX	92	MAP/地圖 21/B-2
Farm House 農圃	✿	XX	96	MAP/地圖 22/C-3
Forum 富臨	✿	XX	99	MAP/地圖 21/B-2
Ho Hung Kee 何洪記	⊕	🍜	117	MAP/地圖 21/B-3
Hunan Garden (Causeway Bay) 洞庭樓 (銅鑼灣)		XxX	121	MAP/地圖 21/B-3
Jade Garden (Hysan Avenue) 翠園 (希慎道)		XX	129	MAP/地圖 22/C-3

Name			Page	Map
Jade Garden (Lockhart Road) 翠園 (駱克道)	⊕	✗	130	MAP/地圖 21/B-2
Kung Tak Lam (Causeway Bay) 功德林 (銅鑼灣)		✗✗	134	MAP/地圖 21/B-2
Lawry's The Prime Rib		✗✗✗	138	MAP/地圖 22/C-3
Modern China (Causeway Bay) 金滿庭 (銅鑼灣)		✗	165	MAP/地圖 21/B-3
Regal Palace 富豪金殿	✿	✗✗✗	186	MAP/地圖 22/D-3
Se Wong Yee 蛇王二	⊕	🥢	193	MAP/地圖 21/B-2
Shanghai Lu Yang Cun 上海綠楊邨		✗✗	195	MAP/地圖 21/B-2
Snow Garden (Causeway Bay) 雪園 (銅鑼灣)		✗✗	202	MAP/地圖 22/C-3
Sushi Shota 壽司翔太		✗	210	MAP/地圖 21/B-2
Tai Ping Koon (Causeway Bay) 太平館 (銅鑼灣)	⊕	✗	211	MAP/地圖 21/B-3
Tai Woo (Causeway Bay) 太湖海鮮城 (銅鑼灣)	⊕	✗✗	213	MAP/地圖 21/B-2
The Drawing Room	✿	✗✗	224	MAP/地圖 22/C-3
Wasabisabi 山葵		✗	242	MAP/地圖 21/B-3
Wu Kong Shanghai (Causeway Bay) 滬江 (銅鑼灣)	⊕	✗✗	245	MAP/地圖 21/B-3
Xinjishi Shanghai 新吉士		✗	247	MAP/地圖 22/C-3

Central/中環

Name			Page	Map
Agnès b. Le Pain Grillé (Central)		✗✗	58	MAP/地圖 16/D-2
Amber	✿✿	✗✗✗✗	59	MAP/地圖 16/C-3
Café Siam	⊕	✗	65	MAP/地圖 17/A-1
Caprice	✿✿✿	✗✗✗✗✗	66	MAP/地圖 16/C-1
Celebrity Cuisine 名人坊	✿	✗✗	67	MAP/地圖 15/B-2
Chez Patrick (Soho)		✗✗	74	MAP/地圖 15/B-2
Chilli Fagara 麻辣燙	⊕	✗	76	MAP/地圖 15/B-3
Cuisine Cuisine 國金軒		✗✗✗	84	MAP/地圖 16/C-2
Da Ping Huo 大平伙	⊕	✗	85	MAP/地圖 15/B-2
DiVino		✗	88	MAP/地圖 17/A-2
Dot Cod		✗✗	91	MAP/地圖 16/D-3
Gaia		✗✗✗	103	MAP/地圖 15/B-2

Happy Valley/跑馬地

North Point/北角

Sheung Wan/上環

Tai Koo Shing/太古城

Tin Hau/天后

Kin's Kitchen 留家廚房	✿	✗	133	MAP/地圖 23/A-3

Wan Chai/灣仔

Bo Innovation	✿	✗✗	64	MAP/地圖 19/B-3
Cépage	✿	✗✗✗	69	MAP/地圖 19/A-3
Che's 車氏粵菜軒	✿	✗	71	MAP/地圖 19/B-2
Cheung Kee 祥記飯店	✿	✗	73	MAP/地圖 19/B-2
Chez Patrick (Wan Chai)		✗✗	75	MAP/地圖 19/A-3
Cinecittà		✗✗✗	79	MAP/地圖 19/A-3
Crystal Jade La Mian Xiao Long Bao (Wan Chai) 翡翠拉麵小籠包 (灣仔)	✿	✗	82	MAP/地圖 20/C-3
Dynasty (Wan Chai) 滿福樓 (灣仔)	✿	✗✗✗	94	MAP/地圖 19/B-1
Eighteen Brook 十八溪		✗✗	95	MAP/地圖 19/B-2
Fook Lam Moon (Wan Chai) 福臨門 (灣仔) ✿✿		✗✗✗	98	MAP/地圖 19/B-3
Fu Sing 富聲		✗✗	101	MAP/地圖 20/D-2
Golden Bauhinia 金紫荊		✗✗	105	MAP/地圖 19/B-1
Grissini		✗✗✗	109	MAP/地圖 19/B-1
Hang Zhou 杭州酒家	✿	✗✗	112	MAP/地圖 20/C-2,3
Lei Garden (Wan Chai) 利苑酒家 (灣仔)	✿	✗✗	147	MAP/地圖 20/D-2
Liu Yuan Pavilion 留園雅敍	✿	✗✗	152	MAP/地圖 19/B-2
Olala (St. Francis Street) 一碗麵 (聖佛蘭士街)	✿	₈⫼	170	MAP/地圖 19/A-3
1/5 Nuevo	✿	✗	171	MAP/地圖 19/A-3
One Harbour Road 港灣壹號		✗✗✗✗	172	MAP/地圖 19/B-1
Ovologue 祇月		✗✗	175	MAP/地圖 19/B-3
Queen's Palace 帝后殿	✿	✗✗	185	MAP/地圖 19/B-3
Sang Kee 生記		✗✗	190	MAP/地圖 19/B-2
Tanyoto Hotpot (Wan Chai) 譚魚頭火鍋 (灣仔)		✗✗	219	MAP/地圖 19/B-3
The Pawn		✗	226	MAP/地圖 19/B-3
Uno Más	✿	✗	239	MAP/地圖 19/B-2
Wing Wah 永華雲吞麵家		₈⫼	244	MAP/地圖 19/B-2
Xi Yan Sweets 囍宴 甜·藝		₈⫼	248	MAP/地圖 19/A-3

| Yat Tung Heen (Wan Chai) 逸東軒 (灣仔) | ✿ | ХХ | 251 | MAP/地圖 20/C-2 |
| Yeung's Noodle 楊記麵家 | | 🍜 | 255 | MAP/地圖 20/C-2 |

Kowloon/九龍

Hung Hom/紅磡

Harbour Grill		ХХХ	113	MAP/地圖 10/D-3
Hoi Yat Heen 海逸軒		ХХХ	118	MAP/地圖 10/D-3
Senzuru 千鶴		Х	191	MAP/地圖 10/C-3
Tasty (Hung Hom) 正斗粥麵專家 (紅磡)	🔄	🍜	221	MAP/地圖 10/D-3

Jordan/佐敦

Lung Kee (Temple Street) 龍記 (廟街)		🍜	156	MAP/地圖 9/B-3
Tam Chai Yunnan Noodles (Jordan Road) 譚仔雲南米線 (佐敦道)		🍜	216	MAP/地圖 9/B-3
Xin Dan Ji 新斗記		Х	246	MAP/地圖 9/B-3
Yat Tung Heen (Jordan) 逸東軒 (佐敦)		ХХ	250	MAP/地圖 9/B-2

Kowloon Bay/九龍灣

Crystal Jade La Mian Xiao Long Bao (Kowloon Bay) 翡翠拉麵小籠包 (九龍灣)	🔄	Х	80	MAP/地圖 13/B-3
Lei Garden (Kowloon Bay) 利苑酒家 (九龍灣)	🔄	ХХ	141	MAP/地圖 13/B-3
Oriental Lily 喜百合	🔄	ХХ	174	MAP/地圖 13/A-3
Shanghai Xiao Nan Guo (Kowloon Bay) 上海小南國 (九龍灣)		ХХ	196	MAP/地圖 13/A-3
Siu Shun Village Cuisine 肇順名滙河鮮專門店	🔄	ХХ	201	MAP/地圖 13/A-3

Kwun Tong/觀塘

| Lei Garden (Kwun Tong) 利苑酒家 (觀塘) | 🔄 | ХХ | 142 | MAP/地圖 14/C-1 |

Mong Kok/旺角

Good Hope Noodles 好旺角麵家		🍜	108	MAP/地圖 9/B-1
Lei Garden (Mong Kok) 利苑酒家 (旺角)	✿	ХХ	143	MAP/地圖 9/B-1
Ming Court 明閣	✿ ✿	ХХХ	163	MAP/地圖 9/B-2
Tim Ho Wan 添好運	✿	🍜	231	MAP/地圖 9/B-2

Tokoro   ✗✗   233   MAP/地圖 9/B-2

San Po Kong/新蒲崗

Tak Lung 得龍   ⌂   🍴   215   MAP/地圖 6/A-2

Sham Shui Po/深水埗

Lau Sum Kee (Fuk Wing Street)
劉森記麵家 (福榮街)   🍴   137   MAP/地圖 7/B-2

Yung Kee Siu Choi Wong 容記小菜王   ⌂   🍴   259   MAP/地圖 7/B-2

Tsim Sha Tsui/尖沙咀

Angelini   ✗✗✗   60   MAP/地圖 12/D-2

Aspasia   ✗✗✗   61   MAP/地圖 12/C-1

BLT Steak   ✗   63   MAP/地圖 11/A-3

Celestial Court 天寶閣   ✗✗   68   MAP/地圖 12/C-3

Chesa 瑞樵閣   ✗✗   72   MAP/地圖 11/B-3

Crystal Jade La Mian Xiao Long Bao (TST)
翡翠拉麵小籠包 (尖沙咀)   ⌂   🍴   81   MAP/地圖 11/A-2

Cucina   ✗✗   83   MAP/地圖 11/A-3

Din Tai Fung 鼎泰豐   ✿   ✗   87   MAP/地圖 11/B-2

Dong Lai Shun 東來順   ✗✗   90   MAP/地圖 12/D-2

Dynasty (Tsim Sha Tsui) 滿福樓 (尖沙咀)   ✗✗   93   MAP/地圖 12/C-3

Fook Lam Moon (Kowloon) 福臨門 (九龍) ✿   ✗✗✗   97   MAP/地圖 12/C-1

Gaddi's 吉地士   ✗✗✗✗   102   MAP/地圖 11/B-3

Hing Kee 避風塘興記   ⌂   ✗   116   MAP/地圖 11/B-1

House of Jasmine 八月居   ✗✗   120   MAP/地圖 11/A-2

Hutong 胡同   ✿   ✗✗   124   MAP/地圖 11/B-2

Inagiku (Kowloon) 稻菊 (九龍)   ✗✗   126   MAP/地圖 12/D-2

Joia   ✗✗   131   MAP/地圖 9/A-3

La Brasserie 林柏軒   ✗✗   135   MAP/地圖 11/A-2

Lei Garden (Elements) 利苑酒家 (圓方) ✿   ✗✗   139   MAP/地圖 9/A-3

Lei Garden (Tsim Sha Tsui)
利苑酒家 (尖沙咀)   ✿   ✗✗   146   MAP/地圖 12/D-2

Le Soleil   ⌂   ✗✗   148   MAP/地圖 12/D-2

Morton's of Chicago   ✿   ✗✗   166   MAP/地圖 12/C-3

Nobu		✗✗	169	MAP/地圖 12/C-3
Oyster & Wine Bar		✗✗	176	MAP/地圖 12/C-3
Peking Garden (Kowloon) 北京樓 (九龍)		✗✗	180	MAP/地圖 11/B-3
Prince 王子飯店		✗✗✗	184	MAP/地圖 11/B-2
Sabatini		✗✗✗	189	MAP/地圖 12/D-2
Shanghai Xiao Nan Guo (TST) 上海小南國 (尖沙咀)		✗✗	197	MAP/地圖 12/D-2
Shang Palace 香宮	❀❀	✗✗✗	198	MAP/地圖 12/D-2
Spasso		✗✗	203	MAP/地圖 11/A-2
Spoon by Alain Ducasse		✗✗✗	204	MAP/地圖 12/C-3
Spring Deer 鹿鳴春	㊙	✗	205	MAP/地圖 12/C-2
Spring Moon 嘉麟樓		✗✗✗	206	MAP/地圖 11/B-3
Tai Woo (Tsim Sha Tsui) 太湖海鮮城 (尖沙咀)		✗✗	214	MAP/地圖 11/B-1
T'ang Court 唐閣	❀❀	✗✗✗✗	218	MAP/地圖 11/B-2
The Royal Garden 帝苑軒		✗✗	228	MAP/地圖 12/D-2
The Steak House		✗✗✗	230	MAP/地圖 12/C-3
Unkai 雲海		✗✗	238	MAP/地圖 12/C-3
Yan Toh Heen 欣圖軒	❀	✗✗✗	249	MAP/地圖 12/C-3
Yè Shanghai (Kowloon) 夜上海 (九龍)	❀	✗✗✗	254	MAP/地圖 11/A-3
Yunyan 雲陽閣	㊙	✗✗	260	MAP/地圖 12/C-1

East New Territories/新界東部

Chuen Kee Seafood 全記海鮮菜館		✗	78	MAP/地圖 28/B-2
Fung Lum 楓林小館	㊙	✗✗	100	MAP/地圖 5/A-2
Lei Garden (Sha Tin) 利苑酒家 (沙田)		✗✗	145	MAP/地圖 5/B-1
Loaf On 六福菜館	❀	🍜	153	MAP/地圖 28/B-2
Sha Tin 18 沙田18		✗✗	199	MAP/地圖 3/B-1

West New Territories/新界西部

Chiu Chow Garden (Tsuen Wan) 潮江春 (荃灣)		✗✗	77	MAP/地圖 4/B-1
Ming Kee 明記	㊙	🍜	164	MAP/地圖 1/A-1
Tai Wing Wah 大榮華	㊙	✗	212	MAP/地圖 2/B-1
Yue Kee 裕記	㊙	🍜	256	MAP/地圖 8/A-1

RESTAURANTS BY CUISINE TYPE
餐廳 — 以菜式分類

American/美式

Union J		✗	237	MAP/地圖 17/B-2

Asian and Western/亞洲及西式

Cucina		✗✗	83	MAP/地圖 11/A-3

British/英式

The Pawn		✗	226	MAP/地圖 19/B-3

Cantonese/粵菜

Celebrity Cuisine 名人坊	❁	✗✗	67	MAP/地圖 15/B-2
Celestial Court 天寶閣		✗✗	68	MAP/地圖 12/C-3
Che's 車氏粵菜軒	☻	✗	71	MAP/地圖 19/B-2
Cuisine Cuisine 國金軒		✗✗✗	84	MAP/地圖 16/C-2
Dynasty (Tsim Sha Tsui) 滿福樓 (尖沙咀)		✗✗	93	MAP/地圖 12/C-3
Dynasty (Wan Chai) 滿福樓 (灣仔)	❁	✗✗✗	94	MAP/地圖 19/B-1
Eighteen Brook 十八溪		✗✗	95	MAP/地圖 19/B-2
Farm House 農圃	❁	✗✗	96	MAP/地圖 22/C-3
Fook Lam Moon (Kowloon) 福臨門 (九龍)	❁	✗✗✗	97	MAP/地圖 12/C-1
Fook Lam Moon (Wan Chai) 福臨門 (灣仔)	❁❁	✗✗✗	98	MAP/地圖 19/B-3
Forum 富臨	❁	✗✗	99	MAP/地圖 21/B-2
Fung Lum 楓林小館	☻	✗✗	100	MAP/地圖 5/A-2
Fu Sing 富聲		✗✗	101	MAP/地圖 20/D-2
Golden Bauhinia 金紫荊		✗✗	105	MAP/地圖 19/B-1
Golden Leaf 金葉庭	❁	✗✗✗	106	MAP/地圖 18/B-2
Hoi Yat Heen 海逸軒		✗✗✗	118	MAP/地圖 10/D-3
House of Jasmine 八月居		✗✗	120	MAP/地圖 11/A-2
Island Tang 港島廳	❁	✗✗✗	127	MAP/地圖 16/D-3

Jade Garden (Hysan Avenue) 翠園 (希慎道)		🍴🍴	129	MAP/地圖 22/C-3
Jade Garden (Lockhart Road) 翠園 (駱克道)	🌝	🍴	130	MAP/地圖 21/B-2
Kin's Kitchen 留家廚房	🌝	🍴	133	MAP/地圖 23/A-3
Lei Garden (Elements) 利苑酒家 (圓方)	❀	🍴🍴	139	MAP/地圖 9/A-3
Lei Garden (IFC) 利苑酒家 (國際金融中心)		🍴🍴	140	MAP/地圖 16/C-2
Lei Garden (Kowloon Bay) 利苑酒家 (九龍灣)	🌝	🍴🍴	141	MAP/地圖 13/B-3
Lei Garden (Kwun Tong) 利苑酒家 (觀塘)	🌝	🍴🍴	142	MAP/地圖 14/C-1
Lei Garden (Mong Kok) 利苑酒家 (旺角)	❀	🍴🍴	143	MAP/地圖 9/B-1
Lei Garden (North Point) 利苑酒家 (北角)	❀	🍴🍴	144	MAP/地圖 23/A-2
Lei Garden (Sha Tin) 利苑酒家 (沙田)		🍴🍴	145	MAP/地圖 5/B-1
Lei Garden (Tsim Sha Tsui) 利苑酒家 (尖沙咀)	❀	🍴🍴	146	MAP/地圖 12/D-2
Lei Garden (Wan Chai) 利苑酒家 (灣仔)	❀	🍴🍴	147	MAP/地圖 20/D-2
Lin Heung Kui 蓮香居	🌝	🍜	149	MAP/地圖 15/A-1
Lin Heung Tea House 蓮香樓	🌝	🍴	150	MAP/地圖 15/B-2
Loaf On 六福菜館	❀	🍜	153	MAP/地圖 28/B-2
Luk Yu Tea House 陸羽茶室	🌝	🍴	155	MAP/地圖 17/B-1
Lung King Heen 龍景軒	❀❀❀	🍴🍴🍴🍴	157	MAP/地圖 16/C-1
Man Ho 萬豪殿		🍴🍴	161	MAP/地圖 18/B-2
Man Wah 文華廳		🍴🍴🍴	162	MAP/地圖 16/D-3
Ming Court 明閣	❀❀	🍴🍴🍴	163	MAP/地圖 9/B-2
One Harbour Road 港灣壹號		🍴🍴🍴🍴	172	MAP/地圖 19/B-1
Regal Palace 富豪金殿	❀	🍴🍴🍴	186	MAP/地圖 22/D-3
Sang Kee 生記		🍴🍴	190	MAP/地圖 19/B-2
Ser Wong Fun 蛇王芬		🍜	192	MAP/地圖 17/A-1
Se Wong Yee 蛇王二	🌝	🍜	193	MAP/地圖 21/B-2
Shang Palace 香宮	❀❀	🍴🍴🍴	198	MAP/地圖 12/D-2
Spring Moon 嘉麟樓		🍴🍴🍴	206	MAP/地圖 11/B-3
Summer Palace 夏宮	❀	🍴🍴🍴	207	MAP/地圖 18/A-2
Tai Wing Wah 大榮華	🌝	🍴	212	MAP/地圖 2/B-1
Tai Woo (Causeway Bay) 太湖海鮮城 (銅鑼灣)	🌝	🍴🍴	213	MAP/地圖 21/B-2

Tai Woo (Tsim Sha Tsui) 太湖海鮮城 (尖沙咀)		✕✕	214	MAP/地圖 11/B-1
Tak Lung 得龍	⌂	⅄	215	MAP/地圖 6/A-2
T'ang Court 唐閣	✿✿	✕✕✕	218	MAP/地圖 11/B-2
The Royal Garden 帝苑軒		✕✕	228	MAP/地圖 12/D-2
The Square 翠玉軒	✿	✕✕✕	229	MAP/地圖 16/D-2
Tim's Kitchen 桃花源小廚	✿✿	✕	232	MAP/地圖 15/B-2
Xin Dan Ji 新斗記		✕	246	MAP/地圖 9/B-3
Yan Toh Heen 欣圖軒	✿	✕✕✕	249	MAP/地圖 12/C-3
Yat Tung Heen (Jordan) 逸東軒 (佐敦)		✕✕	250	MAP/地圖 9/B-2
Yat Tung Heen (Wan Chai) 逸東軒 (灣仔)	✿	✕✕	251	MAP/地圖 20/C-2
Yue Kee 裕記	⌂	⅄	256	MAP/地圖 8/A-1
Yung Kee (Central) 鏞記 (中環)	✿	✕✕	258	MAP/地圖 17/B-2
Zen 采蝶軒		✕✕✕	261	MAP/地圖 18/B-2

Cantonese and Sichuan/粵菜及川菜

Golden Valley 駿景軒	⌂	✕✕	107	MAP/地圖 26/A-3

Chinese/中式

Crystal Jade La Mian Xiao Long Bao (Kowloon Bay) 翡翠拉麵小籠包 (九龍灣)	⌂	✕	80	MAP/地圖 13/B-3
Crystal Jade La Mian Xiao Long Bao (TST) 翡翠拉麵小籠包 (尖沙咀)	⌂	⅄	81	MAP/地圖 11/A-2
Crystal Jade La Mian Xiao Long Bao (Wan Chai) 翡翠拉麵小籠包 (灣仔)	⌂	✕	82	MAP/地圖 20/C-3
Dong Lai Shun 東來順		✕✕	90	MAP/地圖 12/D-2
Hunan Garden (Causeway Bay) 洞庭樓 (銅鑼灣)		✕✕✕	121	MAP/地圖 21/B-3
Hunan Garden (Central) 洞庭樓 (中環)		✕✕✕	122	MAP/地圖 16/C-2
Modern China (Causeway Bay) 金滿庭 (銅鑼灣)		✕	165	MAP/地圖 21/B-3
Ren Bai 任白		✕	187	MAP/地圖 15/B-3
Shanghai Garden 紫玉蘭		✕✕✕	194	MAP/地圖 18/A-1
Sha Tin 18 沙田18		✕✕	199	MAP/地圖 3/B-1
Shui Hu Ju 水滸居		✕✕	200	MAP/地圖 15/B-3
Xi Yan Sweets 囍宴 甜 · 藝		⅄	248	MAP/地圖 19/A-3

Yellow Door Kitchen 黃色門廚房		⚒	252	MAP/地圖 17/A-1
Yung Kee Siu Choi Wong 容記小菜王	🅐	🍜	259	MAP/地圖 7/B-2

Chinese and Western/中式及西式

Tai Ping Koon (Causeway Bay) 太平館 (銅鑼灣)	🅐	⚒	211	MAP/地圖 21/B-3

Chinese contemporary/時尚中式

Hutong 胡同	❀	⚒⚒	124	MAP/地圖 11/B-2
Ovologue 祇月		⚒⚒	175	MAP/地圖 19/B-3
Prince 王子飯店		⚒⚒⚒	184	MAP/地圖 11/B-2
Yun Fu 雲府		⚒⚒	257	MAP/地圖 17/B-2

Chiu Chow/潮洲菜

Chiu Chow Garden (Tsuen Wan) 潮江春 (荃灣)		⚒⚒	77	MAP/地圖 4/B-1
Hung's Delicacies 阿鴻小吃	❀	🍜	123	MAP/地圖 23/B-1
Lippo Chiuchow 力寶軒		⚒⚒	151	MAP/地圖 18/A-2

Dim sum/點心

Dim Sum 譽滿坊		🍜	86	MAP/地圖 26/B-3
Tim Ho Wan 添好運	❀	🍜	231	MAP/地圖 9/B-2

European contemporary/時尚歐陸式

Harlan's		⚒⚒	114	MAP/地圖 16/C-2
Mandarin Grill + Bar 文華扒房+酒吧	❀	⚒⚒⚒⚒	160	MAP/地圖 16/D-3
Watermark		⚒⚒	243	MAP/地圖 16/D-1

French/法式

Agnès b. Le Pain Grillé (Central)		⚒⚒	58	MAP/地圖 16/D-2
Caprice	❀❀❀	⚒⚒⚒⚒	66	MAP/地圖 16/C-1
Chez Patrick (Soho)		⚒⚒	74	MAP/地圖 15/B-2
Chez Patrick (Wan Chai)		⚒⚒	75	MAP/地圖 19/A-3
Gaddi's 吉地士		⚒⚒⚒⚒	102	MAP/地圖 11/B-3
La Brasserie 林柏軒		⚒⚒	135	MAP/地圖 11/A-2
On Lot 10	🅐	⚒	173	MAP/地圖 15/B-2

Petrus 珀翠	✿✿	XXXX	182 MAP/地圖 18/A-2
The Press Room	X	227 MAP/地圖 15/B-2

French contemporary/時尚法式

Amber	✿✿	XXX	59 MAP/地圖 16/C-3
Cépage	✿	XX	69 MAP/地圖 19/A-3
Harvey Nichols		XX	115 MAP/地圖 16/C-3
L'Atelier de Joël Robuchon	✿✿	XX	136 MAP/地圖 16/D-3
Pierre	✿	XXX	183 MAP/地圖 16/D-3
Spoon by Alain Ducasse		XXX	204 MAP/地圖 12/C-3

Fusion/多國菜

Bo Innovation	✿	XX	64 MAP/地圖 19/B-3

Hakkanese/客家菜

Hakka Yé Yé 客家爺爺		X	111 MAP/地圖 17/A-2

Hang Zhou/杭州菜

Hang Zhou 杭州酒家	✿	XX	112 MAP/地圖 20/C-2,3

Hotpot/火鍋

Tanyoto Hotpot (Wan Chai) 譚魚頭火鍋 (灣仔)		XX	219 MAP/地圖 19/B-3

Indian/印度菜

Tandoor	☺	XX	217 MAP/地圖 17/A-1

International/國際菜

D17		XX	92 MAP/地圖 21/B-2
Harbour Grill		XXX	113 MAP/地圖 10/D-3
Paul's Kitchen	☺	X	177 MAP/地圖 15/B-2
The Lounge		XX	225 MAP/地圖 16/C-1

Italian/意式

Aspasia		XXX	61 MAP/地圖 12/C-1
Cinecittà		XXX	79 MAP/地圖 19/A-3

Italian and French contemporary/意式及時尚法式

Italian contemporary/時尚意式

Japanese/日式

Japanese contemporary/時尚日式

Nobu	ⅩⅩ	169	MAP/地圖 12/C-3
Roka	ⅩⅩ	188	MAP/地圖 18/B-2
Wasabisabi 山葵	Ⅹ	242	MAP/地圖 21/B-3
Zuma	ⅩⅩ	262	MAP/地圖 16/C-3

Mediterranean/地中海菜

1/5 Nuevo	🚗	Ⅹ	171	MAP/地圖 19/A-3

Noodles/麵食

Kau Kee 九記	🍜	132	MAP/地圖 15/B-2
Lung Kee (Temple Street) 龍記 (廟街)	🍜	156	MAP/地圖 9/B-3
Mak An Kee Noodle (Wing Kut Street) 麥奀記(忠記)麵家 (永吉街)	🚗 🍜	158	MAP/地圖 16/C-2
Mak's Noodle 麥奀雲吞麵世家	🍜	159	MAP/地圖 17/A-1
Olala (St. Francis Street) 一碗麵 (聖佛蘭士街)	🚗 🍜	170	MAP/地圖 19/A-3
Tam Chai Yunnan Noodles (Jordan Road) 譚仔雲南米線 (佐敦道)	🍜	216	MAP/地圖 9/B-3
Wing Wah 永華雲吞麵家	🍜	244	MAP/地圖 19/B-2
Yeung's Noodle 楊記麵家	🍜	255	MAP/地圖 20/C-2

Noodles and Congee/粥麵

Chee Kei 池記		🍜	70	MAP/地圖 21/B-3
Good Hope Noodles 好旺角麵家		🍜	108	MAP/地圖 9/B-1
Ho Hung Kee 何洪記	🚗	🍜	117	MAP/地圖 21/B-3
Lau Sum Kee (Fuk Wing Street) 劉森記麵家 (福榮街)		🍜	137	MAP/地圖 7/B-2
Tasty (Happy Valley) 正斗粥麵專家 (跑馬地)	🚗	Ⅹ	220	MAP/地圖 26/A-3
Tasty (Hung Hom) 正斗粥麵專家 (紅磡)	🚗	🍜	221	MAP/地圖 10/D-3
Tasty (IFC) 正斗粥麵專家 (國際金融中心)	🚗	🍜	222	MAP/地圖 16/C-2
Tsim Chai Kee (Queen's Road) 沾仔記 (皇后大道中)		🍜	234	MAP/地圖 15/B-2
Tsim Chai Kee (Wellington Street) 沾仔記 (威靈頓街)		🍜	235	MAP/地圖 17/A-1

Pekingese/京菜

Cheung Kee/祥記飯店	⊕	🍴	73	MAP/地圖 19/B-2
Oriental Lily 喜百合	⊕	🍴🍴	174	MAP/地圖 13/A-3
Peking Garden (Admiralty) 北京樓 (金鍾)		🍴🍴	178	MAP/地圖 18/B-2
Peking Garden (Central) 北京樓 (中環)		🍴🍴🍴	179	MAP/地圖 16/D-3
Peking Garden (Kowloon) 北京樓 (九龍)		🍴🍴	180	MAP/地圖 11/B-3
Peking Garden (Tai Koo Shing) 北京樓 (太古城)		🍴🍴🍴	181	MAP/地圖 25/B-1
Spring Deer 鹿鳴春	⊕	🍴	205	MAP/地圖 12/C-2

Seafood/海鮮

Chuen Kee Seafood 全記海鮮菜館		🍴	78	MAP/地圖 28/B-2
Dot Cod		🍴🍴	91	MAP/地圖 16/D-3
Hing Kee 避風塘興記	⊕	🍴	116	MAP/地圖 11/B-1
Lobster Bar and Grill 龍蝦吧		🍴🍴	154	MAP/地圖 18/A-2
Ming Kee 明記	⊕	🍜	164	MAP/地圖 1/A-1
Oyster & Wine Bar		🍴🍴	176	MAP/地圖 12/C-3

Shanghainese/上海菜

Din Tai Fung 鼎泰豐	✿	🍴	87	MAP/地圖 11/B-2
Liu Yuan Pavilion 留園雅敘	⊕	🍴🍴	152	MAP/地圖 19/B-2
Queen's Palace 帝后殿	⊕	🍴🍴	185	MAP/地圖 19/B-3
Shanghai Lu Yang Cun 上海綠楊邨		🍴🍴	195	MAP/地圖 21/B-2
Shanghai Xiao Nan Guo (Kowloon Bay) 上海小南國 (九龍灣)		🍴🍴	196	MAP/地圖 13/A-3
Shanghai Xiao Nan Guo (TST) 上海小南國 (尖沙咀)		🍴🍴	197	MAP/地圖 12/D-2
Snow Garden (Causeway Bay) 雪園 (銅鑼灣)		🍴🍴	202	MAP/地圖 22/C-3
Wu Kong Shanghai (Causeway Bay) 滬江 (銅鑼灣)	⊕	🍴🍴	245	MAP/地圖 21/B-3
Xinjishi Shanghai 新吉士		🍴	247	MAP/地圖 22/C-3
Yè Shanghai (Admiralty) 夜上海 (金鍾)		🍴🍴🍴	253	MAP/地圖 18/B-2
Yè Shanghai (Kowloon) 夜上海 (九龍)	✿	🍴🍴🍴	254	MAP/地圖 11/A-3

Shun Tak/信德菜

Siu Shun Village Cuisine 肇順名匯河鮮專門店	⊕	XX	201	MAP/地圖 13/A-3

Sichuan/川菜

Chilli Fagara 麻辣燙	⊕	X	76	MAP/地圖 15/B-3
Da Ping Huo 大平伙	⊕	X	85	MAP/地圖 15/B-2
Yunyan 雲陽閣	⊕	XX	260	MAP/地圖 12/C-1

Spanish (Tapas)/西班牙菜(小菜)

Uno Más	⊕	X	239	MAP/地圖 19/B-2

Steakhouse/扒房

BLT Steak		X	63	MAP/地圖 11/A-3
Lawry's The Prime Rib		XXX	138	MAP/地圖 22/C-3
Morton's of Chicago	✤	XX	166	MAP/地圖 12/C-3
The Steak House		XXX	230	MAP/地圖 12/C-3

Swiss/瑞士菜

Chesa 瑞樵閣		XX	72	MAP/地圖 11/B-3

Thai/泰式

Café Siam	⊕	X	65	MAP/地圖 17/A-1
Thai Basil		X	223	MAP/地圖 18/B-2

Vegetarian (Shanghainese)/素食(上海菜)

Kung Tak Lam (Causeway Bay) 功德林 (銅鑼灣)		XX	134	MAP/地圖 21/B-2

Vietnamese/越南菜

Le Soleil	⊕	XX	148	MAP/地圖 12/D-2

RESTAURANTS PARTICULARLY PLEASANT
上佳的餐廳

Agnès b. Le Pain Grillé (Central)		XX	58	MAP/地圖 16/D-2
Amber	✿✿	XxX	59	MAP/地圖 16/C-3
Caprice	✿✿✿	XxXxX	66	MAP/地圖 16/C-1
Cépage	✿	XxX	69	MAP/地圖 19/A-3
Chee Kei 池記		🍜	70	MAP/地圖 21/B-3
Chesa 瑞樵閣		XX	72	MAP/地圖 11/B-3
Cucina		XX	83	MAP/地圖 11/A-3
Da Ping Huo 大平伙	⊛	X	85	MAP/地圖 15/B-2
Dim Sum 譽滿坊		🍜	86	MAP/地圖 26/B-3
Domani		XX	89	MAP/地圖 18/A-2
Golden Leaf 金葉庭	✿	XxX	106	MAP/地圖 18/B-2
Harlan's		XX	114	MAP/地圖 16/C-2
Hutong 胡同	✿	XX	124	MAP/地圖 11/B-2
Inagiku (IFC) 稻菊 (國際金融中心)		XX	125	MAP/地圖 16/C-1
Island Tang 港島廳	✿	XxX	127	MAP/地圖 16/D-3
L'Atelier de Joël Robuchon	✿✿	XX	136	MAP/地圖 16/D-3
Lobster Bar and Grill 龍蝦吧		XX	154	MAP/地圖 18/A-2
Lung King Heen 龍景軒	✿✿✿	XxXx	157	MAP/地圖 16/C-1
Mandarin Grill + Bar 文華扒房+酒吧	✿	XxXx	160	MAP/地圖 16/D-3
Man Wah 文華廳		XxX	162	MAP/地圖 16/D-3
Ming Court 明閣	✿✿	XxX	163	MAP/地圖 9/B-2
Olala (St. Francis Street) 一碗麵 (聖佛蘭士街)	⊛	🍜	170	MAP/地圖 19/A-3
1/5 Nuevo	⊛	X	171	MAP/地圖 19/A-3
Petrus 珀翠	✿✿	XxXxX	182	MAP/地圖 18/A-2
Pierre	✿	XxXx	183	MAP/地圖 16/D-3
Shang Palace 香宮	✿✿	XxX	198	MAP/地圖 12/D-2

RESTAURANTS
WITH PRIVATE ROOMS
具備私人房間的餐廳

Agnès b. Le Pain Grillé (Central)		XX	58	MAP/地圖 16/D-2
Amber	✿✿	XXX	59	MAP/地圖 16/C-3
Aspasia		XxX	61	MAP/地圖 12/C-1
At Corner		X	62	MAP/地圖 21/B-2
Bo Innovation	✿	XX	64	MAP/地圖 19/B-3
Caprice	✿✿✿	XXXXX	66	MAP/地圖 16/C-1
Celebrity Cuisine 名人坊	✿	XX	67	MAP/地圖 15/B-2
Celestial Court 天寶閣		XX	68	MAP/地圖 12/C-3
Cépage	✿	XxX	69	MAP/地圖 19/A-3
Che's 車氏粵菜軒	✿	X	71	MAP/地圖 19/B-2
Chez Patrick (Soho)		XX	74	MAP/地圖 15/B-2
Chez Patrick (Wan Chai)		XX	75	MAP/地圖 19/A-3
Chiu Chow Garden (Tsuen Wan) 潮江春 (荃灣)		XX	77	MAP/地圖 4/B-1
Cinecittà		XxX	79	MAP/地圖 19/A-3
Crystal Jade La Mian Xiao Long Bao (Kowloon Bay) 翡翠拉麵小籠包 (九龍灣)	✿	X	80	MAP/地圖 13/B-3
Crystal Jade La Mian Xiao Long Bao (TST) 翡翠拉麵小籠包 (尖沙咀)	✿	및	81	MAP/地圖 11/A-2
Crystal Jade La Mian Xiao Long Bao (Wan Chai) 翡翠拉麵小籠包 (灣仔)	✿	X	82	MAP/地圖 20/C-3
Cuisine Cuisine 國金軒		XxX	84	MAP/地圖 16/C-2
Din Tai Fung 鼎泰豐	✿	X	87	MAP/地圖 11/B-2
Dong Lai Shun 東來順		XX	90	MAP/地圖 12/D-2
Dot Cod		XX	91	MAP/地圖 16/D-3
Dynasty (Tsim Sha Tsui) 滿福樓 (尖沙咀)		XX	93	MAP/地圖 12/C-3
Dynasty (Wan Chai) 滿福樓 (灣仔)	✿	XxX	94	MAP/地圖 19/B-1
Eighteen Brook 十八溪		XX	95	MAP/地圖 19/B-2

Lei Garden (Elements) 利苑酒家 (圓方)	✿	XX	139	MAP/地圖 9/A-3
Lei Garden (IFC) 利苑酒家 (國際金融中心)		XX	140	MAP/地圖 16/C-2
Lei Garden (Kowloon Bay) 利苑酒家 (九龍灣)	⊛	XX	141	MAP/地圖 13/B-3
Lei Garden (Kwun Tong) 利苑酒家 (觀塘)	⊛	XX	142	MAP/地圖 14/C-1
Lei Garden (Mong Kok) 利苑酒家 (旺角)	✿	XX	143	MAP/地圖 9/B-1
Lei Garden (North Point) 利苑酒家 (北角)	✿	XX	144	MAP/地圖 23/A-2
Lei Garden (Sha Tin) 利苑酒家 (沙田)		XX	145	MAP/地圖 5/B-1
Lei Garden (Tsim Sha Tsui) 利苑酒家 (尖沙咀)	✿	XX	146	MAP/地圖 12/D-2
Lei Garden (Wan Chai) 利苑酒家 (灣仔)	✿	XX	147	MAP/地圖 20/D-2
Lippo Chiuchow 力寶軒		XX	151	MAP/地圖 18/A-2
Liu Yuan Pavilion 留園雅敍	⊛	XX	152	MAP/地圖 19/B-2
Loaf On 六福菜館	✿	୳	153	MAP/地圖 28/B-2
Luk Yu Tea House 陸羽茶室	⊛	X	155	MAP/地圖 17/B-1
Lung King Heen 龍景軒	✿✿✿	XXXX	157	MAP/地圖 16/C-1
Mandarin Grill + Bar 文華扒房+酒吧	✿	XXXX	160	MAP/地圖 16/D-3
Man Ho 萬豪殿		XX	161	MAP/地圖 18/B-2
Man Wah 文華廳		XXX	162	MAP/地圖 16/D-3
Ming Court 明閣	✿✿	XXX	163	MAP/地圖 9/B-2
Modern China (Causeway Bay) 金滿庭 (銅鑼灣)		X	165	MAP/地圖 21/B-3
Morton's of Chicago	✿	XX	166	MAP/地圖 12/C-3
Naozen なお膳		X	167	MAP/地圖 17/B-2
Nicholini's 意寧谷		XXXX	168	MAP/地圖 18/B-2
Nobu		XX	169	MAP/地圖 12/C-3
One Harbour Road 港灣壹號		XXXX	172	MAP/地圖 19/B-1
On Lot 10	⊛	X	173	MAP/地圖 15/B-2
Oriental Lily 喜百合	⊛	XX	174	MAP/地圖 13/A-3
Oyster & Wine Bar		XX	176	MAP/地圖 12/C-3
Peking Garden (Admiralty) 北京樓 (金鐘)		XX	178	MAP/地圖 18/B-2
Peking Garden (Central) 北京樓 (中環)		XXX	179	MAP/地圖 16/D-3

Peking Garden (Kowloon) 北京樓（九龍）		XX	180	MAP/地圖 11/B-3
Peking Garden (Tai Koo Shing) 北京樓（太古城）		XXX	181	MAP/地圖 25/B-1
Petrus 珀翠	✿✿	XXXXX	182	MAP/地圖 18/A-2
Pierre	✿	XXXX	183	MAP/地圖 16/D-3
Prince 王子飯店		XXX	184	MAP/地圖 11/B-2
Queen's Palace 帝后殿	☺	XX	185	MAP/地圖 19/B-3
Regal Palace 富豪金殿	✿	XXX	186	MAP/地圖 22/D-3
Sabatini		XXX	189	MAP/地圖 12/D-2
Senzuru 千鶴		X	191	MAP/地圖 10/C-3
Shanghai Garden 紫玉蘭		XXX	194	MAP/地圖 18/A-1
Shanghai Lu Yang Cun 上海綠楊邨		XX	195	MAP/地圖 21/B-2
Shanghai Xiao Nan Guo (Kowloon Bay) 上海小南國（九龍灣）		XX	196	MAP/地圖 13/A-3
Shanghai Xiao Nan Guo (TST) 上海小南國（尖沙咀）		XX	197	MAP/地圖 12/D-2
Shang Palace 香宮	✿✿	XXX	198	MAP/地圖 12/D-2
Sha Tin 18 沙田18		XX	199	MAP/地圖 3/B-1
Shui Hu Ju 水滸居		XX	200	MAP/地圖 15/B-3
Siu Shun Village Cuisine 肇順名匯河鮮專門店	☺	XX	201	MAP/地圖 13/A-3
Snow Garden (Causeway Bay) 雪園（銅鑼灣）		XX	202	MAP/地圖 22/C-3
Spasso		XX	203	MAP/地圖 11/A-2
Spoon by Alain Ducasse		XXX	204	MAP/地圖 12/C-3
Spring Moon 嘉麟樓		XXX	206	MAP/地圖 11/B-3
Summer Palace 夏宮	✿	XXX	207	MAP/地圖 18/A-2
Sushi Kuu 壽司喰		X	209	MAP/地圖 17/B-2
Tai Wing Wah 大榮華	☺	X	212	MAP/地圖 2/B-1
Tai Woo (Causeway Bay) 太湖海鮮城（銅鑼灣）	☺	XX	213	MAP/地圖 21/B-2
Tai Woo (Tsim Sha Tsui) 太湖海鮮城（尖沙咀）		XX	214	MAP/地圖 11/B-1
Tak Lung 得龍	☺	☕	215	MAP/地圖 6/A-2
Tandoor	☺	XX	217	MAP/地圖 17/A-1

RESTAURANTS WITH A VIEW
有景觀的餐廳

Agnès b. Le Pain Grillé (Central)

⚔14 ☎🍴 🍇

Located within the celebrated fashion store, Agnès b. and decorated to resemble a private, yet luxurious, French country home from the 19C. It's divided into three rooms: Paris, Antibes, and Lyon; each with its own character and personality. Chic it most certainly is, to match its elegant clientele. Not surprisingly, the menu is French, with a Mediterranean bias. The impressive wine list features over 100 champagnes.

餐廳位於Agnès b時裝店內，裝潢模仿十九世紀私人奢華法國田園家居。餐廳分為三個空間：Paris、Antibes和Lyon；每個都具有獨特個性風格。餐廳的時尚風格毋庸置疑，配合其高貴客源。菜單一如所料，是帶有地中海風格的法國菜。酒牌上更有超過100種香檳可供選擇。

■ ADDRESS/地址

TEL.2805 0798

Shop 3096-3097, Podium Level 3, IFC Mall, 8 Finance Street, Central

中環金融街8號國際金融中心商場3樓3096-3097號舖

www.agnesb-lepaingrille.com

■ ANNUAL AND WEEKLY CLOSING
　休息日期

Closed Lunar New Year

年初一休息

■ OPENING HOURS, LAST ORDER
　營業時間，最後點菜時間

Lunch/午膳 12:00-15:00 (L.O.)
Dinner/晚膳 19:00-22:30 (L.O.)

■ PRICE/價錢

Lunch/午膳 　set/套餐 　　　$258-318
　　　　　　à la carte/點菜 $300-650
Dinner/晚膳 à la carte/點菜 $300-650

Amber

A tasteful mix of contemporary and Art Deco styling greets diners here. There's much ebony on show, complemented by the original ceiling decoration comprising 3,500 copper tubes: none of it is too fancy. But the food presented here is the real treat. Seriously prepared French contemporary cuisine is based on well-sourced seasonal produce. The comprehensive wine list is 1200 bottles long; the service is flawless.

迎接顧客的是有品味的當代和Art Deco設計。這裡遍佈著黑檀木,以天花板原形襯托,相映3,500 條銅管一任何部分都不會太花巧。食物確實是十分美味。時尚法國菜烹調認真,採用了不同原產地的季節性產品。內容充實的酒牌長達1200種,服務更近乎完美。

■ ADDRESS/地址

TEL.2132 0066

7F, The Landmark Mandarin Oriental Hotel, 15 Queen's Road, Central
中環皇后大道中15號置地文華東方酒店7樓
www.mandarinoriental.com/landmark

■ ANNUAL AND WEEKLY CLOSING
　休息日期
Closed Sunday
週日休息

■ OPENING HOURS, LAST ORDER
　營業時間,最後點菜時間
Lunch/午膳 12:00-14:30 (L.O.)
Dinner/晚膳 18:30-22:30 (L.O.)

■ PRICE/價錢

Lunch/午膳	set/套餐	$518-1,488
	à la carte/點菜	$850-1,500
Dinner/晚膳	set/套餐	$1,088-1,488
	à la carte/點菜	$850-1,500

Angelini

There are few distinguishing features to this restaurant other than the view (a window seat is desirable) and the food which is straightforward and allows the natural flavours to shine. Although other Italian regions are represented, it is the cooking of Campania that gets the upper hand with specialities such as Amalfi-style scialatielli with clams, zucchini and basil. Here is a chef who is extremely passionate about the dishes he produces.

這家餐廳最具特色的地方可説是其優美景觀(窗口座位尤其能飽覽美景),以及簡單的菜式和天然的食材。雖然其他意大利地區的菜式亦有提供,但這裡以坎帕尼亞區的菜式最為突出,阿瑪菲海岸風味蜆配短扁身麵伴青瓜及羅勒香草是當中的表表者。此外,這裡更有一位極其熱愛烹飪的廚師。

■ ADDRESS/地址

TEL.2733 8750

Mezzanine Level, Kowloon Shangri-La Hotel, 64 Mody Road, East Tsim Sha Tsui, Kowloon

九龍尖東麼地道64號九龍香格里拉酒店閣樓

www.shangri-la.com

■ OPENING HOURS, LAST ORDER
　營業時間,最後點菜時間
Lunch/午膳 12:00-15:00 (L.O.)
Dinner/晚膳 18:30-22:30 (L.O.)

■ PRICE/價錢

Lunch/午膳	set/套餐	$218
	à la carte/點菜	$370-1,130
Dinner/晚膳	set/套餐	$780
	à la carte/點菜	$370-1,130

Aspasia

Named after the Greek beauty renowned for her cosmopolitan style and good taste, this restaurant aims to project a similar image. There is subtle Louis XV styling here, mixed with bold animal designs and original artwork on the walls. The cuisine, though, is resolutely Italian with a roll-call of antipasti, pastas and both fish and meat dishes. Their jazz band, Dada, perform on the floor above.

店名 Aspasia是古希臘一位代表創新、帶領潮流的女士名字,亦符合這家餐廳希望帶出的感覺。餐廳裝潢帶有路易十五風格,混合牆上強烈的動物圖案及原創藝術。餐飲方面則貫徹義大利風格,頭盤、義大利麵、魚及肉的主菜。餐廳的爵士樂隊Dada於上層演出。

■ ADDRESS/地址
TEL.3763 8800
1F, The Luxe Manor Hotel, 39 Kimberley Road, Tsim Sha Tsui, Kowloon
九龍尖沙咀金巴利道39號帝樂文娜公館1樓
www.aspasia.com.hk

■ OPENING HOURS, LAST ORDER
營業時間,最後點菜時間
Lunch/午膳 12:00-14:30 (L.O.)
Dinner/晚膳 18:30-23:30 (L.O.)

■ PRICE/價錢
Lunch/午膳 à la carte/點菜 $490-690
Dinner/晚膳 à la carte/點菜 $490-690

At Corner

♿ ⯇ 🚗10

Elevator doors open onto a giant TV screen, setting the tone
for a trendy, fashionable restaurant. The tables along the
wall offer window views over Kowloon; the ones further in
are more secluded for intimacy. There's minimalist under-
statement here, though it's of a more Western style than
Japanese. The menus, though, could only come from one
country: classics such as sushi, sashimi and tempura are
served without fuss or experimentation.

餐廳電梯門前的巨型電視屏幕，與這所時尚入流餐廳的格調融為一體。近牆邊
的餐桌坐擁維港景色，其他位置則讓人有較多私人的空間。餐廳環境氣氛似是
西式多於日式，這樣說只是流於表面，因為餐牌上的菜式全是來自同一個國
家：日本，如壽司、刺身、天婦羅等經典菜式，毫不造作，恰到好處。

■ ADDRESS/地址

TEL.2576 6777
9F, World Trade Centre, 280
Gloucester Road, Causeway Bay
銅鑼灣告士打道280號世界貿易中心9樓
www.heaplace.com

■ OPENING HOURS, LAST ORDER
營業時間，最後點菜時間
Lunch/午膳 12:00-14:30 (L.O.)
Dinner/晚膳 18:00-22:30 (L.O.)

■ PRICE/價錢
Lunch/午膳   set/套餐 $100
               à la carte/點菜 $150-350
Dinner/晚膳 à la carte/點菜 $150-350

BLT Steak

In this instance those initials stand for Bistro Laurent Tou-rondel, a New York celebrity chef. His restaurant specialises in prime beef from the US and Australia, all USDA certified and naturally aged. Choose your cut, from a Porterhouse to a rib-eye, a sauce and sides. There are a few lighter options for those intimidated by a 16oz New York strip. Its terrace overlooking The Star ferry quay and Victoria Harbour is a 'prime' spot.

BLT取紐約名廚(Bistro)Laurent　Tourondel之名，餐廳以來自美國及澳洲頂級牛排為主，全部通過美國農產部認證，自然生長。你可選擇喜歡食用的部份，從大脊骨牛排到肉眼排任君選擇，並配上自選醬汁及配菜。你亦可選擇較輕盈的16oz紐約無骨西冷扒。其平台花園是「搶 手」熱點，可觀賞天星碼頭及維多利亞港景致。

■ ADDRESS/地址
TEL.2730 3508
Shop G62, GF, Ocean Terminal, Harbour City, Tsim Sha Tsui, Kowloon
九龍尖沙咀海運大廈海港城地下G62號舖
www.diningconcepts.com.hk

■ OPENING HOURS, LAST ORDER
　營業時間，最後點菜時間
12:00-23:00 (L.O.)

■ PRICE/價錢
Lunch/午膳　à la carte/點菜 $340-770
Dinner/晚膳　à la carte/點菜 $340-770

Bo Innovation

"X-treme Chinese cuisine" is how this modern fusion restaurant describes itself. Owner-chef Alvin Leung and his team in the open kitchen create dishes that are highly innovative, delicate and inventive. He also deconstructs recognisable Chinese flavour combinations in a playful way. For the full experience, try the small tasting plates of the Chef's Menu. The lift on Ship Street takes you up to a glass-encased room with a terrace.

這家現代餐廳以「X-treme Chinese cuisine」自居,主力是中菜但同時融合了其他地方的菜式。餐廳老闆兼廚師梁經倫(Alvin)和他的團隊滿腦子新主意,在開放式廚房炮製極其創新精緻、獨一無二的菜式。另一方面,他打破了中菜味道的定義,以大膽的方式創造新的組合。品嚐主廚套餐的推薦小菜,享受全面的美食體驗。這家設有露台的玻璃外牆餐廳,在船街搭升降機即可到達。

■ ADDRESS/地址
TEL.2850 8371
2F, J Residence, 18 Ship Street, Wan Chai
灣仔船街18號嘉蓄軒2樓
www.boinnovation.com

■ ANNUAL AND WEEKLY CLOSING
休息日期
Closed 3 days Lunar New Year, Saturday lunch and Sunday
農曆新年3天、週六午膳及週日休息

■ OPENING HOURS, LAST ORDER
營業時間,最後點菜時間
Lunch/午膳 12:00-14:00 (L.O.)
Dinner/晚膳 19:00-22:00 (L.O.)

■ PRICE/價錢
Lunch/午膳	set/套餐	$200-1,080
Dinner/晚膳	set/套餐	$680-1,080

Café Siam

This simple no-nonsense Thai operation packs in a loyal following on a daily basis. So get there early, sit upstairs by the window and order yourself a nice cocktail while you decide what to eat. The key elements of the authentic menu are the curries and the seafood which are bursting with flavour and freshness. You'll emerge afterwards feeling very well looked after by the young, diligent team.

這家簡單的泰國餐廳每天都熟客滿座。因此,請提早到達,在樓上雅座近窗邊位置坐低,在點菜的同時,不妨享用一杯雞尾酒。菜餚原汁原味,主打菜式包括各種咖哩和海鮮,既新鮮又味美。餐廳的年輕侍應幹勁十足,服務令人賓至如歸。

■ ADDRESS/地址
TEL.2851 4803
40-42 Lyndhurst Terrace, Central
中環擺花街40-42號
www.cafesiam.com.hk

■ OPENING HOURS, LAST ORDER
營業時間,最後點菜時間
12:00-22:30 (L.O.)

■ PRICE/價錢

Lunch/午膳	set/套餐	$73-88
	à la carte/點菜	$200-350
Dinner/晚膳	set/套餐	$168
	à la carte/點菜	$200-350

Caprice

✿✿✿

Lamb from Sisteron, duck from Challans and chicken from Bresse highlight straightaway that much superb quality produce used here is imported directly from France: the resulting dishes demonstrate great finesse and imagination. Every aspect of the spacious dining room displays strong interest. There are lovely views of the harbour, of the wine cellar and of the open kitchen with its jewelled canopy. The service shows great attention to detail.

Sisteron地區的羊肉、Challans地區的鴨肉和Bresse地區的雞肉充分反映這家餐廳從法國直接進口名貴材料、炮製優質法國菜的特色。所有菜式均以高超手藝與無窮巧思炮製而成，寬敞的飯廳每個角度都顯示著獨特的風格。環視四周可見維港兩岸美景、酒櫃和帳蓬鑲滿寶飾的開放式廚房。服務周到細心。

■ ADDRESS/地址

TEL.3196 8860

6F, Four Seasons Hotel, 8 Finance Street, Central
中環金融街8號四季酒店平臺6樓
www.fourseasons.com/hongkong

■ OPENING HOURS, LAST ORDER
　營業時間，最後點菜時間
Lunch/午膳　12:00-14:30 (L.O.)
Dinner/晚膳　18:00-22:30 (L.O.)

■ PRICE/價錢

Lunch/午膳	set/套餐	$420
	à la carte/點菜	$800-1,100
Dinner/晚膳	set/套餐	$880-1,280
	à la carte/點菜	$800-1,100

Celebrity Cuisine
名人坊

🍽16 ☎🍴

Limited capacity and a host of regulars mean that booking ahead is vital at this very discreet restaurant concealed within the Lan Kwai Fong hotel. Those regulars come for authentic Cantonese cuisine that is also delicate and sophisticated. The menu may be quite short but there are usually plenty of specials; highlights include chicken with Huadiao rice wine, ox tongue and, one of the chef's own creations, 'bird's nest in chicken wing'.

餐廳座位有限,但常客眾多,對這家考慮周到的餐廳來說,提早預約是必須的。餐廳隱藏在蘭桂坊酒店內,常客都因其精緻具特色的正宗廣東菜而來。餐牌可能頗短,但提供大量特選菜式,包括花雕焗飛天雞及紅燒牛脷。其中,由主廚創作的是燕窩釀鳳翼。

■ ADDRESS/地址
TEL.3650 0066
1F, Lan Kwai Fong Hotel, 3 Kau U Fong, Central
中環九如坊3號蘭桂坊酒店1樓

■ ANNUAL AND WEEKLY CLOSING
　　休息日期
Closed 3 days Lunar New Year
農曆新年3天

■ OPENING HOURS, LAST ORDER
　　營業時間,最後點菜時間
Lunch/午膳　12:00-14:30 (L.O.)
Dinner/晚膳　18:00-23:00 (L.O.)

■ PRICE/價錢
Lunch/午膳　à la carte/點菜 $200-600
Dinner/晚膳　à la carte/點菜 $300-800

Celestial Court
天寶閣

Although this traditional Chinese restaurant is of grand pro-portions, it's common for diners to queue for a table. The refinement of the silk and wood decoration is offset by the noisy reality, courtesy of a low ceiling. A large range of Can-tonese and Chinese specialities includes hand-prepared dim sum, skilfully served at lunch; their steamed shrimp dump-ling with bamboo shoot is renowned. Particular attention is paid to seasonal creations.

雖然這家傳統中國餐廳地方龐大，但食客排隊候座亦是見怪不怪。由於樓底較淺，絲綢和木材裝飾的優雅被嘈雜的環境抵消了。粵菜和中國菜的選擇很多，包括午飯時間供應的人手製點心。筍尖鮮蝦餃王是這裡的名菜。特別留意季節性菜式。

■ ADDRESS/地址

TEL.2369 1111
2F, Sheraton Hotel, 20 Nathan Road, Tsim Sha Tsui, Kowloon
九龍尖沙咀彌敦道20號喜來登酒店2樓
www.sheraton.com/hongkong

■ OPENING HOURS, LAST ORDER
營業時間，最後點菜時間
Lunch/午膳 11:30-15:00 (L.O.)
Dinner/晚膳 18:00-23:30 (L.O.)

■ PRICE/價錢
Lunch/午膳　à la carte/點菜 $ 350-900
Dinner/晚膳　à la carte/點菜 $ 350-900

Cépage

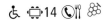

A sophisticated restaurant from the same stable as Les Amis in Singapore. Three floors of stylish design offer the chic diner something special; subtle lighting, crisp linen and Limoges porcelain but also a relaxed atmosphere. The cuisine is contemporary, with French and Italian to the fore, using fine ingredients from around the world. Service is charming without being stuffy and the wine list is one of the most impressive in Hong Kong.

新加坡得獎餐廳集團Les Amis開設的特色餐廳。樓高三層的時尚設計為新潮食客提供不一樣的選擇：柔和燈光、清雅麻布及第里摩(Limoges)瓷器之外，還有讓人放鬆的氣氛。餐飲風格現代，有新派法國及義大利菜，以世界各地的精美食材炮製。優良爽快的服務亦讓人激賞，酒牌提供的選擇之多，更是全港數一數二。

■ ADDRESS/地址
TEL.2861 3130
23 Wing Fung Street, Wan Chai
灣仔永豐街23號
www.lesamis.com.sg

■ ANNUAL AND WEEKLY CLOSING
　　休息日期
Closed Sunday
週日休息

■ OPENING HOURS, LAST ORDER
　　營業時間，最後點菜時間
Lunch/午膳　12:00-14:30 (L.O.)
Dinner/晚膳　19:00-22:30 (L.O.)

■ PRICE/價錢

Lunch/午膳	set/套餐	$390
	à la carte/點菜	$730-1,630
Dinner/晚膳	set/套餐	$880-1,340
	à la carte/點菜	$730-1,630

Chee Kei
池記

The only problem to overcome here is getting in and out of the place: the word has spread about Chee Kei and space is tight. Noise levels are high, with staff in headscarves joining in the general merriment. An extensive menu includes a choice between five types of noodle and a selection of congee. The congee with crab is a best seller, while wonton are generously filled and flavoursome. The big hit for dessert is red bean soup with sweet tofu.

這裡唯一不方便之處是出入問題，池記一向以地方細小但食客多而被受注目。戴著頭巾的員工，為嘈雜環境更添一份歡鬧氣氛。菜式選擇繁多，包括五類麵線和多種款式的粥。最熱賣的包括金衣蟹皇粥，而雲吞更是皮薄餡多，味道濃郁。甜品方面，最受歡迎的甜品是紅豆沙豆腐花。

■ ADDRESS/地址
TEL.2890 8616
84 Percival Street, Causeway Bay
銅鑼灣波斯富街84號

■ OPENING HOURS, LAST ORDER
營業時間，最後點菜時間
11:00-23:30 (L.O.)

■ PRICE/價錢
Lunch/午膳　à la carte/點菜 $ 27-34
Dinner/晚膳　à la carte/點菜 $ 52-92

Che's
車氏粵菜軒

 35

This unremarkable looking little restaurant is very popular with the local businessmen who come here in their droves for the house speciality: crispy pork buns. But there are lots of other reasons to visit: the dim sum at lunch, the extensive menu of classic dishes, simpler offerings such as congee or braised clay pot dishes and the chilled mango to end. The service is prompt and efficient: another reason why it's so popular at lunchtimes.

這家小餐館可能並不起眼，但其實在本地商界人士間卻享負盛名，對其馳名脆皮叉燒包趨之若鶩。除此之外，午市點心、選擇豐富的經典名菜、簡單菜式如粥或瓦　煲仔菜，加上一道冰凍芒果便是個完美結束。服務快速且有效率：這也是令餐廳在午餐時分座無虛席的原因。

■ ADDRESS/地址
TEL.2528 1123
4F, 54-62 Lockhart Road, Wan Chai
灣仔駱克道54-62號4樓

■ OPENING HOURS, LAST ORDER
    營業時間，最後點菜時間
Lunch/午膳 11:30-15:00 (L.O.)
Dinner/晚膳 18:00-22:15 (L.O.)

■ PRICE/價錢

Lunch/午膳	set/套餐	$550-900
	à la carte/點菜	$150-700
Dinner/晚膳	set/套餐	$550-900
	à la carte/點菜	$150-700

Chesa
瑞樵閣

For over forty years, the cuisine of Switzerland has found a charming niche here. An imposing wood door leads you into an intimate Swiss-style chalet with wooden objects left, right and centre. The experienced chef is proud of his cheese specialities: fondue Vaudoise (traditional fondue), or raclette du Valais (hot melted cheese with potatoes, pickled onions and gherkins). For dessert, chocolate fondue or Swiss chocolate mousses are de rigueur!

瑞士美食在香港穩佔一席位超過四十年。壯觀的木門帶領你到親切的瑞士農舍，裡面四處都有木製的裝飾。經驗豐富的廚師對他的芝士作品十分自豪：沃州芝士火鍋(傳統芝士火鍋)或瓦萊州烤芝士(熱熔的芝士配馬鈴薯、醃洋蔥及青瓜)。至於甜品，巧克力火鍋或瑞士巧克力慕絲是兩大必吃！

■ ADDRESS/地址
TEL.2920 2888
1F, The Peninsula Hotel, Salisbury Road, Tsim Sha Tsui, Kowloon
九龍尖沙咀梳士巴利道半島酒店1樓
www.peninsula.com

■ OPENING HOURS, LAST ORDER
營業時間，最後點菜時間
Lunch/午膳 12:00-14:30 (L.O.)
Dinner/晚膳 18:30-22:30 (L.O.)

■ PRICE/價錢
Lunch/午膳   set/套餐 $280
               à la carte/點菜 $415-705
Dinner/晚膳 à la carte/點菜 $415-705

Cheung Kee
祥記飯店

Things almost seem to spill out onto the colourful street at this compact establishment spread over two small rooms. As they've been going since 1948 and have quite a local following, you'd better book to ensure a place. The extremely good-value menu features honest and earthy dishes that include seafood, casseroles and chicken. But it's the Peking duck that remains the must-have dish. Keep some room for the banana fritters too.

這家設有兩間餐室設備俱全的餐館食客如雲，擁擠情況有如把人客擠寫於多彩多姿的街道上。這家自1948年創業的老店一向有不少忠實食客，如欲前往，最好先行預約，以免向隅。菜餚價錢超值，菜式樸實地道，包括海鮮、砂鍋、雞，而北京填鴨更是不可不吃的招牌菜。注意別吃太飽，留點胃口嚐嚐高力豆沙！

■ ADDRESS/地址
TEL.2529 0707
1F, 75 Lockhart Road, Wan Chai
灣仔駱克道75號1樓

■ OPENING HOURS, LAST ORDER
營業時間，最後點菜時間
12:00-23:30 (L.O.)

■ PRICE/價錢
Lunch/午膳　à la carte/點菜 $150-250
Dinner/晚膳　à la carte/點菜 $150-250

Chez Patrick (Soho)

14

Tucked away in a characterful pedestrianised street where the local market takes place, this is a little corner of France. The restaurant is neatly decorated throughout in black, grey and white. A short set-price menu is supplemented by suggestions of the day that might includes foie gras and smoked salmon terrine. Monsieur Patrick in fact prepares the smoked ingredients himself.

在熙來攘往的街市行人尊用區街角裡暗藏着法國風情。餐廳裝潢以黑、灰、白為主色。定價餐單菜式不多，但附有每日精選菜式，有時包括鵝肝或煙三文魚批。事實上，煙燻食材均由法籍主人Patrick親自烹煮。

■ ADDRESS/地址
TEL.2541 1401
26 Peel Street, Soho, Central
中環卑利街26號
www.chezpatrick.hk

■ ANNUAL AND WEEKLY CLOSING
　　休息日期
Closed Sunday
週日休息

■ OPENING HOURS, LAST ORDER
　　營業時間，最後點菜時間
Lunch/午膳 12:00-14:30 (L.O.)
Dinner/晚膳 18:45-22:30 (L.O.)

■ PRICE/價錢
Lunch/午膳　set/套餐　　$ 199-329
Dinner/晚膳　set/套餐　　$ 499-599

Chez Patrick (Wan Chai)

Located in a discreet little street with two levels, Chez Patrick's elegant black and white decor attempts to bring the atmosphere of a typical Parisian apartment to Wan Chai. Waiters crying "bon appétit" as glasses of Cognac, Armagnac and Calvados chink to the sound of French music helps complete a successful Gallic transplant. The romantic ambience is enhanced with a candle lighting on each table; the cuisine is reassuringly traditional.

Chez Patrick位處一條不顯眼的小街，樓高兩層，優雅的黑白裝飾嘗試為灣仔帶來典型巴黎公寓的味道。縈繞的法國音樂，襯托著盛載著干邑、雅馬邑、和蘋果酒的酒杯碰杯聲，服務員並同時大喊「bon appétit」，營造完美的法國氣氛。每張枱上都有點亮燭光，增添餐廳的浪漫情調。餐廳供應的絕對是傳統的菜餚。

■ ADDRESS/地址

TEL.2527 1408
8-9 Sun Street, Wan Chai
灣仔日街8-9號
www.chezpatrick.hk

■ ANNUAL AND WEEKLY CLOSING
　休息日期
Closed 4 days Lunar New Year and Sunday except Public Holidays
農曆新年4天及週日(公眾假期除外)休息

■ OPENING HOURS, LAST ORDER
　營業時間，最後點菜時間
Lunch/午膳 12:00-14:30 (L.O.)
Dinner/晚膳 19:00-22:00 (L.O.)

■ PRICE/價錢
Lunch/午膳　set/套餐　　$199
Dinner/晚膳　set/套餐　　$499

Chilli Fagara
麻辣燙

Chillies are a passion here! The window's filled with them, as well as orange flames, which act as a forewarning! Rich red walls create an intimate atmosphere. The heat is turned up as you progress from mild 'natural' dishes through to the likes of red hot chilli prawn – only for the very brave. Caramelized banana and chrysanthemum tea cool things down at the end. A sweet ambience prevails as the small team ensures all runs smoothly.

這裡充滿辣椒的激情！窗口充滿著辣椒，而橙色的火焰就像是預警！濃豔的紅牆營造親切的氣氛，當你從溫和的「普 通」菜式吃到辣椒蝦之類的菜餚時，便會渾身發熱！當然，只有夠膽的人才會一嚐後者。最後可用拔絲香蕉及菊花茶涼快下來。為數不多的員工，和諧的團隊合作，令餐廳運作順暢，更顯溫馨。

■ ADDRESS/地址

TEL.2893 3330

Shop E, GF, 51A Graham Street, Soho, Central

中環嘉咸街51A地下舖

www.chillifagara.com

■ ANNUAL AND WEEKLY CLOSING
　　休息日期

Closed 8 days Lunar New Year

農曆新年8天

■ OPENING HOURS, LAST ORDER
　　營業時間，最後點菜時間

Lunch/午膳 11:30-14:00 (L.O.)

Dinner/晚膳 17:00-23:00 (L.O.)

■ PRICE/價錢

Lunch/午膳　set/套餐　　　$78

Dinner/晚膳　à la carte/點菜 $220-400

Chiu Chow Garden (Tsuen Wan)
潮江春 (荃灣)

✕✕

⛶70

Although it may take a little while to travel to the end of the MTR line, you will find this Maxim group restaurant will still be busy during peak hours. Chiu Chow Garden is situated in a shopping centre that is conveniently integrated to Tsuen Wan station. Instead of ordering from the main menu, opt for the little sheets of colourful papers which offer a range of dim sums and small dishes at great prices.

要前往港鐵線的終點可能得花點時間，但你會發現，美心集團旗下的這家餐廳於繁忙時段依然擠滿食客。潮江春所處的商場直通港鐵荃灣站。與其從主餐牌點菜，倒不如拿取不同顏色的點心小菜紙——價錢相宜。

■ ADDRESS/地址
TEL.2498 3381
Shop 10-12, 2F, Luk Yeung Galleria, 22-66 Wai Tsuen Road, Tsuen Wan, New Territories
新界荃灣蕙荃路22-66號綠楊坊2樓 10-12號舖
www.maxims.com.hk

■ OPENING HOURS, LAST ORDER
營業時間，最後點菜時間
Lunch/午膳　08:00-16:00 (L.O.)
Dinner/晚膳　18:00-23:00 (L.O.)

■ PRICE/價錢
Lunch/午膳　set/套餐　　　　$75-160
　　　　　　à la carte/點菜 $40-700
Dinner/晚膳　à la carte/點菜 $160-700

Chuen Kee Seafood
全記海鮮菜館

Two family-run restaurants overlook a pleasant harbour to distant islands; choose the one with the rooftop terrace and the quay-side (plastic) seats. An extraordinary range of seafood is available from adjacent fishmongers': cuttlefish, bivalve, crab and lobster, mollusc, shrimps, prawns... Go to the tank, select your meal, and minutes later it appears in front of you, steamed, poached, or wok fried. Then settle back and watch the boats go by.

這兩家餐廳是家族生意，位置優越，可觀賞海港及離島。天台陽台那一家，以及碼頭邊的塑膠座位備受推介。這裡海鮮種類繁多，包括墨魚、貝殼、 蟹、龍蝦、賴尿蝦、大蝦小蝦等等。你可以到魚缸挑選你的海鮮， 蒸、 燉、炒也好，幾分鐘後便會奉到餐桌上，成為你的食物。然後你便可輕鬆地細賞船艇來來往往。

■ ADDRESS/地址
TEL.2792 6938
53 Hoi Pong Street, Sai Kung
西貢海傍街53號

■ OPENING HOURS, LAST ORDER
營業時間，最後點菜時間
11:00-23:00 L.O. 22:30

■ PRICE/價錢
Lunch/午膳　set/套餐　　　$ 174
　　　　　　à la carte/點菜 $ 130-300
Dinner/晚膳　set/套餐　　　$ 174
　　　　　　à la carte/點菜 $ 130-300

Cinecittà

This big, modern restaurant has one outstanding feature: a big screen showing Italian movies – well, it's not called Cinecitta for nothing! And if you tire of the films, there's always the food – Roman specialities and traditional Italian dishes are respected here, accompanied by warm, smiley service. Taglioni, green ravioli and tortelloni are bases for tasty specialities, while many Italian wines appear from a spectacular glass cellar.

播著意大利電影的闊螢幕是這家寬闊的現代餐廳令人注目的特徵-名副其實的Cinecitta！如果你對電影沒甚興趣，這裡還有美食一羅馬特色菜及意大利菜餚備受喜愛。此外，這裡的服務親切，服務員笑面迎人。美食首推Taglioni(意大利麵條)、嫩菜雲吞及其他自製雲吞，而壯觀的玻璃酒窖提供的意大利酒更是目不暇給。

■ ADDRESS/地址
TEL.2529 0199
GF, Starcrest Building, 9 Star Street, Wan Chai
灣仔星街9號星域軒地下
www.elite-concept.com

■ ANNUAL AND WEEKLY CLOSING
  休息日期
Closed Saturday lunch and Sunday lunch
週六、日午膳休息

■ OPENING HOURS, LAST ORDER
  營業時間，最後點菜時間
Lunch/午膳 12:00-15:00 (L.O.)
Dinner/晚膳 18:00-23:30 (L.O.)
■ PRICE/價錢
Lunch/午膳 set/套餐 $168
       à la carte/點菜 $250-500
Dinner/晚膳 à la carte/點菜 $250-500

Crystal Jade La Mian Xiao Long Bao (Kowloon Bay)
翡翠拉麵小籠包 (九龍灣)

Slightly smaller than the other establishments in this group; this restaurant, with its mix of round tables and booths, gets particularly busy during lunch but the young, efficient and attentive serving team appear to have no trouble at all! Although famous for their pork dumplings, they also make a splendid steam fish with bean paste and some great appetisers as well. Dishes are prepared using good ingredients and prices are sensible.

此店與集團其他分店相比顯得略小，設有圓桌及卡座，在午飯時分總是忙不過來——幸而年輕、有效率、細心的服務團隊對此駕輕就熟！雖然小籠包是其名菜，但豉汁蒸魚及其他出色前菜亦毫不遜色。食材優質，價格合理。

■ ADDRESS/地址
TEL.2305 9990
Shop 520, 5F, Telford Plaza II,
Kowloon Bay
九龍灣德福廣場2期520號舖

■ ANNUAL AND WEEKLY CLOSING
　休息日期
Closed 2 days Lunar New Year
農曆新年休息2天

■ OPENING HOURS, LAST ORDER
　營業時間，最後點菜時間
11:00-23:00 (L.O.)

■ PRICE/價錢
Lunch/午膳　à la carte/點菜 $ 100-250
Dinner/晚膳　à la carte/點菜 $ 100-250

Crystal Jade La Mian Xiao Long Bao (TST)
翡翠拉麵小籠包 (尖沙咀)

Could this be Harbour City Mall's most popular eatery? Very probably. It's a modern cafeteria that buzzes all day - if your party is less than four strong, you'll be eating communally with strangers. The food – a mix of Northern Chinese and Sichuan, prepared in a sizzling semi-open kitchen – is very fresh, aromatic and tasty. Signature dishes include steamed pork dumpling with warm soup, or la Mian hand-made noodles with shrimp and cashew nuts.

這裡是海港城裡最受歡迎的食肆嗎？很可能是。這是家整天繁忙的餐廳，如果同行少於四人，你們很可能要和人併桌而坐。食物混合了中國北方菜式和四川菜，在熱烘烘的半開放式廚房烹調，非常新鮮，既香又美味。招牌菜包括上海小籠包、四川擔擔拉麵。

■ ADDRESS/地址
TEL.2622 2699
Shop 3328, 3F, Gateway Arcade, Harbour City, Canton Road, Tsim Sha Tsui, Kowloon
九龍尖沙咀廣東道海港城港威商場3樓
3328號舖

■ OPENING HOURS, LAST ORDER
營業時間，最後點菜時間
11:00-23:00 L.O. 22:30

■ PRICE/價錢
Lunch/午膳　à la carte/點菜 $100-250
Dinner/晚膳　à la carte/點菜 $100-250

Crystal Jade La Mian Xiao Long Bao (Wan Chai)
翡翠拉麵小籠包 (灣仔)

This relative newcomer to the dining scene has already established a reputation for its Shanghai dumplings and noodles. The modern, slightly retro looking diner, with its plush booths, has light flooding through its third floor location. The place positively buzzes with atmosphere and there is a distinct air of satisfaction from its customers. Being a pre-eminent member of the group, they also specialise in shark fin.

這位餐飲界的新貴在上海小籠包及麵食上已享負盛名。餐廳裝潢在現代中帶點懷舊，設有絲絨卡座，雖然位於三樓依然吸引不少食客。餐廳氣氛熱鬧，從中清楚感受到顧客的滿足。作為集團的新星，魚翅亦是餐廳的主打。

■ ADDRESS/地址
TEL.2573 8844
Shop 310, 3F, Tai Yau Plaza, Wan Chai
灣仔大有廣場3樓310號舖

■ ANNUAL AND WEEKLY CLOSING
　休息日期
Closed 2 days Lunar New Year
農曆新年休息2天

■ OPENING HOURS, LAST ORDER
　營業時間，最後點菜時間
11:00-22:30 (L.O.)

■ PRICE/價錢
Lunch/午膳　à la carte/點菜 $ 100-300
Dinner/晚膳　à la carte/點菜 $ 100-300

Cucina

A chill-out atmosphere, great views and design focusing on beautiful natural materials all add up to a relaxed but fashionable interior. Factor in an extremely diverse menu that includes Chinese noodles, pan Asian combinations and a hefty dollop of Italian dishes, and you end up with something uniquely interesting. Not only do the chefs dazzle you with their technique, they also suggest wines to go with what they're cooking.

餐廳氣氛輕鬆，景色壯麗，設計更採用美麗的自然素材，交織成輕鬆而時尚的室內空間。餐單讓人目不暇給，菜式極為多樣化，囊括中式麵點、亞洲菜和多不勝數的意大利菜式，食客定能選擇獨特迷人的美食。主廚烹調技巧出色，讓你大開眼界，亦會推介配搭佳餚的美酒。

■ ADDRESS/地址

TEL.2113 0808

6F, Marco Polo Hotel, Harbour City,
Canton Road, Tsim Sha Tsui, Kowloon
九龍尖沙咀廣東道海港城馬哥孛羅酒店6樓
www.cucinahk.com

■ OPENING HOURS, LAST ORDER
   營業時間，最後點菜時間
Lunch/午膳 12:00-15:00 L.O. 14:30
Dinner/晚膳 18:00-23:00 L.O. 22:30

■ PRICE/價錢
Lunch/午膳   set/套餐 $ 180-220
             à la carte/點菜 $ 250-1,300
Dinner/晚膳 à la carte/點菜 $ 600-1,300

Cuisine Cuisine
國金軒

This fashionably decorated room easily seats 200 people; but before you're escorted to your table, with its fine harbour view, select a fish from the tank, to be served with their own specially-brewed soy sauce. This place is light and airy at lunchtime but more intimately lit at night. Cantonese specialities include sautéed crystal king prawns, braised shark fin with crab claws and steamed egg white and honey-glazed barbecue pork.

國金軒毗鄰亮明居，裝潢極盡奢華，且能輕易容納約二百人。你可以從容地先在魚缸挑選鮮魚，然後國金軒會用自製醬油清蒸，再在侍應帶領下施然走到飽覽醉人海景的餐桌。午飯時間的氣氛輕鬆悠閒，晚上則燈光璀璨。粵菜精選包括水晶大蝦球，荷香茗燻雞及蜜餞叉燒皇。

■ ADDRESS/地址
TEL.2393 3933
Shop 3101, Podium Level 3, IFC Mall, 8 Finance Street, Central
中環金融街8號國際金融中心商場3樓3101號舖
www.cuisinecuisine.hk

■ OPENING HOURS, LAST ORDER
營業時間，最後點菜時間
Lunch/午膳 12:00-14:30 (L.O.)
Dinner/晚膳 18:00-22:30 (L.O.)

■ PRICE/價錢
Lunch/午膳   set/套餐 $298-398
             à la carte/點菜 $250-1,300
Dinner/晚膳 à la carte/點菜 $250-1,300

Da Ping Huo
大平伙

This charming, hidden restaurant is ideal for those wanting something a little different. It is run by a couple from Sichuan: he is an artist and his wife a singer. Here she cooks a nightly 12 course menu, using authentic and family-style Sichuan recipes while he welcomes the guests into his modern and elegant restaurant which he created himself. And at the end of the meal, he'll usually sing one or two folk songs.

這家獨具魅力卻鮮為人知的餐廳讓追求不平凡的人士有更多選擇。餐廳由一對來自四川的夫婦經營：丈夫是藝術家，太太則是歌手。太太負責烹調十二道菜的晚餐，以正宗四川家庭菜譜炮製，丈夫則負責招待賓客進入由他親自設計，既現代又優雅的餐廳。杯盤狼藉之際，他通常會高歌一兩首民謠。

■ ADDRESS/地址
TEL.2559 1317
LG, Hilltop Plaza, 49 Hollywood Road, Central
中環荷李活道49號鴻豐商業中心地下低層

■ ANNUAL AND WEEKLY CLOSING
　　休息日期
Closed 1 week Lunar New Year, Easter, mid-August, Christmas and Sunday
農曆新年7天、復活節、8月中、聖誕節及週日休息

■ OPENING HOURS, LAST ORDER
　　營業時間，最後點菜時間
Dinner/晚飯 18:30-21:00 (L.O.)

■ PRICE/價錢
Dinner/晚膳　set/套餐　　$280

Dim Sum
譽滿坊

Get here early to beat the loyal Happy Valley following. There's a cosy and homely charm here defined by closely set tables: peek across at nearby diners to see what they've ordered. Start with the steamed dumplings, Leong Har Gao and Siu Mai. Top three dim sums in the luxury section are Yu Chee Gao, abalone Siu Mai and Koon Yin Gao. Also worth trying are Loong Har Tong (lobster bisque) and Goon Tong Gao (soup with giant Chinese dumpling).

早一點抵埗，在跑馬地的信眾到來前搶先入座。這裡餐桌排列緊密，既舒適又有在家中的感覺：你可以偷偷看鄰座的食客點了甚麼。先試燕液蝦餃、竹笙龍蝦餃和鮑翅燒賣，而比較昂貴的有最受歡迎的三大點心一鮮蝦魚翅餃、BB鮑燒賣和官燕鮮蝦餃。此外，竹笙龍蝦湯和鮑翅灌湯餃亦值得一試。

■ ADDRESS/地址

TEL.2834 8893
63 Shing Woo Road, Happy Valley
跑馬地成和道63號

■ ANNUAL AND WEEKLY CLOSING
　　休息日期
Closed Lunar New Year
年初一休息

■ OPENING HOURS, LAST ORDER
　　營業時間，最後點菜時間
Lunch/午膳　11:00-16:30 (L.O.)
Dinner/晚膳　18:00-22:30 (L.O.)

■ PRICE/價錢
Lunch/午膳　à la carte/點菜 $ 105-240
Dinner/晚膳　à la carte/點菜 $ 135-280

Din Tai Fung
鼎泰豐

📦14 🚫🍴

Mr Yang opened up his dumpling shop in Taiwan back in 1958 and focused on delivering service, price and quality; there are now branches in all major Asian cities. Fresh, handmade Shanghai dumplings are their speciality and they are extremely good; the steamed pork ones being especially tasty. Queues are the norm here, but don't worry: a team of 130 smart and efficient staff serve at least 1000 people a day and take it all in their stride.

楊先生在1958年於台灣開辦其第一家小籠包店,特別注重服務、價格及品質; 如今,已在所有主要亞洲城市開辦分店。新鮮手包的上海小籠包是餐廳主打, 令人食指大動;蒸豬肉餡更是美味。店前總擠滿排隊等候的人,但不用擔心: 由130名員工組成精明有效率的服務團隊,每天服務最少一千名客人,令人賓 至如歸。

■ ADDRESS/地址

TEL.2730 6928
Shop 130 & Restaurant C, 3F,
Silvercord, 30 Canton Road, Tsim Sha
Tsui, Kowloon
九龍尖沙咀廣東路30號新港中心3樓C130號舖

■ ANNUAL AND WEEKLY CLOSING
    休息日期
Closed 3 days Lunar New Year
農曆新年休息3天

■ OPENING HOURS, LAST ORDER
    營業時間,最後點菜時間
11:30-22:30 (L.O.)

■ PRICE/價錢
Lunch/午膳   à la carte/點菜 $90-160
Dinner/晚膳   à la carte/點菜 $90-160

DiVino

This belongs to a stable of reliable Italian restaurants dotted around Hong Kong. It's simpler than the others and is really more of a wine bar, boasting a list of over 150 Italian wines, many of which are available by the glass. It offers a casual and relaxed atmosphere in a stylish and inviting atmosphere. The cuisine is authentic Italian with a wide range of dishes. Platters for sharing are often the popular choice.

DiVino是本港具質素的義大利餐廳之一，設計較其他餐廳簡單，主要是以供應葡萄酒為主的酒吧，提供超過150種義大利酒的名單，大部份提供杯裝。餐廳提供輕鬆自在的氣氛，既時尚又吸引。餐飲是正宗義大利菜，有一系列主配菜可供選擇。可供多人分享的拼盤是人氣之選。

■ ADDRESS/地址
TEL.2167 8883
73 Wyndham Street, Central
中環雲咸街73號
www.divino.com.uk

■ ANNUAL AND WEEKLY CLOSING
　休息日期
Closed Sunday lunch
週日午膳休息

■ OPENING HOURS, LAST ORDER
　營業時間，最後點菜時間
Lunch/午膳 12:00-15:00 (L.O.)
Dinner/晚膳 18:00-23:00 (L.O.)

■ PRICE/價錢
Lunch/午膳　set/套餐　　　$170
Dinner/晚膳　à la carte/點菜 $350-600

Domani

The talented Italian chef puts his own interpretation on classic combinations and in doing so creates some of the more original Italian cooking found in Hong Kong, with seafood being the speciality. The room, within a glass structure on Pacific Place offering good views and natural light, is elegantly furnished, with an open kitchen and a wave patterned ceiling. The wine list is comprehensive and there is an appealing weekly lunch menu.

才華洋溢的義籍廚師以自創風格詮釋傳統組合，並透過此法成功打造全港最原汁原味的義大利菜之一，以海鮮菜式為招牌菜。房間在太古廣場的玻璃部份當中，提供絕佳景觀及自然光，且經過精緻裝潢，附有開放式廚房及波浪形天花。酒牌提供不少選擇，每週午市套餐亦相當吸引。

■ ADDRESS/地址

TEL.2111 1197
Shop 406, Level 4, Pacific Place, 88 Queensway, Admiralty
金鐘金鐘道88號太古廣場4樓406號舖
www.domani.hk

■ OPENING HOURS, LAST ORDER
營業時間，最後點菜時間
Lunch/午膳 12:00-15:00 (L.O.)
Dinner/晚膳 19:00-23:00 (L.O.)

■ PRICE/價錢

Lunch/午膳	set/套餐	$310-350
	à la carte/點菜	$550-780
Dinner/晚膳	set/套餐	$980
	à la carte/點菜	$550-780

Dong Lai Shun
東來順

The first Dong Lai Shun was founded over a hundred years ago in Peking, and has been successfully transplanted to the basement of the Royal Garden hotel. Its décor is contemporary with distinct Asian nuances, such as panels and paintings; there's a water feature which creates a relaxing atmosphere. The mix of Beijing and Huaiyang recipes includes hot pot, Peking duck and 'shuan yang rou': paper thin slices of inner Mongolian black-headed mutton.

享譽百載的東來順始創於北京，其後成功遷移到帝苑酒店地庫層。餐廳的裝修揉合了現代和傳統格調；鮮明細緻的亞洲特色，從牆板和壁畫便可略窺一二。這裡的人工噴泉更營造了輕鬆的氣氛。食物方面，餐廳的北京和淮陽菜共冶一爐，包括火鍋、北京填鴨，以及「涮羊肉」：採用內蒙黑頭白羊的上乘部分，肉質薄如紙，軟如棉。

■ ADDRESS/地址
TEL.2733 2020
B2F, The Royal Garden Hotel, 69 Mody Road, East Tsim Sha Tsui, Kowloon
九龍尖東麼地道69號帝苑酒店地庫2樓
www.rghk.com.hk

■ OPENING HOURS, LAST ORDER
營業時間，最後點菜時間
Lunch/午膳 11:30-14:30 (L.O.)
Dinner/晚膳 18:00-22:30 (L.O.)

■ PRICE/價錢

Lunch/午膳	set/套餐	$88-110
	à la carte/點菜	$250-680
Dinner/晚膳	set/套餐	$280-480
	à la carte/點菜	$250-680

Dot Cod

⏷20

That this is owned by the Hong Kong Cricket Club has some bearing on the atmosphere which can get quite raucous, especially if you end up sitting near the bar when there's a match on. If you're after a more genteel time, ask for a table in the back room. The menu here of course majors on seafood but there are salads, grills and pasta dishes as well. Anyone concerned about fish sustainability should consult the menu or ask the staff.

Dot Cod是香港木球會旗下對外開放的會所餐廳，因此氣氛有時頗為狂熱，尤其是球賽舉行期間，愈近酒吧區，愈是喧鬧。如果你想享受寧靜時光，建議要求廳後面的座位。餐單主要是海鮮菜式，此外還有沙律、烤肉和意大利麵可供選擇。如果你關注海鮮的新鮮程度，可以參考餐單或向餐廳職員查詢。

■ ADDRESS/地址
TEL.2810 6988
B4F, Prince's Building, 10 Charter Road, Central
中環遮打道10號太子大廈地庫4樓
www.dotcod.com

■ ANNUAL AND WEEKLY CLOSING
　休息日期
Closed Sunday and Public Holidays
週日及公眾假期休息

■ OPENING HOURS, LAST ORDER
　營業時間，最後點菜時間
Lunch/午膳　12:00-14:30 (L.O.)
Dinner/晚膳　18:00-22:30 (L.O.)

■ PRICE/價錢
Lunch/午膳　set/套餐　　　　　$238
　　　　　　à la carte/點菜 $340-530
Dinner/晚膳　à la carte/點菜 $340-530

D17

You have the option of watching the chefs in the open kitchen from the seafood counter or the plush and intimate dining room that seats a maximum of 35. The food is a blend of French and Italian with some contemporary twists; there is even the occasional Asian note. There are original seafood creations to start and classic grills to follow. The whole operation is overseen by a highly diligent serving team.

你可以選擇從海鮮吧桌觀看開放式廚房內觀看大廚烹調,或是豪華緊密的飯廳,最多可容納三十五人。食物融合了法國和義大利風格,加上現代巧思變化;有時甚至帶點亞洲風味。嚐過原創海鮮創作後,尚有經典烤肉。餐廳運作由極其勤勞的服務團隊包辦。

■ ADDRESS/地址

TEL.3907 0090

17F, Continental Diamond Plaza, 525 Hennessy Road, Causeway Bay
銅鑼灣軒尼詩道525號恆和鑽石大廈17樓
www.givemefive.hk

■ ANNUAL AND WEEKLY CLOSING
   休息日期
Closed Lunar New Year
年初一休息

■ OPENING HOURS, LAST ORDER
   營業時間,最後點菜時間
Lunch/午膳 12:00-14:30 (L.O.)
Dinner/晚膳 18:00-22:30 (L.O.)

■ PRICE/價錢
Lunch/午膳   set/套餐 $ 128-238
              à la carte/點菜 $ 250-500
Dinner/晚膳   à la carte/點菜 $ 250-500

Dynasty (Tsim Sha Tsui)
滿福樓 (尖沙咀)

Suckling pig and barbecued pork are the highlights of the traditionally Cantonese menu that also incorporates other specialities, including braised sliced abalone with goose webs and mango and pomelo sago sweet soup. The restaurant's interior is themed to recreate the charms of a Chinese tea house and has interesting crockery to match. The friendly and attentive service is of note.

乳豬和叉燒是滿福樓的名菜，但傳統的廣東菜譜上亦不乏其他精選菜色，包括鮮鮑扣鵝掌與楊枝甘露。餐館的裝潢以突出中國茶樓的魅力為主，並配以精美餐具。友善而細心的服務值得留意。

■ ADDRESS/地址
TEL.2734 6688
4F, Renaissance Kowloon Hotel,
22 Salisbury Road, Tsim Sha Tsui,
Kowloon
九龍尖沙咀梳士巴利道22號萬麗酒店4樓

■ OPENING HOURS, LAST ORDER
　營業時間，最後點菜時間
Lunch/午膳 11:30-14:30 (L.O.)
Dinner/晚膳 18:30-23:00 (L.O.)

■ PRICE/價錢
Lunch/午膳 　à la carte/點菜 $180-1,200
Dinner/晚膳 　à la carte/點菜 $210-1,200

Dynasty (Wan Chai)
滿福樓 (灣仔)

The flying fairy motif is on everything but is used to good effect to highlight the Cantonese menu's signature dishes, which are well worth trying: traditional plates of barbecue pork, roast pigeon, and steamed crab claw, along with family-style dishes of boiled rice in clay pots with chicken and salted fish. Desserts are done particularly well. Dine beside the convincing-looking palm trees, here on the third floor of the hotel.

天外飛仙的主題無處不在，用以點出粵菜菜單中值得一試的招牌菜更為適合：古法叉燒拼盤、燒乳鴿、蒸蟹鉗，還有住家風味的鹹魚雞粒煲仔飯。甜品特別出色。雖然身處酒店三樓，你仍可在幾可亂真的棕櫚樹旁用餐。

■ ADDRESS/地址

TEL.2584 6971

3F, Renaissance Harbour View Hotel, 1 Harbour Road, Wan Chai

灣仔港灣道1號萬麗海景酒店3樓

www.renaissancehotels.com/HKGHV

■ OPENING HOURS, LAST ORDER

營業時間，最後點菜時間

Lunch/午膳 12:00-15:00 (L.O.)
Dinner/晚膳 18:30-23:00 (L.O.)

■ PRICE/價錢

Lunch/午膳	set/套餐	$690-880
	à la carte/點菜	$300-650
Dinner/晚膳	set/套餐	$690-880
	à la carte/點菜	$300-650

Eighteen Brook
十八溪

Handily placed if you want to reach Wan Chai from mainland Hong Kong, the restaurant is close to the Star Ferry pier. An elevator brings you to the eighth floor of the convention plaza, where you will find an aquarium at the door but, alas, an absence of good views inside. Well-distanced tables; a gourmet destination, with specialities like sliced prawn with green crab and egg white, or steamed conpoy rice with sliced chicken, yunnan ham and mushroom.

餐廳毗鄰灣仔天星碼頭，從九龍半島到這裡十分便利。乘搭電梯直達會展廣場八樓，便可看見大門的魚缸，但可惜餐廳內沒有景觀。餐桌間距離適中，提供的美食包括珊瑚貴妃鮮蝦片、或者竹籠蟹子瑤柱麒麟雞飯。

■ ADDRESS/地址
TEL.2827 8802
8F, Convention Plaza, 1 Harbour Road, Wan Chai
灣仔港灣道1號會展廣場8樓

■ OPENING HOURS, LAST ORDER
營業時間，最後點菜時間
Lunch/午膳 11:30-15:00 (L.O.)
Dinner/晚膳 17:30-23:30 (L.O.)

■ PRICE/價錢
Lunch/午膳   set/套餐 $ 168
              à la carte/點菜 $ 300-450
Dinner/晚膳 set/套餐 $ 415
              à la carte/點菜 $ 300-450

Farm House
農圃

In a sleek business building, this contemporary-style dining room has private rooms leading off as well as a huge aquarium running the length of one entire wall. The Cantonese menu uses exceedingly fresh ingredients and includes such specialities as shark's fin soup, abalone and chicken wings all of which are exceedingly tasty and well-priced. The staffs are very courteous and professional.

這家飯店位處線條流麗的商業大廈當中，並備有富現代感的獨立餐室和沿著牆身一路延伸的巨型水族箱。粵菜選用特級新鮮材料炮製而成，名菜有魚翅羹、鮑魚和雞翼，味道超凡，價錢相宜。員工非常專業有禮。

■ ADDRESS/地址

TEL.2881 1331
1F, Phase 1, Ming An Plaza, 8 Sunning Road, Causeway Bay
銅鑼灣新寧道民安廣場1期1樓
www.farmhouse.com.hk

■ OPENING HOURS, LAST ORDER
 營業時間，最後點菜時間
Lunch/午膳 11:00-15:00 L.O. 14:45
Dinner/晚膳 18:00-24:00 L.O. 23:00

■ PRICE/價錢
Lunch/午膳 set/套餐 $230
     à la carte/點菜 $210-1,000
Dinner/晚膳 set/套餐 $300
     à la carte/點菜 $210-1,000

Fook Lam Moon (Kowloon)
福臨門 (九龍)

This Kowloon branch may have fewer business people among its customers than the one in Wanchai but it shares the same principles: fresh, seasonal ingredients treated with the utmost care. The result is that this refined Cantonese cooking has been attracting a loyal following since the restaurant opened in 1972. The family owners are always around and their staff share their zeal for maintaining high standards of food and service.

與灣仔店相比，光顧此九龍分店的商務人士可能較少，但原則一致：以新鮮、時令材料精心炮製。得出的是極其精緻的粵菜，難怪自1972年開業迄今吸引不少忠實捧場客。開辦酒家的家族成員經常駐守，酒家員工亦同樣秉承對高品質餐飲及服務的追求。

■ ADDRESS/地址
TEL.2366 0286
53-59 Kimberley Road, Tsim Sha Tsui, Kowloon
九龍尖沙咀金巴利道53-59號
www.fooklammoon-grp.com

■ ANNUAL AND WEEKLY CLOSING
休息日期
Closed 3 days Lunar New Year
農曆年休息3天

■ OPENING HOURS, LAST ORDER
營業時間，最後點菜時間
Lunch/午膳 11:30-14:30 (L.O.)
Dinner/晚膳 18:00-22:30 (L.O.)

■ PRICE/價錢

Lunch/午膳	set/套餐	$ 1,500-2,500
	à la carte/點菜	$ 300-2,000
Dinner/晚膳	set/套餐	$ 1,500-2,500
	à la carte/點菜	$ 300-2,000

Fook Lam Moon (Wan Chai)
福臨門 (灣仔)

&♿ ☞ ⛶100 ☎⏧

Newly renovated and spread over three floors, this has been owned by the same family for several generations. The care and attention they've invested is clearly visible in the refinement of the Cantonese cooking. Ingredients don't come any more natural or fresher, there's complete respect for seasonality and a ban on any artificial flavourings. The welcome is warm and the service efficient.

全新裝潢的店面佔地三層,由同一家族數代相傳。提供極盡精緻的廣東菜色,背後付出的心血可見一斑。選用最當造(時 令)的新鮮材料,更嚴禁使用人工添加劑,確保原汁原味。服務員的歡迎之聲令人倍感溫暖,服務亦具效率。

■ ADDRESS/地址
TEL.2866 0663
35-45 Johnston Road, Wan Chai
灣仔莊士敦道35-45號
www.fooklammoon-grp.com

■ ANNUAL AND WEEKLY CLOSING
　休息日期
Closed 3 days Lunar New Year
農曆新年休息3天

■ OPENING HOURS, LAST ORDER
　營業時間,最後點菜時間
Lunch/午膳 11:30-14:30 (L.O.)
Dinner/晚膳 18:00-22:30 (L.O.)

■ PRICE/價錢
Lunch/午膳　set/套餐　　$400-2,750
　　　　　　à la carte/點菜 $800-2,750
Dinner/晚膳　set/套餐　　$400-2,750
　　　　　　à la carte/點菜 $800-2,750

Forum
富臨

You cannot fail to notice the pictures of owner-chef Yeung Koon Yat. For over thirty years he's been attracting everyone from world leaders to locals to his Forum restaurant, thanks largely to his celebrated speciality: abalone. His fried bird's nest and shark's fin soup are noteworthy too but it is for the abalone cooked in a clay pot that many come. The restaurant is spread over three floors, with seating for around 150.

你肯定會留意到世界御廚楊貫一的照片。三十多年來，光顧他的客人從世界領導人到本地食客包羅萬有，這大概應歸功於他的拿手名菜：阿一鮑魚。大部分客人都為其砂鍋鮑魚慕名而來，而皇冠燕盞及紅燒翅也相當不俗。飯店佔地三層，可容納約一百五十人。

■ ADDRESS/地址
TEL.2891 2555
485 Lockhart Road, Causeway Bay
銅鑼灣駱克道485號

■ OPENING HOURS, LAST ORDER
　營業時間，最後點菜時間
Lunch/午膳　11:00-15:00 (L.O.)
Dinner/晚膳　18:00-23:00 (L.O.)

■ PRICE/價錢

Lunch/午膳	set/套餐	$1,400-2,600
	à la carte/點菜	$400-2,000
Dinner/晚膳	set/套餐	$1,400-2,600
	à la carte/點菜	$600-2,000

Fung Lum
楓林小館

Located opposite the station and known for its striking façade, this is the original Fung Lum; the famed replica in Los Angeles was a hit in the 1980s. The recipes remain untarnished to this day, with the seafood being highly recommended, particularly the baked shrimps with salt and lobster and the crab with black beans. Regulars believe the pigeon is a must. If ordering several dishes, just ask for them to be paced accordingly.

位於車站對面的楓林小館正面的設計讓人印象深刻；這是原汁原味的楓林；洛杉磯著名的複製品在一九八零年代曾一度讓人瘋靡。今天菜單依然毫不遜色，尤其推薦海鮮，如鹽焗蝦、龍蝦、豆醬焗蟹。常客相信不能缺少一道乳鴿。如果點了好幾道菜，可交由店員編排次序。

■ ADDRESS/地址

TEL.2692 1175

45-47 Tsuen Nam Road, Tai Wai,
Sha Tin, New Territories
新界沙田大圍村南道45-47號

■ ANNUAL AND WEEKLY CLOSING
　　休息日期
Closed 2 days Lunar New Year
農曆新年休息2天

■ OPENING HOURS, LAST ORDER
　　營業時間，最後點菜時間
Lunch/午膳 11:00-15:00 (L.O.)
Dinner/晚膳 18:00-22:30 L.O. 22:00

■ PRICE/價錢
Lunch/午膳　à la carte/點菜 $240-600
Dinner/晚膳　à la carte/點菜 $240-600

Fu Sing
富聲

Taking the lift up in this stylish modern building will bring you out directly into the plush spacious restaurant with its smart carpeting and wall plates. The service is very attentive and the cooking is equally precise with its broad range of Cantonese dishes. Among the recommendations are stewed abalone and goose web as well as braised cow tail in red wine. Plenty of fresh juices are available and there's a fine collection of cognacs.

進入設計時尚、富現代感的大樓後,升降機帶你直達富麗堂皇、佔地寬廣的餐廳,牆紙和地毯的鋪設均見心思。服務非常周到,烹調方法亦獨具特色,備有一系列粵菜可供選擇。推介菜式包括炆鮑魚鵝掌和紅酒燉牛尾。除了各種鮮榨果汁,店內亦提供精選法國干邑白蘭地。

■ ADDRESS/地址

TEL.2893 0881

1F, 353 Lockhart Road, Sunshine Plaza, Wan Chai
灣仔駱克道353號三湘大廈1樓

■ OPENING HOURS, LAST ORDER
　營業時間,最後點菜時間
Lunch/午膳 11:00-15:00 (L.O.)
Dinner/晚膳 18:00-23:00 (L.O.)

■ PRICE/價錢

Lunch/午膳	set/套餐	$320-680
	à la carte/點菜	$250-450
Dinner/晚膳	set/套餐	$320-680
	à la carte/點菜	$250-450

Gaddi's
吉地士

Gaddi's is truly an institution in the city. A private lift whisks you to this legend celebrating over fifty years of fine dining. Live music and old-style British formality accompanies the French classical cuisine. If you want to make an evening of it you should try the tasting menu. Gaddi's celebrates a by-gone elegance where the proper meaning of dining is taken very seriously. For the gentlemen, don't forget to bring a jacket.

吉地士是城內有名的食府。私人電梯迅速把你把帶到這個超過五十年的優質餐飲傳奇之地。現場音樂和古老英國禮節配襯著經典法國菜。如果想享受美好的晚餐，便要品嚐吉地士的tasting menu。餐廳保留著一種昔日的典雅，餐飲的真正意義得以尊重。男士們，謹記帶上一件西裝外套。

■ ADDRESS/地址

TEL.2920 2888

1F, The Peninsula Hotel, Salisbury Road, Tsim Sha Tsui, Kowloon
九龍尖沙咀梳士巴利道半島酒店1樓
www.peninsula.com

■ OPENING HOURS, LAST ORDER
營業時間，最後點菜時間
Lunch/午膳　12:00-14:30 (L.O.)
Dinner/晚膳　19:00-22:30 (L.O.)

■ PRICE/價錢

Lunch/午膳	set/套餐	$428
	à la carte/點菜	$1,000-1,300
Dinner/晚膳	set/套餐	$1,388
	à la carte/點菜	$1,000-1,300

Gaia

Classy Italian restaurant with a subdued and sober atmosphere enhanced by ambient music, a lovely terrace and, in the evening, the romantic addition of a glowing candle at each table. The welcoming manager ensures that you have a meal to remember. Fresh ingredients from Italy help create memorable dishes such as homemade pasta tossed in a rabbit-stew style ragout, or sautéed veal chop with porcini mushrooms and goose liver sauce.

這優質的意大利餐廳，在音樂襯托下，宜人的平台花園，氣氛典雅而莊嚴。尤其在傍晚時分，每張桌上點起蠟燭，增添浪漫氣氛。好客的經理確保客人對這一餐留下深刻印象。餐廳採用從意大利運來的新鮮材料，烹調令人難忘的菜餚。例如蔬菜雜燴拌自製意大利麵，或嫩煎小牛扒配磨菇及鵝肝醬。

■ ADDRESS/地址
TEL.2167 8200
GF, Grand Millennium Plaza, 181
Queen's Road, Central
中環皇后大道中181號新紀元廣場地下
www.gaiaristorante.com

■ ANNUAL AND WEEKLY CLOSING
   休息日期
Closed Lunar New Year
年初一休息

■ OPENING HOURS, LAST ORDER
   營業時間，最後點菜時間
Lunch/午膳 12:00-15:00 (L.O.)
Dinner/晚膳 18:00-23:00 (L.O.)

■ PRICE/價錢
Lunch/午膳 set/套餐 $248
               à la carte/點菜 $370-700
Dinner/晚膳 à la carte/點菜 $370-700

Goccia

Stairs from the stylish bar lead up to this elegant dining room, with its dramatic contemporary artwork and clubby atmosphere. A quiet terraced area is where you'll find the pizza oven. Most ingredients are imported directly from Italy, including fish and seafood, the signature specialities of Goccia. A lot of effort has gone into the wine list, which offers more than 150 choices and almost 40 by the glass.

位於地下的酒吧散發著時尚的味道，拾級而上就會進入風格鮮明高雅的飯廳，擁有現代藝術品裝飾，氣氛猶如俱樂部。安靜宜人的戶外陽台更設有薄餅爐。絕大部分食材均從意大利空運而來，包括魚類及海鮮，都是餐廳的招牌菜。想必在酒牌也花了不少心思——提供超過150種選擇，將近40種提供杯裝。

■ ADDRESS/地址
TEL.2167 8181
73 Wyndham Street, Central
中環雲咸街73號
www.goccia.com.uk

■ ANNUAL AND WEEKLY CLOSING
   休息日期
Closed Saturday lunch, Sunday lunch and Public Holidays lunch
週六、日午膳及公眾假期午膳休息

■ OPENING HOURS, LAST ORDER
   營業時間，最後點菜時間
Lunch/午膳 12:00-14:30 (L.O.)
Dinner/晚膳 18:00-23:00 (L.O.)

■ PRICE/價錢
Lunch/午膳   set/套餐 $175-266
            à la carte/點菜 $360-550
Dinner/晚膳 à la carte/點菜 $360-550

Golden Bauhinia
金紫荊

🚾 👉 **P** 🍴14

Conveniently located for visitors to the Hong Kong Convention and Exhibition Centre (and not far from the ferry pier either), this large dining room may be monochrome in tone but it is ideally positioned for admiring the Bauhinia sculpture. Specialities include steamed bean curd with shrimp and scallop in fish soup, and sautéed prawns with honey beans and fungus. Great care is taken with the service.

前往香港會議展覽中心的人士可輕易找到這家餐廳,離碼頭亦是咫尺之遙。偌大的餐廳配色可能較為單一,但欣賞金紫荊雕像則是一流位置。特色小菜包括:海皇魚湯浸豆腐及蜜豆愉耳炒蝦球。服務非常細心。

■ ADDRESS/地址
TEL.2582 7728
Hong Kong Convention and Exhibition Centre, Golden Bauhinia Square, Expo Drive East, Wan Chai
灣仔博覽道1號金紫荊廣場香港會議展覽中心地下

■ OPENING HOURS, LAST ORDER
營業時間,最後點菜時間
Lunch/午膳 12:00-14:45 (L.O.)
Dinner/晚膳 18:30-22:45 (L.O.)

■ PRICE/價錢
Lunch/午膳   à la carte/點菜 $250-800
Dinner/晚膳   à la carte/點菜 $250-800

Golden Leaf
金葉庭

The extremely popular Golden Leaf is elegantly dressed with panels, sculptured wood, antique art pieces and chandeliers. It is to this cosy oriental environment that customers come to enjoy the chef's recommendations, such as the steamed, fresh crab claw with minced ginger and rice wine or the poached chicken with chicken essence. A bargain set lunch menu and an appealing selection of dim sum are also available.

非常受歡迎的金葉庭以高雅屏風、木雕、古董藝術品及吊燈裝飾。客人都愛身處此溫暖而具東方特色的環境，享受廚師推介的菜式，如蒸薑米酒鮮蟹鉗，或是貴妃雞。此外，亦有午飯特惠套餐及一系列吸引點心可供選擇。

■ ADDRESS/地址
TEL.2521 3838
5F, Conrad Hotel, Pacific Place, 88 Queensway, Admiralty
金鐘金鐘道88號太古廣場港麗酒店5樓
www.conradhotels.com

■ OPENING HOURS, LAST ORDER
　營業時間，最後點菜時間
Lunch/午膳　11:30-15:00 (L.O.)
Dinner/晚膳　18:00-23:00 (L.O.)

■ PRICE/價錢

Lunch/午膳	set/套餐	$ 368-500
	à la carte/點菜	$ 350-1,000
Dinner/晚膳	set/套餐	$ 498-598
	à la carte/點菜	$ 350-1,000

Golden Valley
駿景軒

Not only is The Emperor hotel fortunate to be close to the famous race course, it also has this fine traditional restaurant. They serve classic Cantonese and Sichuan cuisine, the menu equally divided between the two varieties. It's a regular haunt of many a famous face and avid race goers whom enjoy the archetypal surroundings. From delicate dim sum to fiery hotpots, the choice is exhaustive.

英皇駿景酒店座落於跑馬地，鄰近著名馬場。除了坐擁極佳的地理位置外，酒店更設有駿景軒這家精緻的傳統中菜廳。餐廳提供傳統粵菜及川菜，選擇平均。不少名流及馬場常客經常現身，享受保留傳統的環境。從精美點心到火鍋，選擇層出不窮。

■ ADDRESS/地址
TEL.2961 3330
The Emperor Hotel, 1 Wang Tak
Street, Happy Valley
跑馬地宏德街1號英皇駿景酒店
www.emperorhotel.com.hk

■ OPENING HOURS, LAST ORDER
營業時間，最後點菜時間
12:00-22:00 (L.O.)

■ PRICE/價錢
Lunch/午膳　à la carte/點菜　$ 160-450
Dinner/晚膳　à la carte/點菜　$ 160-450

Good Hope Noodles
好旺角麵家

Choosing what you want to eat here is easy – just watch the chefs preparing food in the two tiny kitchens – wontons and noodles in one, congee in the other - as you wait for a table. Beef, pork knuckles or fish ball with noodles? It all very fresh and tasty, which explains its perennially popularity with those locals, who have been coming here for years. Two generations of owners keep the place looking clean and bright.

要決定吃什麼非常容易——在等待座位時看看廚師在兩個小廚房裡如何烹調食物吧——雲吞麵或是粥類。牛腩、豬手還是魚蛋麵？全都新鮮美味，難怪全年深受本地食客捧場，多年不斷。兩代店主致力保持店面清潔明亮。

■ ADDRESS/地址
TEL.2393 9036
146 Sai Yeung Choi Street, Mong Kok, Kowloon
九龍旺角西洋菜街146號

■ ANNUAL AND WEEKLY CLOSING
休息日期
Closed Lunar New Year
年初一休息

■ OPENING HOURS, LAST ORDER
營業時間，最後點菜時間
11:00-03:00 (L.O.)

■ PRICE/價錢
Lunch/午膳　à la carte/點菜 $22-70
Dinner/晚膳　à la carte/點菜 $22-70

Grissini

If you fancy a romantic dinner with views to match, then this smart Italian restaurant with its candle-lit tables is just the job. The range of authentic dishes captures the length and breadth of Italy's regions and manages to be both traditional and imaginative. Equal space is given to pasta, risotto, meat and fish. You'll find it hard restricting yourself to just one of the exquisite grissini that lend the place its name.

假如你嚮往在醉人夜景下享受燭光晚餐，這家時尚的餐廳定是必然之選。真材實料的菜式囊括意大利不同地域的尊長，兼具傳統特色和創意。意大利麵，意大利燴飯，肉類和魚類菜式均有不少選擇。這店的名詞來自意大利一種長條麵包，也是餐廳裡忍不住要吃的美食。

■ ADDRESS/地址
TEL.2584 7722
Grand Hyatt Hotel, 1 Harbour Road, Wan Chai
灣仔港灣道1號君悅酒店
www.hongkong.grand.hyatt.com

■ ANNUAL AND WEEKLY CLOSING
　　休息日期
Closed Saturday lunch
週六午膳休息

■ OPENING HOURS, LAST ORDER
　　營業時間，最後點菜時間
Lunch/午膳 12:00-14:30 (L.O.)
Dinner/晚膳 19:00-22:30 (L.O.)

■ PRICE/價錢

Lunch/午膳	set/套餐	$ 280-540
	à la carte/點菜	$ 640-850
Dinner/晚膳	set/套餐	$ 540
	à la carte/點菜	$ 640-850

Gusto

20

The impressive array of appetising pastries on display in the window should be sufficient to entice you into this pleasantly bright, modern shop which doubles as an Italian restaurant. Before sampling those desserts, there are some equally tasty and authentic dishes to try, such as squid ink spaghetti with cuttlefish and citrus zest, herb-spiced beef steak with grilled vegetables or sea bass with prosciutto.

刺激食慾的美味糕餅展示在櫥窗上，應足以吸引你進入這家光線充足的現代店內，它同時亦是一家義大利餐廳。在嘗試甜品之前，先嚐嚐同樣出色及正宗的主菜，如魷魚檸檬墨魚汁義大利麵、香草牛扒伴烤蔬菜及黑鱸伴煙燻五香火腿。

■ ADDRESS/地址
TEL.2147 3768
Shop 201-203, 2F, Nexxus Building,
41 Connaught Road (entrance on 77
Des Voeux Road), Central
中環干諾道中41號盈置大廈2樓201-203號
舖(正門位於德輔道77號)
www.gusto.hk

■ OPENING HOURS, LAST ORDER
營業時間，最後點菜時間
Lunch/午膳 11:30-15:00 (L.O.)
Dinner/晚膳 19:00-22:30 (L.O.)

■ PRICE/價錢
Lunch/午膳   set/套餐 $170-200
             à la carte/點菜 $370-480
Dinner/晚膳 à la carte/點菜 $400-570

Hakka Yé Yé
客家爺爺

The food of the Hakka people is very much sophisticated peasant cookery, relying largely on pork and chicken. Specialities here include braised pork belly with preserved vegetables and Emperor chicken. The small contemporary room is simply furnished but the charming team go out of their way to explain the distinctive characteristics of their authentic and reasonably-priced regional cuisine.

客家菜的特色是農家菜，大部分食材選用豬肉和雞肉。這裡的推介菜式包括西施梅菜扣肉和霸爺雞。地方小巧裝潢現代精緻，親切友善的員工用獨有方式介紹原汁原味的客家菜，且價錢合理。

■ ADDRESS/地址
TEL.2537 7060
2F, Parekh House, 63 Wyndham Street, Central
中環雲咸街63號巴力大廈2樓
www.yeyegroup.com

■ ANNUAL AND WEEKLY CLOSING
   休息日期
Closed Sunday and Public Holidays
週日及公眾假期休息

■ OPENING HOURS, LAST ORDER
   營業時間，最後點菜時間
Lunch/午膳 12:00-14:15 (L.O.)
Dinner/晚膳 18:30-22:15 (L.O.)

■ PRICE/價錢
Lunch/午膳   set/套餐 $ 92
              à la carte/點菜 $ 160-250
Dinner/晚膳   à la carte/點菜 $ 160-250

Hang Zhou
杭州酒家

36 (C)

The owner-chef has his fresh ingredients delivered directly from Hang Zhou every afternoon and you can certainly tell when you bite into those delicious fried river prawns with Longjing tea leaves; the braised pork belly is also worth trying. The chef inherited his obvious passion for food and the delicate cuisine of Hang Zhou from his father (who is also a famous chef in town) and strives to keep his cooking authentic.

餐廳主廚兼老闆堅持每天下午由杭州運來新鮮食材。你不難察覺這點：嚐嚐鮮美的龍井河蝦仁吧，東坡肉同樣值得一試。廚師從其父親身上遺傳了對飲食及杭州美食的熱愛（其父同為城中名廚），並努力維持正宗煮法。

■ ADDRESS/地址

TEL.2591 1898

1F, Chinachem Johnston Plaza,
178-186 Johnston Road, Wan Chai

灣仔莊士敦道178-186號華懋莊士敦廣場
1樓

■ OPENING HOURS, LAST ORDER
營業時間，最後點菜時間
Lunch/午膳 11:30-14:30 L.O. 14:15
Dinner/晚膳 17:30-22:30 L.O. 22:15

■ PRICE/價錢
Lunch/午膳   set/套餐 $70-90
           à la carte/點菜 $114-194
Dinner/晚膳   à la carte/點菜 $200-1,800

Harbour Grill

The décor here is elegant and comfortable and suits a romantic evening just as well as a more formal business lunch. The international menu shows ambition, placing classical French dishes alongside grills incorporating Wagyu and Japanese Kobe beef. Specialities include scallops seared with pork belly and the Bouillabaisse (traditional seafood soup flavoured with saffron). An extensive wine list has been well chosen.

此處的裝修優雅舒適，不論共度醉人黃昏，或是與客人食午餐都適合不過。國際化的菜式充份表現酒店的野心：傳統法國菜佐以燒烤和牛及日本神戶牛柳。特別推介包括煎帶子伴脆極黑豬腩肉配糖燴香梨和法式海鮮濃湯（傳統海鮮湯，以番紅花調味）。酒類選擇繁多，且經精心挑選。

■ ADDRESS/地址
TEL.2996 8433
GF, Harbour Plaza Hotel, 20 Tak Fung Street, Whampoa Garden, Hung Hom, Kowloon
九龍紅磡黃埔花園德豐街20號海逸酒店地下
www.harbour-plaza.com/hphk

■ OPENING HOURS, LAST ORDER
營業時間，最後點菜時間
Lunch/午膳 12:00-14:00 (L.O.)
Dinner/晚膳 18:00-22:00 (L.O.)

■ PRICE/價錢
Lunch/午膳 à la carte/點菜 $550-1,150
Dinner/晚膳 à la carte/點菜 $550-1,150

Harlan's

& ⟨ ⏱24 ◑¶ ⊗

"Where dining is an experience" says the sign on the door and, inside, not only do all tables have lovely harbour views, but there's also a broad sweep of contemporary European influences to the cooking. The diverse menu allows pizzas and sandwiches to share space with a range of oysters and freshly sliced hams as well as more substantial dishes. Lighter lunches and afternoon teas are also served. Wines are well chosen.

門上的告示寫道:「在這裡,每次用餐都是一種體驗」,入內一看,全場均可欣賞迷人海港景致,而且菜式充滿當代歐陸風情。令人目不暇給的餐單,從意大利薄餅、三文治到蠔、鮮切火腿片以至較具份量的菜色都應有盡有。餐廳另有提供較輕盈的午餐和下午茶餐。選酒質素一流。

■ ADDRESS/地址
TEL.2805 0566
Shop 2075, Podium Level 2, IFC Mall, 8 Finance Street, Central
中環金融街8號國際金融中心商場2樓2075號鋪
www.harlans.com.hk

■ OPENING HOURS, LAST ORDER
營業時間,最後點菜時間
Lunch/午膳 11:30-14:30 (L.O.)
Dinner/晚膳 18:30-22:30 (L.O.)

■ PRICE/價錢
Lunch/午膳　set/套餐　　　$268
　　　　　à la carte/點菜 $400-800
Dinner/晚膳　à la carte/點菜 $400-800

Harvey Nichols

It's not just the shopping that's chic there: the restaurant is design-led, with a harlequin style ceiling and floor, the colours illuminated by shifting beams of light; and black leather seating with comfortable imitation snakeskin armchairs. And the food? The French cuisine is given a contemporary twist: sashimi scallops, roasted black cod with lobster mashed potatoes or Angus beef with caramelised foie gras. Afternoon tea is also served.

這裡入時的不僅是購物。這家的餐廳設計新穎，天花及地板採用了丑角服裝的風格，移動的燈光照亮顏色。餐廳內有黑色皮革座位及舒適的仿蛇皮扶手椅。至於食物又如何?法國美食被當代大革新：生帶子、烤黑鱈魚伴龍蝦薯蓉，以及安格斯牛肉配焦糖鵝肝。設有下午茶餐。

■ ADDRESS/地址

TEL.3695 3389

4F, The Landmark, 15 Queen's Road Central, Central
中環皇后大道中15號置地廣場4樓

■ ANNUAL AND WEEKLY CLOSING
  休息日期
Closed Lunar New Year and Sunday
年初一及週日休息

■ OPENING HOURS, LAST ORDER
  營業時間，最後點菜時間
Lunch/午膳 12:00-14:30 (L.O.)
Dinner/晚膳 19:00-22:30 (L.O.)

■ PRICE/價錢

Lunch/午膳	set/套餐	$340
Dinner/晚膳	set/套餐	$380
	à la carte/點菜	$470-570

Hing Kee
避風塘興記

Originated from Causeway Bay two generations ago, the family moved their business to Tsim Sha Tsui, where they've made a name for themselves with their Boat People style cuisine; further testimony comes from the celebrity signatures lining the walls. Elder sister heads the serving team; younger brother takes charge in the kitchen. They are famous for their stir-fry crabs with black beans and chili, roast duck and rice noodles in soup and congee.

兩代前已於銅鑼灣開業，家族將餐廳移往尖沙嘴，建立了避風塘特色菜的名聲，牆上貼滿明星簽名，更見證此店美味。招牌菜包括避風塘炒蟹、燒鴨湯河及艇仔粥。

■ ADDRESS/地址
TEL.2722 0022
1F, Bowa House, 180 Nathan Road, Tsim Sha Tsui, Kowloon
九龍尖沙咀彌敦道180號寶華商業大廈1樓

■ ANNUAL AND WEEKLY CLOSING
　　休息日期
Closed 2 days Lunar New Year
農曆新年休息2天

■ OPENING HOURS, LAST ORDER
　　營業時間，最後點菜時間
Dinner/晚膳 18:00-05:00 (L.O.)

■ PRICE/價錢
Dinner/晚膳　à la carte/點菜 $250-500

Ho Hung Kee
何洪記

The owner's parents opened the business in Wan Chai in 1946. The restaurant's been here, near Times Square, since 1974, so Mr Ho advisedly calls it the Original Noodle Shop! His wife claims the noodles won her over before she'd even met her husband. On both sides of the entrance, two little cook stations entice you in with their aromas. Exceptional shrimp won ton boasts a decades-old recipe, while congee with fish is also of legendary status.

東主父母於1946年在灣仔開設此家餐廳。自1974年以來，餐廳一直座落於現時位置，毗鄰時代廣場。因此，何先生特意稱它為「傳統麵店」！他太太聲稱還未與丈夫第一次見面，麵就已經贏得芳心。入口兩邊都有廚師以食物香味引誘你。著名的鮮蝦雲吞以幾十年的祖傳食譜烹調，而魚粥亦是令人讚不絕口的菜式。

■ ADDRESS/地址
TEL.2577 6558
2 Sharp Street, Causeway Bay
銅鑼灣雲東街2號

■ OPENING HOURS, LAST ORDER
　營業時間，最後點菜時間
11:30-23:30 (L.O.)

■ PRICE/價錢
Lunch/午膳　à la carte/點菜 $26-38
Dinner/晚膳　à la carte/點菜 $33-99

Hoi Yat Heen
海逸軒

𝕏𝕏𝕏

    ♿ ← ☞ 🅿 🛗12

This large restaurant has great harbour views and so too do the two private rooms. With live music every night, it serves carefully prepared Cantonese cooking that has been given a contemporary twist. Specialities include oven baked crabmeat with shredded onion on the crab shell and sautéed sliced pork with pear and black vinegar. The very diligent manager heads up an attentive team.

這家餐廳不論主廳與貴賓房，都能俯瞰美麗的維港景色。每晚有現場音樂演奏，配搭大廚精美菜式，為廣東菜添上一絲現代感。特色菜包括：金牌焗釀蟹蓋、桂花梨黑醋脆柳。勤快的經理帶領著出色的服務團隊，這裡絕對能讓你賓至如歸。

■ ADDRESS/地址
TEL.2996 8459
2F, Harbour Plaza Hotel, 20 Tak Fung Street, Whampoa Garden, Hung Hom, Kowloon
九龍紅磡德豐街20號海逸酒店2樓
www.harbour-plaza.com/hphk

■ OPENING HOURS, LAST ORDER
　營業時間，最後點菜時間
Lunch/午膳　11:30-15:00 (L.O.)
Dinner/晚膳　18:00-23:00 (L.O.)

■ PRICE/價錢
Lunch/午膳　à la carte/點菜 $300-1,000
Dinner/晚膳　à la carte/點菜 $300-1,000

H One

There has been a new concept in H One since 2009: two chefs, two menus, two types of cuisine! An Italian chef presents respectfully traditional cuisine from his home country, while a Finish chef prepares more contemporary French dishes. Their one common goal is make your meal memorable. Three modern dining rooms offer three different atmospheres and views (harbour, kitchen or garden terrace).

H One從2009年開始引進新體制：兩個主廚、兩款菜單、兩種煮意！義大利廚師呈獻家鄉傳統菜式，芬蘭廚師則提供當代法國菜，適隨尊便。他們只有一個共同目的：讓你擁有難忘的用餐體驗。三間富現代感的飯廳提供三種不同氣氛及景觀（海景、廚房及平台花園）。

■ ADDRESS/地址
TEL.2805 0638
Shop 4008, Podium Level 4, IFC Mall,
8 Finance Street, Central
中環金融街8號國際金融中心商場4樓
4008號舖
www.h-one.com.hk

■ ANNUAL AND WEEKLY CLOSING
　休息日期
Closed Lunar New Year
年初一休息

■ OPENING HOURS, LAST ORDER
　營業時間，最後點菜時間
Lunch/午膳 12:00-14:30 (L.O.)
Dinner/晚膳 18:30-22:30 (L.O.)

■ PRICE/價錢
Lunch/午膳 set/套餐　　$278-298
　　　　　à la carte/點菜 $450-850
Dinner/晚膳 à la carte/點菜 $450-850

House of Jasmine
八月居

⚔ ⚔

♿ 🏛 **P** 🚃60

When it's not too hot outside, grab a seat on the terrace for fantastic views of the harbour and Hong Kong Island. Inside, though not so dramatic, there's an attractive, contemporary feel to this busy, three-roomed restaurant. One of the rooms, featuring a bar, is particularly pleasant and cosy. What keeps the customers coming is the Cantonese cuisine with modern twists; typically, marinated ox tendon with black vinegar, or prawn on egg custard.

天氣稍涼時，食客可以選擇露天雅座，飽覽維港及港島的璀璨美景；餐廳裡頭雖然不及戶外變化多端，不過裝潢設計富現代感，甚具吸引力，與餐廳的繁忙景象相映成趣。餐廳共分為三間餐室，其中一間設有酒吧，極其舒適愜意。這裡客似雲來的原因，在於其原味粵菜以現代方式呈現，招牌菜包括鎮江牛蹄筋脆及太雕玻璃蝦球。

■ ADDRESS/地址

TEL.2992 0232

Shop 401, 4F, Ocean Centre, Harbour City, Canton Road, Tsim Sha Tsui, Kowloon

九龍尖沙咀廣東道海港城海洋中心4樓401號舖

www.maxims.com.hk

■ OPENING HOURS, LAST ORDER
　營業時間，最後點菜時間

Lunch/午膳　11:00-15:00 L.O. 14:30
Dinner/晚膳　18:00-23:00 L.O. 22:30

■ PRICE/價錢

Lunch/午膳	set/套餐	$238
	à la carte/點菜	$120-600
Dinner/晚膳	set/套餐	$398-568
	à la carte/點菜	$200-600

Hunan Garden (Causeway Bay)
洞庭樓（銅鑼灣）

As you walk in on the 13th floor, you're welcomed near a channel of running water complete with live fish. This leads into a spacious contemporary room with bright chandeliers and painted wood panels on the walls. The Hunan-style cooking uses well-sourced, fresh local ingredients. Specialities include sautéed prawns with fermented beans and chilli and fish fillets with fried minced bean.

甫踏進十三樓，你就會看見水流源源不絕的活魚水槽。繼續往前走，便進入了寬敞時尚的進餐區。璀璨的吊燈點綴加上牆身的漆木板，交織成獨特的風格。湖南菜選料皆採用本地新鮮食材，午飯時段設有一系列的點心，供購物及商務客人選擇。特別推薦有四季豆豉香辣蝦及豆酥魚。

■ ADDRESS/地址
TEL.2506 9288
Shop 1302, 13F, Food Forum, Times Square, 1 Matheson Street, Causeway Bay
銅鑼灣時代廣場食通天13樓1302號舖
www.maxims.com.hk

■ OPENING HOURS, LAST ORDER
營業時間，最後點菜時間
Lunch/午膳 11:30-14:30 (L.O.)
Dinner/晚膳 18:00-23:00 (L.O.)

■ PRICE/價錢
Lunch/午膳 à la carte/點菜 $300-850
Dinner/晚膳 à la carte/點菜 $300-850

Hunan Garden (Central)
洞庭樓 (中環)

XXX

⏹16

This is a large restaurant in a prestigious development. Expensive carpets, floor-to-ceiling glass, huge columns decorated with flowers, and pink and white linen-clad tables announce a refined dining experience. As the cuisine is predominantly Hunan, expect fiery flavours with extensive use of chillies. For more conservative tastes, Cantonese dishes are also offered.

這家寬敞的餐廳位處高級商業地段。價值不菲的地毯、落地玻璃、以鮮花裝飾的龐大圓柱、粉紅色白色的麻質桌布，交織成高雅的餐飲體驗。食物方面以湖南菜為主，大部分菜式都會採用辣椒，因此請做好心理準備！至於口味較為保守的食客，則可選擇粵菜。

■ ADDRESS/地址
TEL.2868 2880
3F, The Forum, Exchange Square, Central
中環交易廣場富臨閣3樓
www.maxims.com.hk

■ OPENING HOURS, LAST ORDER
　營業時間，最後點菜時間
Lunch/午膳 11:30-14:45 (L.O.)
Dinner/晚膳 17:30-23:00 (L.O.)

■ PRICE/價錢
Lunch/午膳　à la carte/點菜 $210-540
Dinner/晚膳　à la carte/點菜 $210-540

Hung's Delicacies
阿鴻小吃

Having been encouraged by regulars in previous establishments, Mr and Mrs Lai have put their all into their own business here in North Point. They are clearly committed to finding the best suppliers and so ensuring the quality of the Cantonese and Chiu Chow dishes. Furthermore, it's served by a delightful little team led by Mrs Lai. The roast meats and bean curd with special sauce and the crispy squid squares are worthy of note.

之前開業得到常客支持，讓黎氏夫婦在此北角店傾盡全力，致力尋找最好的供應商，確保店內的粵菜及潮州菜保持一貫水準。此外，黎太帶領的一小對開朗活潑的服務生為賓客提供服務。鹵水豆腐燒肉及香脆墨魚餅值得留意。

■ ADDRESS/地址
TEL.2570 1108
Shop 4, GF, Ngan Fai Building, 84-94 Wharf Road, North Point
北角和富道84-94號銀輝大廈地下4號舖

■ ANNUAL AND WEEKLY CLOSING
　　休息日期
Closed Lunar New Year and Monday except Public Holidays
年初一及週一(公眾假期除外)休息

■ OPENING HOURS, LAST ORDER
　　營業時間，最後點菜時間
10:00-23:00 (L.O.)

■ PRICE/價錢
Lunch/午膳 　à la carte/點菜 $ 100-150
Dinner/晚膳 　à la carte/點菜 $ 100-150

Hutong
胡同

Come here for dinner to really experience one of Kowloon's hippest establishments. The subtle lighting, the huge array of bird cages and beautiful carved wood panels make it all so atmospheric that one almost forgets the stunning harbour views. The cuisine is pretty exciting too: it puts a modern twist on Cantonese classics and presents them in a stylish way – try the Hutong signature dishes to see it at its best.

來到胡同享受晚餐，你可置身九龍區的時尚尖端。柔和燈光、一列列的鳥籠和精雕細琢的木層板，營造強烈的氣氛，幾乎令人忘卻醉人海港景緻。菜色方面也極具驚喜：為傳統廣東菜進行現代大變身，以時尚風格呈現——嚐嚐胡同盡心設計的出色招牌菜吧。

■ ADDRESS/地址
TEL.3428 8342
28F, One Peking Road, Tsim Sha Tsui, Kowloon
九龍尖沙咀北京道1號28樓
www.aqua.com.hk

■ OPENING HOURS, LAST ORDER
營業時間，最後點菜時間
Lunch/午膳 12:00-15:00 L.O. 14:30
Dinner/晚膳 18:00-24:00 L.O. 23:30

■ PRICE/價錢
Lunch/午膳　à la carte/點菜 $250-400
Dinner/晚膳　à la carte/點菜 $400-1,000

Inagiku (IFC)
稻菊（國際金融中心）

Adjacent to the Four Seasons Hotel in the IFC Mall, this is a delightfully uncluttered contemporary installation with illuminated flooring and large plate glass windows affording fine views. There are separate sushi, teppanyaki and tempura counters and a whole series of special set menus. This is traditional Japanese cooking that has been successfully adapted to suit the local market.

鄰靠中環國際金融中心商場四季酒店，餐廳設計極具時尚風格。射燈地板配上大型落地玻璃，怡人景觀盡收眼底。餐廳設有壽司、鐵板燒及天婦羅吧，更提供一系列的特選套餐。這可算是傳統日式料理進軍本地市場的成功例子。

■ ADDRESS/地址
TEL.2805 0600
4F, Four Seasons Hotel, 8 Finance Street, Central
中環金融街8號四季酒店4樓
www.fourseasons.com/hongkong

■ OPENING HOURS, LAST ORDER
營業時間，最後點菜時間
Lunch/午膳 11:30-14:30 (L.O.)
Dinner/晚膳 18:00-22:30 (L.O.)

■ PRICE/價錢
Lunch/午膳   set/套餐 $300-600
             à la carte/點菜 $350-1,200
Dinner/晚膳   set/套餐 $800-2,000
             à la carte/點菜 $350-1,200

Inagiku (Kowloon)
稻菊 (九龍)

Inagiku has a strong pedigree: the first was established over a century ago in Japan. Décor is elegantly upscale, the Japanese influences a visual pleasure. There are several dining areas: a sushi bar with fish tank, a tempura counter, a teppanyaki area and a few tables in the centre of the room. Not only that, but five separate private rooms, too. The restaurant is renowned for its tempura and teppanyaki. An attractive list of sake is also available.

稻菊來頭殊不簡單，早在百多年前已於日本開業。這裡的裝潢設計典雅高尚，源自日本人對美學的要求，為食客帶來視覺上的享受。餐廳共有幾個用餐區，包括設有魚缸的壽司吧、天婦羅檯、鐵板燒區，以及餐廳中心的幾張餐桌。此外，稻菊還設有五間私人餐室。這裡的天婦羅及鐵板燒享負盛名，而員工亦可為你推介更多菜式。提供一系列清酒名單任君選擇，相當吸引。

■ ADDRESS/地址

TEL.2733 2933
1F, The Royal Garden Hotel, 69 Mody Road, East Tsim Sha Tsui, Kowloon
九龍尖東麼地道69號帝苑酒店1樓
www.rghk.com.hk

■ OPENING HOURS, LAST ORDER
　營業時間，最後點菜時間
Lunch/午膳 12:00-14:30 (L.O.)
Dinner/晚膳 18:00-22:30 (L.O.)

■ PRICE/價錢
Lunch/午膳　set/套餐　　$160-380
　　　　　　à la carte/點菜 $230-1,500
Dinner/晚膳 set/套餐　　$680-950
　　　　　　à la carte/點菜 $230-1,500

Island Tang
港島廳

🍽40 📞🍴

This elegant art deco inspired room, with its chandeliers, rich wood panelling and mirrors, is reminiscent of 40s Hong Kong; and it should come as no surprise to learn that Sir David Tang is behind it. The menu offers a range of sophisticated and delicious Cantonese dishes, from king prawns with lobster sauce and baked crab meat to terrific Peking duck and many other classics. As befits the surroundings, service is slick and professional.

靈感來自裝飾藝術的高雅房間配有吊燈、厚木鑲板及鏡子，重現四十年代香港的光景；此情此景，發現幕後主腦原是鄧永鏘爵士，面對如斯景致，你應毫不意外毫不意外。菜單上提供一系列獨特美味的廣東菜，從龍蝦醬皇帝蝦、焗蟹肉到出色的北京填鴨及其他不同經典菜色。悉心專業的服務與出色的環境相得益彰。

■ ADDRESS/地址
TEL.2526 8798
Shop 222, The Galleria, 9 Queen's Road, Central
中環皇后大道中9號嘉軒廣場222號舖
www.islandtang.com

■ OPENING HOURS, LAST ORDER
營業時間，最後點菜時間
Lunch/午膳 12:00-14:30 (L.O.)
Dinner/晚膳 18:00-22:30 (L.O.)

■ PRICE/價錢
Lunch/午膳　set/套餐　　$ 298-398
　　　　　　à la carte/點菜 $ 300-1,200
Dinner/晚膳　à la carte/點菜 $ 300-1,200

Isola

There's no rest for the staff as they dart between the main dining room with its trendy wavy white wall and the equally large outside terrace which offers a great view on the harbour. The place is invariably packed with people ordering generous plates of pizza, pasta and grilled meats. Considering the speed and volume involved, the kitchen is remarkably consistent. Lively bar on the upper floor, opened until late.

主餐室的波浪形白色牆身非常新穎，露天部份亦相當寬敞，是觀賞海港的絕佳據點。餐廳的人流絡繹不絕，服務員繁忙地穿插店內外替客人落單，一碟又一碟的薄餅、意大利麵和烤肉等。考慮到速度和食物份量，廚房仍能保持一貫水準。上層設有熱鬧的頂層酒吧，營業至夜深。

■ ADDRESS/地址
TEL.2383 8765
Shop 3071-75, Podium Level 3, IFC
Mall, 8 Finance Street, Central
中環金融街8號國際金融中心商場3樓3071-75號舖
www.isolabarandgrill.com

■ OPENING HOURS, LAST ORDER
營業時間，最後點菜時間
Lunch/午膳 12:00-14:30 (L.O.)
Dinner/晚膳 18:30-23:00 (L.O.)

■ PRICE/價錢
Lunch/午膳   set/套餐 $248
           à la carte/點菜 $370-650
Dinner/晚膳 à la carte/點菜 $370-650

Jade Garden (Hysan Avenue)
翠園 (希慎道)

This is the more senior of the two Jade Garden restaurants in Causeway Bay, having been in operation for over thirty years on Hysan Avenue. They specialise in Cantonese cuisine and, while a large part of the menu focuses on shark fin and abalone, they are particularly known for their barbecued meats. It opens early for those with a craving for dim sum.

銅鑼灣兩間翠園中，以這家歷史較悠久。位處希慎道的翠園經營超過三十年。餐廳專門打造精美粵菜，大部分菜式着重魚翅及鮑魚，而最有名的要算是燒肉了。餐廳清晨開始營業，照顧熱愛點心的顧客。

■ ADDRESS/地址
TEL.2577 9332
1 Hysan Avenue, Causeway Bay
銅鑼灣希慎道1號
www.maxims.com.hk

■ OPENING HOURS, LAST ORDER
營業時間，最後點菜時間
Lunch/午膳 07:30-16:30 (L.O.)
Dinner/晚膳 18:00-24:00 L.O. 23:30
■ PRICE/價錢
Lunch/午膳   à la carte/點菜 $150-300
Dinner/晚膳   à la carte/點菜 $300-500

Jade Garden (Lockhart Road)
翠園 (駱克道)

Fancy a quiet dinner in a romantic location? Then don't come here! Jade Garden is located in a very busy street, and the restaurant is just as lively. At lunch, the restaurant is filled with dim sum trolleys; if you don't understand Cantonese then don't be shy to wave the waiter over and peek under the lids yourself. In the evening, take your time to taste one of the chef's specials: fresh shark fin in scrambled egg or the crispy chicken.

想在浪漫的地方寧靜渡過晚膳時光？這裡不會是你的選擇!翠園位處車水馬龍的繁忙街道上，餐廳本身亦同樣生氣勃勃。午飯時間，餐廳內佈滿點心車；如果你不會講廣東話，千萬不要害羞，揚手示意，大可叫服務生走過來讓你直接掀起點心蓋子、看個究竟吧！傍晚時分，你可把握時間嚐廚師精選：古法炒桂花翅或是翠園炸子雞。

■ ADDRESS/地址

TEL.2573 9339

3F, Causeway Bay Plaza II, 463-483
Lockhart Road, Causeway Bay
銅鑼灣駱克道463-483號銅鑼灣廣場第2期
3樓
www.maxims.com.hk

■ OPENING HOURS, LAST ORDER
營業時間，最後點菜時間
07:00-23:00 (L.O.)

■ PRICE/價錢

Lunch/午膳	set/套餐	$ 100-460
	à la carte/點菜	$ 200-350
Dinner/晚膳	set/套餐	$ 170-460
	à la carte/點菜	$ 200-350

Joia

Easy-going restaurant that's especially pleasant at night if you're seated next to the floor-to-ceiling windows under dimmed lights looking out over Civic Square's attractive rooftop courtyard with palm trees. The Italian menus specialise in a light Mediterranean cuisine: the trademark is pasta, though the pizza, too, is very popular here. This is backed up with a good choice of Italian wines, served by a very friendly and attentive team.

餐廳氣氛自然悠閒，晚上坐在落地玻璃窗旁的雅座，燈光微黃；在此細看外面的天台廣場和棕櫚樹，尤其舒適愜意。餐廳提供意大利菜式，主打為輕盈的地中海菜。招牌菜包括各種意大利麵食，比薩薄餅也很受歡迎；佐以意大利美酒享用。侍應招呼周到，提供賓至如歸的服務。

■ ADDRESS/地址
TEL.2382 2323
Roof Garden, 3F, Elements, 1 Austin Road West, Kowloon
九龍柯士甸道西1號圓方3樓花園平台
www.joia.com.hk

■ OPENING HOURS, LAST ORDER
營業時間，最後點菜時間
Lunch/午膳 12:00-14:30 (L.O.)
Dinner/晚膳 18:00-22:30 (L.O.)

■ PRICE/價錢
Lunch/午膳   set/套餐 $238-250
             à la carte/點菜 $330-690
Dinner/晚膳   à la carte/點菜 $330-690

Kau Kee
九記

You'll probably have to line up in the street first to eat here: Kau Kee has been trading since the 1930s and has consequently built up a huge following which includes some well known faces from show business and politics. It's all very basic and you'll have to share your table but the food is delicious. Beef noodles are the speciality; different cuts of meat with a variety of noodles in a tasty broth or spicy sauce. Try also the iced milk tea.

要在九記用膳，你可能要在街上排隊等候：九記自一九三零年代起開始經營，聚集了大量支持者，包括部分政商名人。九記陳設回歸基本，進餐時要和其他人士共用餐桌，但食物極具水準。九記的特色在於其牛肉麵；不同部位的肉塊與美味清湯或辣醬麵的搭配。奶茶亦值得一試。

■ ADDRESS/地址
TEL.N/A
21 Gough Street, Central
中環歌賦街21號

■ ANNUAL AND WEEKLY CLOSING
　休息日期
Closed 10 days Lunar New Year, Sunday and Public Holidays
農曆新年10天、週日及公眾假期休息

■ OPENING HOURS, LAST ORDER
　營業時間，最後點菜時間
Lunch/午膳　12:30-14:15 (L.O.)
Dinner/晚膳　20:30-23:30 (L.O.)

■ PRICE/價錢
Lunch/午膳　à la carte/點菜 $26-68
Dinner/晚膳　à la carte/點菜 $26-68

Kin's Kitchen
留家廚房

The bad news – Kin's Kitchen is hidden away on a noisy, grubby street beneath an expressway. The good news – this buzzing single room boasts two friendly owners who are passionate about food and who eat in some of the world's best restaurants. They've made it a wonderfully informal place that serves tasty Cantonese dishes, including specials like Kin's smoked chicken (smoked in the kitchen), and stuffed duck braised with lotus seed and barley.

壞消息：留家廚房隱藏在一條嘈雜骯髒的街，位處高速公路下面。好消息：這家熱鬧的餐廳是屬於兩位熱衷美食，品嚐過世上最好一些餐廳的菜式的東主。他們為餐廳營造輕鬆的氣氛，並奉上美味的廣東菜，包括留家煙燻雞(在廚房內煙燻)，以及京酥鴨。

■ ADDRESS/地址
TEL.2571 0913
9 Tsing Fung Street, Tin Hau
天后清風街9號
www.yellowdoorkitchen.com.hk

■ ANNUAL AND WEEKLY CLOSING
　休息日期
Closed 3 days Lunar New Year
農曆新年休息3天

■ OPENING HOURS, LAST ORDER
　營業時間，最後點菜時間
Lunch/午膳 11:00-15:00 L.O. 14:30
Dinner/晚膳 18:00-23:00 L.O. 22:30

■ PRICE/價錢
Lunch/午膳　à la carte/點菜 $ 146-298
Dinner/晚膳　à la carte/點菜 $ 146-298

Kung Tak Lam (Causeway Bay)
功德林 (銅鑼灣)

A fresh green colour scheme reflects this restaurant's philosophy of offering bright and vibrant vegetarian food. There are Shanghainese and Sichuan influences on the menu and several of the dishes have punchy and aromatic flavours. Don't be alarmed by the words 'chicken' and 'prawn' appearing on the menu: this is merely a clever use of soy bean products. Merriment fills the room and you'll leave feeling revitalised.

翠綠色系充分體現了這家餐廳致力提供鮮美素菜的哲學。菜色帶有滬菜及川菜特色，其中部分菜色更是香濃出眾。看到菜單上出現「雞」、「蝦」等字眼毋須擔心──全都是精心炮製的大豆製品。室內洋溢歡樂氣氛，你離開餐廳時必會精神煥發。

■ ADDRESS/地址
TEL.2881 9966
10F, World Trade Centre, 280
Gloucester Road, Causeway Bay
銅鑼灣告士打道280號世貿中心10樓

■ OPENING HOURS, LAST ORDER
　營業時間，最後點菜時間
11:00-23:00 (L.O.)

■ PRICE/價錢
Lunch/午膳　set/套餐　　　　$45
　　　　　à la carte/點菜 $150-200
Dinner/晚膳　à la carte/點菜 $150-200

La Brasserie
林柏軒

This basement restaurant adopts the adage 'simply French', and so it is. There's a typically unpretentious brasserie atmosphere, with brown wooden walls, old French furniture and the reassuring aroma of garlic. Classics derive from all across France, including French onion soup gratin with cheese, snails with garlic butter and tartar of beef. Local staff dress as 'garcons de café' and go about their work in a quietly stylish way.

這家地庫餐廳的格言是「simply french」，也名副其實。餐廳氣氛像法國的簡樸餐館一樣，毫不造作；採用了棕色木牆、舊法國傢具，以及大蒜的氣味，更添一點法國味道。經典菜式源自法國各地，包括芝士酥皮焗法式洋蔥湯、蒜茸牛油焗田螺，以及生牛肉他他。當地服務員打扮成「咖啡館男生」一般，以時尚安靜的方式工作。

■ ADDRESS/地址
TEL.2113 7925
Lower lobby, Gateway, Harbour City, 13 Canton Road, Tsim Sha Tsui, Kowloon
九龍尖沙咀廣東道13號海港城港威酒店大堂下層
www.marcopolohotels.com

■ OPENING HOURS, LAST ORDER
營業時間，最後點菜時間
Lunch/午膳 12:00-15:00 L.O. 14:30
Dinner/晚膳 18:30-23:00 L.O. 22:00

■ PRICE/價錢
Lunch/午膳   set/套餐 $ 168-198
          à la carte/點菜 $ 500-800
Dinner/晚膳   à la carte/點菜 $ 500-800

L'Atelier de Joël Robuchon

The hallmark colours of red and black are once again evident at this branch of the Robuchon Empire. The restaurant is divided into two sections: the main one, L'Atelier, offers a ringside seat at the show kitchen while Le Jardin is more discreet and comfortable. On both sides, the French contemporary cuisine focuses on top seasonal ingredients which are simply cooked to preserve their original flavours. Superb wine list

紅黑色的標記清楚顯示這是世紀大廚Robuchon集團旗下的餐廳。餐廳分成兩個主要區域：主區L'Atelier的開放式廚房提供前排座位可供觀賞，而Le Jardin則較沉穩舒適。兩區的當代法國菜，以簡約方法烹調頂級時令食材，保留原汁原味。精選出色美酒。

■ ADDRESS/地址

TEL.2166 9000

Shop 401, 4F, The Landmark,
15 Queen's Road, Central
中環皇后大道中15號置地廣場4樓401號舖
www.robuchon.hk

■ OPENING HOURS, LAST ORDER
營業時間，最後點菜時間
Lunch/午膳 12:00-14:30 (L.O.)
Dinner/晚膳 18:30-22:30 (L.O.)

■ PRICE/價錢

Lunch/午膳	set/套餐	$ 390-1,850
	à la carte/點菜	$ 500-1,500
Dinner/晚膳	set/套餐	$ 560-1,850
	à la carte/點菜	$ 500-1,500

Lau Sum Kee (Fuk Wing Street)
劉森記麵家 (福榮街)

This is one noodle shop that is not afraid of the competition. In a street overflowing with noodle shops, Lau Sum Kee (and its sister shop around the corner) are packed with customers buzzing in and out. Run by the third generation of the family, the noodles are pressed by bamboo and the wontons are freshly made at the shop. Recommendations include wonton noodles, dry prawn roe mix with noodles and pork knuckles mixed with noodles.

這家麵店可謂經得起競爭。在滿佈各家麵店的街上，劉森記麵家（及其轉角位的姐妹店）擠滿來往的食客。此麵店由家族第三代經營，在店內新鮮製造竹昇麵及雲吞。推薦菜式包括雲吞麵、蝦子麵及豬手麵。

■ ADDRESS/地址
TEL.2386 3583
82 Fuk Wing Street, Sham Shui Po, Kowloon
九龍深水埗福榮街82號

■ ANNUAL AND WEEKLY CLOSING
　休息日期
Closed 3 days Lunar New Year
農曆新年休息3天

■ OPENING HOURS, LAST ORDER
　營業時間，最後點菜時間
12:30-23:30 (L.O.)

■ PRICE/價錢
Lunch/午膳　à la carte/點菜 $22-40
Dinner/晚膳　à la carte/點菜 $22-40

Lawry's The Prime Rib

♿ ☐ 20

This famous chain originated in Beverley Hills in 1938 and faithful diners are always drawn by one thing only: finest American roast prime rib of beef served "au jus" and carved directly from the trolley. Here is no exception. There's lobster and shrimp to kick things off and New York cheesecake plus English trifle if you've still got room at the end. Simple as that. Uniformed staff are charming and the list of Napa Valley wines is good.

這家著名的連鎖牛扒餐廳於1938年在比華利山創辦,忠實顧客最重視的只有一件事:原汁原味的烤肉眼牛排、在手推車上直接切肉及奉到桌上。香港分店亦秉承一貫宗旨,頭盤可以是龍蝦和鮮蝦;假如當天胃口佳,還可以品嚐紐約芝士餅和英式冧酒蛋糕作甜點。簡簡單單、並無花巧。侍應制服整齊,活力十足;餐廳亦提供不錯的各種美國加州納帕谷酒。

■ ADDRESS/地址

TEL.2907 2218

4F, The Lee Gardens, 33 Hysan Avenue, Causeway Bay
銅鑼灣希慎道33號利園4樓
www.maxconcepts.com.hk

■ OPENING HOURS, LAST ORDER
　營業時間,最後點菜時間
Lunch/午膳　11:30-14:30 (L.O.)
Dinner/晚膳　18:00-22:30 (L.O.)

■ PRICE/價錢
Lunch/午膳　à la carte/點菜　$ 500-800
Dinner/晚膳　set/套餐　　　$ 344-388
　　　　　　à la carte/點菜　$ 500-800

Lei Garden (Elements)
利苑酒家 (圓方)

Located in the blue-tinted "water" area of this large shopping mall, the décor is more contemporary than some of the other Lei Garden branches. It is composed of different dining rooms one of which offers the striking sight of water cascading down some crystal curtains. The cooking throughout is reliable Cantonese but excels with its broad range of interesting seafood preparations as well as some highly unusual double-boiled tonic soups.

這家裝潢華麗優雅的餐館位於巨大的購物商場中的藍色「水」 區,比其他利苑分店更有時代感。它由不同的飯廳組合而成,其中一間更有流水,從水晶簾如瀑布般落下。菜色是清一色的廣東菜,但以各種方法烹調的海鮮和與別不同的燉湯,都令這裡顯得分外出色。

- ■ ADDRESS/地址
TEL.2196 8133
Shop 2068-70, 2F, Elements, 1 Austin Road West, Kowloon
九龍柯士甸道西1號圓方2樓2068-70號鋪
www.leigarden.com.hk

- ■ OPENING HOURS, LAST ORDER
  營業時間,最後點菜時間
Lunch/午膳 11:30-14:45 (L.O.)
Dinner/晚膳 18:00-22:45 (L.O.)

- ■ PRICE/價錢
Lunch/午膳 à la carte/點菜 $160-1,100
Dinner/晚膳 à la carte/點菜 $160-1,100

Lei Garden (IFC)
利苑酒家 (國際金融中心)

☍☍

♿ 🛁16 ☎🍴

Forward planning is advisable here – not only when booking but also when selecting certain roast meat dishes which require advance notice. An extensive menu also features specialist seafood dishes and the lunchtime favourites include shrimp and flaky pastries filled with shredded turnip. All this is served up by good-natured staff in cleanly contemporary surroundings.

到利苑用餐，無論是預訂座位，還是食燒臘，提早預約都十分重要。這裡菜式繁多，其中以海鮮炮製的佳餚最具特色，而午市時段的美食首推的銀蘿千層酥。格局設計富時代感，潔淨雅致，服務令人賓至如歸。

■ ADDRESS/地址

TEL.2295 0238

Shop 3008-3011, Podium Level 3, IFC Mall, 1 Harbour View Street, Central
中環港景街1號國際金融中心商場第2期3樓3008-3011號舖
www.leigarden.com.hk

■ ANNUAL AND WEEKLY CLOSING
　　休息日期
Closed 3 days Lunar New Year
農曆新年休息3天

■ OPENING HOURS, LAST ORDER
　　營業時間，最後點菜時間
Lunch/午膳 11:30-14:30 (L.O.)
Dinner/晚膳 18:00-22:30 (L.O.)

■ PRICE/價錢

Lunch/午膳	set/套餐	$ 150-300
	à la carte/點菜	$ 150-450
Dinner/晚膳	set/套餐	$ 150-300
	à la carte/點菜	$ 150-450

Lei Garden (Kowloon Bay)
利苑酒家 (九龍灣)

P ⟷40

Conveniently situated in a shopping mall which has a joining walkway to an MTR station, this restaurant is filled with large round tables and comfortable orange chairs. The Cantonese à la carte menu is very appealing; stand-outs include handmade dim sums and fresh fish and seafood straight from the tank; their soup of the day is also worth a mention. All dishes are based on quality ingredients and their careful preparation.

利苑酒家選址便利，位於商場內，有通道直達港鐵站。酒家內滿佈大圓桌及舒適的橘色座椅。廣東菜的單點菜單非常吸引，當中特別特出的包括手工點心、隨時從缸內取出泡製的鮮魚及活海鮮；每日例湯亦值得一提。所有菜色以高品質食材精心製造。

■ ADDRESS/地址
TEL.2331 3306
Shop Unit F2, Telford Plaza, 33 Wai Yip Street, Kowloon Bay, Kowloon
九龍灣偉業街33號德福廣場F2號鋪
www.leigarden.com.hk

■ ANNUAL AND WEEKLY CLOSING
  休息日期
Closed 3 days Lunar New Year
農曆新年休息3天

■ OPENING HOURS, LAST ORDER
  營業時間，最後點菜時間
Lunch/午膳 11:30-15:00 (L.O.)
Dinner/晚膳 18:00-23:00 (L.O.)

■ PRICE/價錢
Lunch/午膳 à la carte/點菜 $160-400
Dinner/晚膳 à la carte/點菜 $160-400

Lei Garden (Kwun Tong)
利苑酒家 (觀塘)

♿ P 🚑20

Avoid the escalators and use the shuttle lift to get to the fifth floor in this confusingly arranged new shopping mall. Once there, it'll seem familiar if you've experienced other Lei Garden branches: the menu is the standard Cantonese but is reliably cooked using fresh ingredients. The place is as frantic as the others but has been partitioned into different seating areas by smart trellis. Try not to sit near the entrance – too noisy.

由於這新建商場的設計混亂且複雜,最好不要使用扶手電梯;升降機可直達5樓。假如你曾光顧利苑的其他分店,你絕不會感到陌生:依然是清一色的廣東菜與可靠的美食及新鮮的材料。當然,這裡同樣擠滿了利苑的忠實擁躉,店內設計簡潔的屏風巧妙地將餐廳分隔成不同的用餐區。入口附近太嘈吵,最好不要選擇那裡的座位。

■ ADDRESS/地址

TEL.2365 3238

Shop L5-8, Level 5, apm, Millennium City 5, 418 Kwun Tong Road, Kwun Tong

觀塘觀塘道418號創紀之城5期apm5樓 L5-8號舖

www.leigarden.com.hk

■ OPENING HOURS, LAST ORDER
營業時間,最後點菜時間
Lunch/午膳 11:30-15:00 (L.O.)
Dinner/晚膳 18:00-23:30 L.O. 23:00

■ PRICE/價錢
Lunch/午膳 à la carte/點菜 $190-400
Dinner/晚膳 à la carte/點菜 $190-400

Lei Garden (Mong Kok)
利苑酒家 (旺角)

Families, shoppers and business people continuously flock to this perennially popular good-sized restaurant so it's essential to book. The smart contemporary décor is spread across the two floors and the upper space has views out onto the busy street. The long and varied Cantonese menu certainly offers very good value and includes such excellent seafood recommendations as giant sea whelk and mantis shrimp sautéed with salt, pepper and garlic.

家庭，購物者與白領一族都對這家餐廳趨之若鶩，其受歡迎程度可見一斑。儘管餐廳已經非常寬敞，沒有事先預約的客人依然難覓座位。富時代感的餐廳共分為兩層，樓上可看到旺角繁華的街景。以廣東菜為主的菜單花樣多變令人目不暇給，菜色物有所值，特別推薦薄殼大䐔螺及椒鹽富貴蝦。

■ ADDRESS/地址
TEL.2392 5184
121 Sai Yee Street, Mong Kok, Kowloon
九龍旺角洗衣街121
www.leigarden.com.hk

■ OPENING HOURS, LAST ORDER
營業時間，最後點菜時間
Lunch/午膳 11:30-15:00 (L.O.)
Dinner/晚膳 18:00-23:30 (L.O.)

■ PRICE/價錢
Lunch/午膳   à la carte/點菜 $160-750
Dinner/晚膳   à la carte/點菜 $160-750

Lei Garden (North Point)
利苑酒家 (北角)

🍽20 🕐🍽

Discreetly tucked away on the first floor of an office block but overlooking a pleasant courtyard garden, things at this branch of the popular chain can get frenetic: the place accommodates up to 300 people. The lengthy Cantonese mirrors what's available at other Lei Gardens with its emphasis on shark's fin, abalone and bird's nest preparations. The dim sum lunchtime selection includes excellent dumplings and deep-fried turnip pastries.

隱藏在商業大廈的一樓,從餐廳望出去可看到一個美麗的後花園一這家受歡迎的連鎖餐廳分店絕對可以滿足瘋狂的食客;寬敞的餐廳足可容納三百人!這裡的菜單與其他利苑分店相差無幾,特別推薦魚翅、鮑魚和燕窩。午市點心包括各式包點與蘿蔔絲酥餅,水準一流。

■ ADDRESS/地址

TEL.2806 0008
1F, Block 9-10, City Garden, North Point
北角城市花園9-10座1樓
www.leigarden.com.hk

■ OPENING HOURS, LAST ORDER
營業時間,最後點菜時間
Lunch/午膳 11:30-14:30 (L.O.)
Dinner/晚膳 18:00-22:30 (L.O.)

■ PRICE/價錢
Lunch/午膳   à la carte/點菜 $ 160-750
Dinner/晚膳 à la carte/點菜 $ 160-750

Lei Garden (Sha Tin)
利苑酒家 (沙田)

This Lei Garden may have been an old name around town for 20 years but it has been recently refurbished. It is located in New Town Plaza Sha Tin, which means that it can get especially busy at weekends when everyone needs refuelling after a day spent shopping. The menu largely follows the theme of others in the group; always ask for the daily special. Pre-ordering the soup and barbecued pork is particularly recommended.

這家利苑酒家已是二十年的老字號，最近更重新裝潢。酒家位於沙田新城市廣場，因此週末購物一整天過後前來小歇一番的茶客更是絡繹不絕。菜單與集團的其他餐廳主題相若；謹記留意是日精選。建議預訂老火湯及叉燒。

■ ADDRESS/地址

TEL.2698 9111
6F, Phase I New Town Plaza, Sha Tin, Kowloon
九龍沙田新城市廣場第1期6樓
www.leigarden.com.hk

■ OPENING HOURS, LAST ORDER
    營業時間，最後點菜時間
Lunch/午膳 11:30-15:00 L.O. 14:45
Dinner/晚膳 18:00-23:30 L.O. 23:00

■ PRICE/價錢
Lunch/午膳   à la carte/點菜 $150-350
Dinner/晚膳   à la carte/點菜 $150-350

Lei Garden (Tsim Sha Tsui)
利苑酒家 (尖沙咀)

The entrance takes you past an intricately carved wooden wall and a series of large fish tanks into a big, bustling, traditional dining room that's brightly lit and comfortable. There's pagoda detailing on the ceiling, bare red-brick walls and an army of staff in attendance. The varied Cantonese menu reiterates what's on offer at the other Lei Gardens using fine quality ingredients and cooking them respectfully.

要進入這家餐廳，你要先經過雕刻精緻的木質牆壁和一列大魚缸，最後來到寬敞熱鬧的傳統客廳。餐廳燈光明亮，座位亦十分舒適；天花上畫有精美寶塔圖案，牆壁上也鋪有紅磚，侍應生就如軍隊一般隨時候命。這裡的廣東菜單與其他利苑分店相若，而同出一轍的就是一級的材料和廚師認真的烹調態度。

■ ADDRESS/地址

TEL.2722 1636

B2F, Houston Centre, 63 Mody Road, East Tsim Sha Tsui, Kowloon
九龍尖東麼地道63號好時中心地庫2樓
www.leigarden.com.hk

■ OPENING HOURS, LAST ORDER
營業時間，最後點菜時間
Lunch/午膳 11:30-14:45 (L.O.)
Dinner/晚膳 18:00-23:00 (L.O.)

■ PRICE/價錢
Lunch/午膳 à la carte/點菜 $80-200
Dinner/晚膳 à la carte/點菜 $160-750

Lei Garden (Wan Chai)
利苑酒家 (灣仔)

An inventory of restaurants in Wan Chai wouldn't be complete without a Lei Garden. This branch has been recently refurbished and boasts an attractive, contemporary Chinese feel. The menu follows the tried and tested formula evident in its sister restaurants. Considerable care is taken in both sourcing the ingredients and in their preparation; specialities include deep-fried rock oyster in port wine and, of course, their famed dim sum.

灣仔的中式酒家名單怎能缺少利苑呢？這家分店最近重新裝潢，無論是選料還是準備菜式方面都見心思。菜單跟隨其他分店行之有效的美味配方，無論是選料還是準備菜式方面都精心準備。特式包括砵酒焗生蠔及著名點心。

■ ADDRESS/地址
TEL.2892 0333
1F, CNT Tower, 338 Hennessy Road, Wan Chai
灣仔軒尼詩道338號北海中心1樓
www.leigarden.com.hk

■ ANNUAL AND WEEKLY CLOSING
　休息日期
Closed 3 days Lunar New Year
農曆新年休息3天

■ OPENING HOURS, LAST ORDER
　營業時間，最後點菜時間
Lunch/午膳 11:30-14:45 (L.O.)
Dinner/晚膳 18:00-22:45 (L.O.)

■ PRICE/價錢
Lunch/午膳　à la carte/點菜 $160-750
Dinner/晚膳　à la carte/點菜 $160-750

Le Soleil

No, not a French restaurant, but a Vietnamese one, over-looking the hotel's atrium from third floor level, which can be an interesting diversion for diners. It feels a bit like sitting on a rooftop veranda as you watch elevators glide up and down. Very friendly service backs up nicely presented dishes – sometimes with an 'Asian fusion' twist – prepared with fresh market ingredients. Prices are keen and the ambience unfailingly hits the spot.

Le Soleil並非法國餐廳,而是一家越南餐廳。餐廳位於酒店三樓,食客可一邊用餐,一邊觀看中庭景象,可算是有趣的另類體驗;看著電梯上下行駛,感覺仿如置身於頂樓露台一樣。服務態度友善,菜式賣相亦相當討好,並選用新鮮食材,有時會融入亞洲元素。價錢相宜,環境格調可謂無懈可擊。

■ ADDRESS/地址

TEL.2733 2033

3F, The Royal Garden Hotel, 69 Mody Road, East Tsim Sha Tsui, Kowloon
九龍尖東麼地道69號帝苑酒店3樓
www.rghk.com.hk

■ OPENING HOURS, LAST ORDER
營業時間,最後點菜時間
Lunch/午膳 11:30-14:30 (L.O.)
Dinner/晚膳 18:00-22:30 (L.O.)

■ PRICE/價錢
Lunch/午膳   set/套餐 $ 128
                 à la carte/點菜 $ 250-600
Dinner/晚膳 à la carte/點菜 $ 250-600

Lin Heung Kui
蓮香居

Opened in May 2009, this huge eatery on two floors aims to build on the success of the famous Lin Heung Tea House in Wellington Street. Modest inside, but hugely popular, the dim sum trolley is a must with customers keen to be the first to choose from its extensive offerings. The main menu offers classic Cantonese dishes with specialities such as Lin Heung special duck house style. The pastry shop below is worth a look on the way out.

佔地甚廣的蓮香居於二零零九年開幕，樓高兩層，秉承威靈頓街蓮香樓的輝煌成績。樸素的內部裝潢擋不住人氣，點心車最讓急不及待從其各式各樣點心中選擇心愛好。菜單上提供傳統廣東菜及特色小菜，如蓮香霸王鴨。離開時路經樓下的中式餅店，亦值得留意。

■ ADDRESS/地址
TEL.2156 9328
2-3F, 40-50 Des Voeux Road West,
Sheung Wan
上環德輔道西40-50號2-3樓

■ OPENING HOURS, LAST ORDER
　營業時間，最後點菜時間
06:00-22:30

■ PRICE/價錢
Lunch/午膳　à la carte/點菜 $ 120-300
Dinner/晚膳　à la carte/點菜 $ 120-300

Lin Heung Tea House
蓮香樓

A famous name for 80 years, this restaurant was lightly renovated in June 2009. Dim sum is served from 6am to late afternoon, while classic Cantonese dishes are offered at night. Don't underestimate this place: many come early for their dim sum and not only do you need to find a table but the favourites, like steamed egg cake, are gone the second those trolleys roll out. Try a few Lin Heung specials in the evening, like the duck and pork ribs.

八十年來聞名四方的蓮香樓於二零零九年六月稍作裝修。清晨六時至下午供應點心，晚上則供應粵菜。不要低估了這茶樓：很多人清早慕名前來品嘗其點心，你不但要忙著佔桌，更要找尋著名美點，如蒸馬拉糕，點心車甫出現就被掃個片甲不留了。晚上可嚐嚐蓮香精選蓮香霸王鴨及招牌醬燒骨。

■ ADDRESS/地址
TEL.2544 4556
160-164 Wellington Street, Central
中環威靈頓街160-164號

■ ANNUAL AND WEEKLY CLOSING
　休息日期
Closed 3 days Lunar New Year
農曆新年休息3天

■ OPENING HOURS, LAST ORDER
　營業時間，最後點菜時間
06:00-23:00

■ PRICE/價錢
Lunch/午膳　à la carte/點菜 $ 120-300
Dinner/晚膳　à la carte/點菜 $ 120-300

Lippo Chiuchow
力寶軒

Lippo Chiuchow has around 300 seats so is hardly the spot for a romantic dinner. But its noisy atmosphere is clearly appealing, as the local office workers who come in for a quick lunch will testify. But the main reason why it is always full – and why bookings are a must – is because the food is very good. Chiuchow – a popular Chinese cuisine – is simple and fresh: smoked duck with green apple or fried chicken with chinjew sauce.

力寶軒設有約300個座位，要吃浪漫晚餐，這裡並不是合適的選擇。但吵鬧的氣氛代表著它受歡迎的程度，中午時分來此用餐的本地白領大可作證。這裡如此有名，座無虛席——更必須訂座——的最主要原因，還是其出色的菜式。這裡的潮州菜(中菜的一種)既簡單又新鮮，推介菜式包括青蘋果煙鴨及碧綠川椒雞。

■ ADDRESS/地址

TEL.2526 1168

Shop 4, GF, Lippo Centre, 89 Queensway, Admiralty

金鐘金鐘道89號力寶中心4號舖

www.lipporestaurant.com

■ OPENING HOURS, LAST ORDER

營業時間，最後點菜時間

Lunch/午膳 11:00-15:00 (L.O.)
Dinner/晚膳 17:00-22:30 (L.O.)

■ PRICE/價錢

Lunch/午膳 à la carte/點菜 $180-800
Dinner/晚膳 à la carte/點菜 $180-800

Liu Yuan Pavilion
留園雅敘

🖥16 ☏🍴

Thanks to being more intimate than most restaurants and having built up a loyal following means that it's advisable to arrive having booked ahead. The light and airy décor is a pleasing environment in which to enjoy some seriously good Shanghainese cuisine. Perhaps start with some steamed pork dumplings and pan-fried pork buns and include hairy crab with salty eggs from the vast seafood choice to follow. Good value for money.

留園雅敘比大多數餐廳提供更貼心服務，造就了一群忠心擁護者。建議提早預約。輕巧通爽的裝潢提供舒適環境，可供享受極為出色的上海佳餚。先試試蒸豬肉餃、生煎包，毛蟹鹹蛋之外更有一系列海鮮可供選擇。物超所值。

■ ADDRESS/地址
TEL.2804 2000
3F, The Broadway, 54-62 Lockhart Road, Wan Chai
灣仔駱克道54-62號博匯大廈3樓

■ OPENING HOURS, LAST ORDER
營業時間，最後點菜時間
Lunch/午膳 12:00-14:30 (L.O.)
Dinner/晚膳 18:00-22:30 (L.O.)

■ PRICE/價錢
Lunch/午膳 à la carte/點菜 $200-400
Dinner/晚膳 à la carte/點菜 $300-600

Loaf On
六福菜館

🛋36 📞🍴

Hidden one block behind the strip of seafood restaurants in Sai Kung is this neat little restaurant, spread over three floors. Their soup of the day depends on what the owner finds and buys from the local fishermen. You can even bring your own seafood and have staff prepare it for you. Besides seafood, Loaf On also offers simple Cantonese dishes like stir-fry prawns with eggs, Loaf On-style chicken and salt and pepper calamari.

這家小菜館隱藏在西貢的海鮮餐廳一帶的後街，佔地三層。是日例湯視乎店主當天從當地漁民處買到的新鮮食材。你甚至可自行攜帶海鮮，交由店員烹調。除了海鮮，六福菜館還提供簡單粵菜如滑蛋蝦仁、風沙雞及椒鹽鮮魷。

■ ADDRESS/地址

TEL.2792 9966
49 See Cheung Street, Sai Kung
西貢市場街49號

■ OPENING HOURS, LAST ORDER
　營業時間，最後點菜時間
11:00-23:00 L.O. 22:30

■ PRICE/價錢
Lunch/午膳　à la carte/點菜 $150-500
Dinner/晚膳　à la carte/點菜 $200-500

Lobster Bar and Grill
龍蝦吧

The clubby atmosphere here derives from the British colonial furniture and décor: you can even enjoy an aperitif or
single malt whisky in a cosy armchair upholstered in Scottish
tartan. Specialities here are of course Maine lobsters (where
you choose which one you want from the large tank) as
well as a variety of oysters, fish and grilled meats. Largely
business-orientated at lunchtime but more relaxed with live
music during the evening.

殖民地英式傢具和裝潢襯托出夜店般的氣氛：你可以躺在舒適的蘇格蘭格仔扶
手椅上享受一杯餐前酒或單一麥芽威士忌。鎮店菜式當然少不了波士頓(緬因
州)龍蝦（可以從大魚缸中挑選），以及一系列蠔，魚及烤肉。午餐時段較多
商務人士，晚上氣氛則較悠閒，有現場樂隊演奏。

■ ADDRESS/地址

TEL.2820 8560
6F, Island Shangri-La Hotel, Pacific
Place, Supreme Court Road, Admiralty
中區法院道太古廣場港島香格里拉大酒店
6樓
www.shangri-la.com

■ OPENING HOURS, LAST ORDER
　營業時間，最後點菜時間
Lunch/午膳 12:00-14:30 (L.O.)
Dinner/晚膳 18:30-22:30 (L.O.)

■ PRICE/價錢
Lunch/午膳　à la carte/點菜 $500-900
Dinner/晚膳　à la carte/點菜 $500-900

Luk Yu Tea House
陸羽茶室

One of the few remaining authentic teahouses in Central, which is why it's usually full with regulars every day. But persevere: it's well worth a visit. The dim sum here is affordable and excellent: no wonder the entire three floors fill up very quickly. Make sure you don't leave without trying the superb egg tarts which are wonderfully fresh. Tang Dynasty scholar and tea fanatic Luk Yuk, after whom this is named, would be proud.

這是一間在中環碩果僅存的正宗茶室，難怪經常擠滿常客，座無虛席。雖則要久候，但不要因此而卻步，用餐後你會發覺絕對不枉此行。這裡的點心價廉物美，佔地三層的茶室一早滿座亦理所當然。來到陸羽茶室，別忘記一嘗新鮮出爐的滋味蛋撻，店名中的唐代學者兼茶聖陸羽也會倍感自豪。

■ ADDRESS/地址
TEL.2523 5464
24-26 Stanley Street, Central
中環士丹利街24-26號

■ ANNUAL AND WEEKLY CLOSING
　休息日期
Closed Lunar New Year
年初一休息

■ OPENING HOURS, LAST ORDER
　營業時間, 最後點菜時間
07:00-22:00 (L.O.)

■ PRICE/價錢
Lunch/午膳　à la carte/點菜 $100-300
Dinner/晚膳　à la carte/點菜 $200-300

Lung Kee (Temple Street)
龍記 (廟街)

This little noodle shop, like its three other branches in Hong Kong, is renowned for is wonton noodles and various meat balls. It is also your typical basic model, with a few round tables, foldable chairs and quick service. The menu is on the wall, with pictures to help along the decision process. The wonton goes without saying, but the pork ball with special sauce would make many a customer come back for more.

這家小小的麵店與本港另外三家分店一樣,以雲吞麵及多種肉丸馳名。店面陳設為常見的基本模式:數張圓桌、摺椅及快速服務。菜單張貼在牆上,並附有圖片助你做出決定。雲吞的美味當然不用多説,其醬爆豬肉丸更令不少食客食過番尋味。

■ ADDRESS/地址

TEL.2770 9108

226 Temple Street, Jordan, Kowloon
九龍佐敦廟街226號

■ ANNUAL AND WEEKLY CLOSING
　休息日期
Closed 1 week Lunar New Year
農曆新年休息7天

■ OPENING HOURS, LAST ORDER
　營業時間,最後點菜時間
11:00-21:00 (L.O.)

■ PRICE/價錢

Lunch/午膳	set/套餐	$ 17
	à la carte/點菜	$ 13-35
Dinner/晚膳	set/套餐	$ 17
	à la carte/點菜	$ 13-35

Lung King Heen
龍景軒

✿✿✿　　　　　　　　　　　　　　　✕✕✕✕

Translated as 'view of the dragon', it now offers a pan-orama of Victoria Harbour whilst the interior is smart and uncluttered, with hand-embroidered silk, columns and glass screens. Ingredients here are of the highest quality – particularly the seafood which is impeccably fresh; all dishes are expertly crafted, nicely balanced and enticingly presented. The serving team is highly professional and describe dishes with great care and obvious pride.

龍景軒名副其實，坐擁動人心弦的維港全景；餐廳內部亦時尚整潔，飾以手工刺繡絲綢、圓柱和玻璃屏幕。食材品質上等，特別是海鮮，絕對新鮮。菜式全是悉心烹調，精心雕琢，賣相一流。服務專業，侍應會細心自豪地介紹菜式。

■ ADDRESS/地址
TEL.3196 8880
4F, Four Seasons Hotel, 8 Finance
Street, Central
中環金融街8號四季酒店4樓
www.fourseasons.com/hongkong

■ OPENING HOURS, LAST ORDER
　營業時間，最後點菜時間
Lunch/午膳 12:00-14:30 (L.O.)
Dinner/晚膳 18:00-22:30 (L.O.)

■ PRICE/價錢
Lunch/午膳　set/套餐　　　　$430
　　　　　　à la carte/點菜 $300-1,300
Dinner/晚膳　set/套餐　　　$1,080
　　　　　　à la carte/點菜 $300-1,300

Mak An Kee Noodle (Wing Kut Street)
麥奀記(忠記)麵家 (永吉街)

This narrow shop, at Des Voeux Road and Wing Kut Street, tucked away behind the market, quickly fills up at lunch break time. The regular clientele will happily move up to allow you to share their tables. The legendary beef and wonton noodles is the speciality of the house; using the best quality raw ingredients, their exquisite bowls are bursting with flavour. Furthermore, this quality comes at prices that represent very good value for money.

這家窄小的麵店位於德輔道與永吉街交界，隱藏在街市後方，午飯時間座無虛席。店內常客很樂意稍移座位，與你共用餐桌。其傳統牛腩雲吞麵甚具特色，用料上乘，泡製出每一碗都香濃美味。此外，更是價格相宜，物超所值。

■ ADDRESS/地址
TEL.2541 6388
37 Wing Kut Street, Central
中環永吉街37號

■ OPENING HOURS, LAST ORDER
營業時間，最後點菜時間
10:30-20:00 (L.O.)

■ PRICE/價錢
Lunch/午膳　à la carte/點菜 $ 35-60
Dinner/晚膳　à la carte/點菜 $ 35-60

Mak's Noodle
麥奀雲吞麵世家

A small place with a famous reputation: Mak Chi Ming's father opened the original Mak's Noodle in 1960, while his granddad was 'king of the won ton' in the 1930s. Fittingly, for a world-renowned name, the premises are very simple. The staff - strict, efficient and overseen by the boss - serve nothing but noodles, with fresh, authentic recipes utilising seasonal vegetables produced to order. Most prized dish is the mouth-watering chutney pork.

地方淺窄的餐廳卻享負盛名：麥志明祖父是30年代的「雲吞麵大王」，父親則於1960年創立了麥奀記老店。作為世界知名的食店，地方亦十分簡潔。員工由老闆監督著，既嚴謹又有效率。餐廳供應的只有麵，採用新鮮食材、正宗食譜，以及季節性蔬菜。最特別的菜式是令人垂涎欲滴的炸醬麵。

■ ADDRESS/地址
TEL.2854 3810
77 Wellington Street, Central
中環威靈頓街77號

■ OPENING HOURS, LAST ORDER
營業時間，最後點菜時間
11:00-19:45 (L.O.)

■ PRICE/價錢
Lunch/午膳   à la carte/點菜 $ 28-60
Dinner/晚膳   à la carte/點菜 $ 28-60

Mandarin Grill + Bar
文華扒房+酒吧

A luminous dining room — Sir Terence Conran's refurbishment has kept the Oriental references; if you want to be seen, this is the place to eat. Alternatively, if you want to see the oyster chefs at work, sit at the bar and watch them — guaranteed freshness! On the other side, behind a window, the kitchen team prepare appealing and contemporary European cuisine. Soufflé lovers adore this place as they have a large selection from which to choose.

明亮的餐廳經過20世紀著名的室內設計師Sir Terence Conran 的裝修後，仍然保留文華東方的味道。如果你的用餐不介意張揚，這家餐廳則十分適合。又或者，如果你想看看師傅如何準備生蠔，坐在吧檯觀看吧，生蠔保證新鮮！餐廳的另一邊，你可透過窗戶看到廚房團隊用心準備令人垂涎三尺的當代歐洲菜。梳乎厘的愛好者鍾情於這個地方，因為這裡的選擇琳瑯滿目。

■ ADDRESS/地址

TEL.2825 4004

1F, Mandarin Oriental Hotel, 5 Connaught Road, Central
中環干諾道中5號文華東方酒店1樓
www.mandarinoriental.com/hongkong

■ ANNUAL AND WEEKLY CLOSING
  休息日期
Closed Saturday lunch and Sunday lunch
週六、日午膳休息

■ OPENING HOURS, LAST ORDER
  營業時間，最後點菜時間
Lunch/午膳 12:00-14:30 (L.O.)
Dinner/晚膳 18:30-22:30 (L.O.)

■ PRICE/價錢

Lunch/午膳	set/套餐	$588
	à la carte/點菜	$650-1,000
Dinner/晚膳	set/套餐	$888
	à la carte/點菜	$650-1,000

Cantonese/粵菜

MAP/地圖　18/B-2

Man Ho
萬豪殿

A recent renovation has updated the décor of these two large and elegant dining rooms, located just below the lobby of the JW Marriott Hotel. But regulars won't be too bothered because, more importantly to them, the food remains as was. That means traditional Cantonese cuisine and the judicious use of fresh, local ingredients in good-value dishes, such as double-boiled fish maws soup with sea whelks and chicken.

最近重新裝潢，令這兩個位於萬豪酒店大堂下層、佔地甚廣的高雅飯廳更添精緻。常客則不會受此影響；對他們來說，食物品質維持一貫高水平更為重要——萬豪殿提供以新鮮本地食材烹製的傳統粵菜，如原盅花膠響螺燉雞。

■ ADDRESS/地址
TEL.2841 3853
3F, JW Marriott Hotel, Pacific Place, 88 Queensway, Admiralty
金鐘金鐘道88號太古廣場萬豪酒店3樓
www.jwmarriotthongkong.com

■ OPENING HOURS, LAST ORDER
　營業時間，最後點菜時間
Lunch/午膳　11:30-14:30 (L.O.)
Dinner/晚膳　18:30-21:30 (L.O.)

■ PRICE/價錢
Lunch/午膳　à la carte/點菜　$280-700
Dinner/晚膳　à la carte/點菜　$280-700

161

Man Wah
文華廳

Man Wah seems to have been untouched by the hotel's modern renovation and exudes a luxuriously intimate and traditional feel. Tables just off the room entrance have the better harbour views, though everyone can appreciate the décor: brass lanterns hang from the wood ceiling and the ornate screen is from the original opening. The Peking duck is a classic, as is the steamed crab claw with winter melon and ginger and the Wagyu beef Cantonese style.

文華似乎沒有被酒店的現代裝修影響，這裡仍然散發著一種豪華的舒適傳統氣息。雖然近門口的餐桌享有較佳的海景，但所有人都可以欣賞這裡的裝潢：木天花板吊著黃銅燈籠，而華麗的屏幕是從開張使用至今。菜單滿是著經典菜式，這裡的北京填鴨是名副其實的美食，薑汁冬瓜蒸蟹拑及粵式和牛亦不遑多讓。

■ ADDRESS/地址

TEL.2825 4003

25F, Mandarin Oriental Hotel, 5 Connaught Road, Central
中環干諾道中5號文華東方酒店25樓
www.mandarinoriental.com/hongkong

■ OPENING HOURS, LAST ORDER
營業時間，最後點菜時間
Lunch/午膳 12:00-14:30 (L.O.)
Dinner/晚膳 18:30-22:30 (L.O.)

■ PRICE/價錢

Lunch/午膳	set/套餐	$428-548
	à la carte/點菜	$300-750
Dinner/晚膳	à la carte/點菜	$300-750

Ming Court
明閣

A fascinating collection of replica Ching Dynasty pottery as well as some fine Chinese landscape paintings lend elegance to this already stylish interior with its curved walls and smart lighting. This is more than matched by the equally sophisticated Cantonese menu with its featured specialities of shark fin flight (4 ways with shark fin) and deep-fried lobster with cheese and simmered abalone with vinegar. The service here is also excellent.

餐廳收藏了一系列清代陶器的仿製品,以及一些筆法細緻的中國山水畫,令本已獨具風格的裝潢更顯高雅。牆身呈弧形,燈光亦經過精心設計。這樣的環境與同樣匠心獨運的粵菜菜譜配合得天衣無縫。精選菜式包括魚紅翅肆式薈(四種魚翅烹調法)及脆芝士龍蝦伴醋香鮑魚天使麵。服務態度更是一流。

■ ADDRESS/地址
TEL.3552 3300
6F, Langham Place Hotel, 555
Shanghai Street, Mong Kok, Kowloon
九龍旺角上海街555號朗豪酒店6樓
www.hongkong.langhamplacehotels.com

■ OPENING HOURS, LAST ORDER
營業時間,最後點菜時間
Lunch/午膳 11:00-14:30 (L.O.)
Dinner/晚膳 18:00-22:30 (L.O.)

■ PRICE/價錢

Lunch/午膳	set/套餐	$398
	à la carte/點菜	$200-600
Dinner/晚膳	set/套餐	$398-798
	à la carte/點菜	$200-600

Ming Kee
明記

Lau Fau Shan, in the west of New Territories, is famed for its oyster farms and Ming Kee is one of several seafood restaurants on its main street. But it stands out from others for the consistent quality of popular dishes, such as stir-fry prawns in soy sauce, oysters cooked in port and Ming Kee-style fried rice. Or choose your seafood from the shop next door and the waiters will give you the cooking options. Reservations are a must at weekends.

位於新界西的流浮山向來以養蠔場聞名，明記就是大街上著名的海鮮酒家之一。明記較其他同業更為優勝之處，在於能維持其招牌名菜的水準，如豉油皇大海蝦、砵酒焗生蠔及招牌炒飯。你亦可在旁邊的海鮮店自行挑選材料，讓服務生建議烹調方式。週末必須預約。

■ ADDRESS/地址
TEL.2472 1408
40, Ching Tai Street, Lau Fau Shan, New Territories
新界流浮山正大街40號

■ OPENING HOURS, LAST ORDER
營業時間，最後點菜時間
Lunch/午膳 11:00-14:30 (L.O.)
Dinner/晚膳 16:30-22:30 (L.O.)

■ PRICE/價錢
Lunch/午膳 à la carte/點菜 $200-600
Dinner/晚膳 à la carte/點菜 $200-600

Modern China (Causeway Bay)
金滿庭 (銅鑼灣)

🍴

🪑18 🕐🍴

Two statues of ancient Chinese soldiers stand guard at the entrance to this Northern Chinese establishment housed on one of the 4 floors of a bustling food forum and with its own direct lift access. Inside, the atmosphere is lively and noisy and diners are allowed a clear view into the spotless kitchen to see good-value specialities from the areas of Shanghai, Sichuan and Beijing being prepared. Booking is essential.

兩座中國古代士兵雕像昂然屹立於門前；金滿庭位於佔地四層的食通天美食廣場，人流旺盛，設有專屬升降機供顧客使用。店內同樣是一片熙來攘往，廚房只隔一道透明玻璃，顧客可清楚看見一塵不染的廚房烹調來自上海、四川、北京等地的名菜。必須預先訂座。

■ ADDRESS/地址
TEL.2506 2525
Shop 1002, 10F, Food Forum, Times Square, 1 Matheson Street, Causeway Bay
銅鑼灣勿地臣街1號時代廣場食通天10樓1002號舖
www.modernchinarestaurant.com

■ ANNUAL AND WEEKLY CLOSING
　休息日期
Closed Lunar New Year
年初一休息

■ OPENING HOURS, LAST ORDER
　營業時間，最後點菜時間
Lunch/午膳 11:45-14:45 (L.O.)
Dinner/晚膳 17:45-22:45 (L.O.)

■ PRICE/價錢
Lunch/午膳 　à la carte/點菜 $200-800
Dinner/晚膳 　à la carte/點菜 $200-800

Morton's of Chicago

♿ ≺ 📷12 ❧

This buzzing outpost of the legendary Illinois steakhouse allows you to feast on all the classic dishes – only with Victoria Harbour sparkling as the backdrop. As well as old favourites such as Caesar salad and shrimp cocktail, all the prime cuts are available using both American and Australian aged beef. But beware: portions are massive and two of you may care to share a double Porterhouse steak!

這家享負盛名的美國伊利諾扒房總是鬧哄哄，在此食客可以品嘗到所有經典美食，同時飽覽維多利亞港的閃爍夜景。除了凱撒沙律和大蝦雞尾酒等招牌美食，這裡更提供美國和澳洲頂級的各種牛扒。請注意：這裡的牛扒份量十足，一塊雙份上等腰肉牛扒已足夠二人享用！

■ ADDRESS/地址

TEL.2732 2343

4F, Sheraton Hotel, 20 Nathan Road,
Tsim Sha Tsui, Kowloon
九龍尖沙咀彌敦道20號喜來登酒店4樓
www.mortons.com

■ ANNUAL AND WEEKLY CLOSING
  休息日期

Closed 1 January and Lunar New Year
1月1日及年初一休息

■ OPENING HOURS, LAST ORDER
  營業時間，最後點菜時間
Dinner/晚膳 17:30-23:00 (L.O.)

■ PRICE/價錢
Dinner/晚膳 à la carte/點菜 $ 600-900

Naozen
なお膳

📷20 🚇 ☎🍴

A simple, sober Japanese restaurant in an easy-to-find location. There are two rooms, one at the front and one at the back; as you enter, you can watch the chef in front of you preparing sushi and sashimi. Upstairs are three tatami rooms for private dining (take off your shoes when you come up here). The menu features almost all types of Japanese cuisine: sushi, sashimi, tempura, soba and seasonal recipes. Bargain prices at lunch are available.

這是一家簡單沉著的日本餐廳，位置容易尋找。餐廳包括兩個房間，一間在前面，另一間在後面。進入餐廳時，可以看到師傅在你面前準備壽司和魚生。樓上有三間榻榻米房間供私人用餐，到這裡時便要脫鞋。菜式選擇包括各種日本料理：壽司、刺身、天婦羅、蕎麥麵及時令特選菜式。午餐時段更有特惠價格。

■ ADDRESS/地址
TEL.2877 6668
21-25 Wellington Street, Central
中環威靈頓街21-25號
www.naozen.com

■ ANNUAL AND WEEKLY CLOSING
　休息日期
Closed Lunar New Year and Sunday lunch
年初一及週日午膳休息

■ OPENING HOURS, LAST ORDER
　營業時間，最後點菜時間
Lunch/午膳 11:30-14:30 (L.O.)
Dinner/晚膳 18:00-22:30 (L.O.)

■ PRICE/價錢

Lunch/午膳	set/套餐	$ 110-240
	à la carte/點菜	$ 200-700
Dinner/晚膳	set/套餐	$ 320-780
	à la carte/點菜	$ 200-700

Nicholini's
意寧谷

This stylish circular room has large windows that offer a peak between the adjoining tower blocks, allowing views over the bay. At the back is a large Venetian scene and some intriguing glass sculptures which lend an air of opulence to the formal feel. The cooking mixes traditional Northern Italian recipes and contemporary influences; don't miss the excellent pasta. Recommended dishes include three-way scallops and the wild mushroom lasagne.

這家時尚的圓形餐廳擁有寬大的窗戶，於鄰近摩天大樓中鶴立雞群，坐擁維港美景。餐廳後方的巨型威尼斯佈景和迷人的玻璃塑像，散發著豪華莊重的氣息。烹調方式融合北義大利傳統煮法及現代元素；切勿錯過其出色義大利麵！推薦菜式包括三式帶子及焗野菌千層麵。

■ ADDRESS/地址
TEL.2521 3838
8F, Conrad Hotel, Pacific Place, 88 Queensway, Admiralty
金鐘金鐘道88號太古廣場港麗酒店8樓
www.conradhotels.com

■ ANNUAL AND WEEKLY CLOSING
　休息日期
Closed Saturday lunch
週六午膳休息

■ OPENING HOURS, LAST ORDER
　營業時間，最後點菜時間
Lunch/午膳　12:00-15:00 (L.O.)
Dinner/晚膳　18:30-23:00 (L.O.)

■ PRICE/價錢
Lunch/午膳　set/套餐　　　　$395
　　　　　　à la carte/點菜 $500-1,000
Dinner/晚膳　set/套餐　　$688-788
　　　　　　à la carte/點菜 $500-1,000

Nobu

The ceiling here has patterns of undulating sea urchin spines and behind the bar, there are views of cherry blossoms at this branch of the über-fashionable Nobu brand. Sadly, the service is not so spot on. At lunch, bento boxes are very popular. At dinner, Mr. Matsuhisa's beguiling blend of Japanese and South American tastes continues to work its fashionable magic by featuring sushi and sashimi, excellent quality seafood and fine salsas.

天花板有呈波浪狀的海膽刺，而酒吧後面則有櫻花美景一走在時代尖端的設計盡在享譽國際的Nobu餐廳，然而服務尚有改善空間。午餐時間的便當盒非常受歡迎，而晚餐方面，主廚松久信幸融合日本和南美風味，炮製的嶄新口味更是迷人。菜式包括壽司、刺身、頂級海鮮及辛香番茄醬。

■ ADDRESS/地址

TEL.2313 2340

2F, Intercontinental Hotel, 18 Salisbury Road, Tsim Sha Tsui, Kowloon

九龍尖沙咀梳士巴利道18號洲際酒店2樓

■ OPENING HOURS, LAST ORDER
　營業時間，最後點菜時間

Lunch/午膳 12:00-14:30 (L.O.)
Dinner/晚膳 18:00-23:00 (L.O.)

■ PRICE/價錢

Lunch/午膳	set/套餐	$ 130-588
	à la carte/點菜	$ 250-1,200
Dinner/晚膳	set/套餐	$ 688-1,188
	à la carte/點菜	$ 250-1,200

Olala (St. Francis Street)
一碗麵 (聖佛蘭士街)

Olala has this corner of chic Wan Chai covered, with its brasserie, charcuterie shop and traiteur. But it is the immaculately kept noodle shop on the corner that is the best of the bunch. Its creator, Mr Chow, has a passion for fine ingredients and imports many of them from Europe. The bones from the Iberico hams form the basis of the big bowls of noodles which are becoming legendary, along with the braised beef variety too.

一碗麵位處灣仔時尚一角，有啤酒店、熟食店、熟食外燴(traiteur)。但其位於街角的麵店才是真正中心，客人的不二之選。創辦人周老闆對精緻原料有一番追求，不少原料更由歐洲進口。西班牙黑毛豬風腿骨是大碗麵的基本材料，已成傳奇，還有炆牛腩可供選擇。

■ ADDRESS/地址

TEL.2294 0426
33 St. Francis Street, Wan Chai
灣仔聖佛蘭士街33號

■ OPENING HOURS, LAST ORDER
營業時間，最後點菜時間
11:30-22:30 (L.O.)

■ PRICE/價錢
Lunch/午膳　à la carte/點菜 $80-150
Dinner/晚膳　à la carte/點菜 $100-250

1/5 Nuevo

Behind the modern glass façade you'll find a stylish bar but head beyond, to the rear dining room. Here, red drapes and arty nude photos add to the sensual and intimate feel. The open-plan kitchen delivers very good value international cooking at lunch which is geared towards local business types. The dinner à la carte menu offers more Mediterranean influences, especially from Spain and Italy. The cooking is crisp, light, fresh and satisfying.

1/5 Nuevo擁有時尚的玻璃外觀，型格酒吧的後方便是餐室，這裡的紅色窗簾和藝術性的裸照營造了感性的氣氛。這間開放式廚房的餐廳在午市時段供應物有所值的國際菜式，食客亦以本地商務客人為主。晚餐散叫的菜單涵蓋較多地中海菜式，尤其是西班牙菜和意大利菜。菜餚清新輕盈，既新鮮又豐足。

■ ADDRESS/地址
TEL.2529 2300
9 Star Street, Wan Chai
灣仔星街9號
www.elite-concept.com

■ ANNUAL AND WEEKLY CLOSING
　休息日期
Closed Sunday lunch
週日午膳休息

■ OPENING HOURS, LAST ORDER
　營業時間，最後點菜時間
Lunch/午膳 12:00-14:30 L.O. 14:00
Dinner/晚膳 18:00-24:00 L.O. 22:45

■ PRICE/價錢
Lunch/午膳　à la carte/點菜 $ 118-168
Dinner/晚膳　à la carte/點菜 $ 220-300

One Harbour Road
港灣壹號

One Harbour Road may be set in a hotel, but its beautifully refined ambience will make you think you're on the terrace of an elegant 1930s Taipan mansion. The bright and airy feel comes courtesy of split-level dining offering views of the harbour. A profusion of plants, large lotus pond and sound of running water soften the bold statement of the huge pillars. Renowned Cantonese menus offer a wide variety of well-prepared meat and fish dishes.

雖然港灣壹號位於酒店內，但這裡的優雅氣氛，令你恍如置身於30年代的優雅大班府第。分層用餐讓你同時飽覽海景，享受明亮又通風的環境。茂盛的植物、大型蓮花池，以及潺潺的流水聲，軟化了龐大柱子給人的感覺。這裡的著名粵菜包括準備妥當、種類繁多的肉類和魚類菜式。

■ ADDRESS/地址
TEL.2584 7722
8F, Grand Hyatt Hotel, 1 Harbour Road, Wan Chai
灣仔港灣道一號君悅酒店8樓
www.hongkong.grand.hyatt.com

■ OPENING HOURS, LAST ORDER
營業時間，最後點菜時間
Lunch/午膳 12:00-14:30 (L.O.)
Dinner/晚膳 18:30-22:30 (L.O.)

■ PRICE/價錢
Lunch/午膳	set/套餐	$ 400-500
	à la carte/點菜	$ 300-990
Dinner/晚膳	set/套餐	$ 770
	à la carte/點菜	$ 330-990

On Lot 10

Having just 12 seats inside and 8 on the terrace makes this one of the smallest French restaurants in town. But what it lacks in size it makes up for in quality. The passionate chef tours the markets daily to compile his good value menu of traditional Gallic home cooking; specialities include whole fish with crushed potatoes and roasted chicken with black truffle and sweet peas. Choice is limited at lunch so dinner is the best time to visit.

這家全港最小巧的法國餐廳只提供十二個室內座位及八個花園雅座，但其高品質讓它絲毫不顯遜色。充滿熱情的主廚每天穿梭市場，準備其獨具傳統法國家常菜風格的實惠菜單；店內特色法國菜包括原條魚焗薯蓉、黑松露茵蜜糖豆烤雞。中午時段選擇有限，建議於晚餐時段光顧。

■ ADDRESS/地址
TEL.2155 9210
34 Gough Street, Central
中環歌賦街34號

■ OPENING HOURS, LAST ORDER
營業時間，最後點菜時間
Lunch/午膳 12:15-14:45 (L.O.)
Dinner/晚膳 18:00-22:30 (L.O.)

■ PRICE/價錢
Lunch/午膳　set/套餐　　　$110-130
Dinner/晚膳　à la carte/點菜 $280-370

Oriental Lily
喜百合

♿ P ⌗24

Ask for help at the entrance, because there is a bewildering array of escalators and lifts. The journey is worth it though, as the restaurant is surprisingly plush, with chandeliers and deep carpets; the best seats are hidden behind an impressive curtain of steel. Expect authentic Pekingese dishes, with classics such as Peking duck and deep-fried prawns with chilli sauce. Specialities such as Beggars chicken are well worth pre-ordering.

在入口尋求協助吧——一列電梯和升降機可能令你不知所措。不過一切都是值得的：餐廳豪華得令人驚嘆，設有華麗吊燈及地毯，最好的座位隱藏在鋼帘後。在這裡，你可享受到正宗北京菜，經典如北京填鴨及北京宮爆蝦球。馳名菜式如富貴雞建議預訂——你會發現物有所值。

■ ADDRESS/地址
TEL.2629 5038
13F, MegaBox, 38 Wang Chiu Road, Kowloon Bay, Kowloon
九龍灣宏照道38號MegaBox13樓
www.maxims.com.hk

■ OPENING HOURS, LAST ORDER
營業時間，最後點菜時間
Lunch/午膳　11:30-15:00 L.O. 14:45
Dinner/晚膳　17:30-23:30 L.O. 23:15

■ PRICE/價錢
Lunch/午膳　à la carte/點菜 $160-310
Dinner/晚膳　à la carte/點菜 $160-310

Ovologue
祇月

The ground floor of this recently converted 'tong lau' building houses a fashionable destination restaurant that's best seen in the evening. Try to sit in the far room, with its images of old Hong Kong projected onto its walls. The contemporary interior is matched by the food and features strong Sichuan and Shanghainese influences. Follow the 'rules' set down in the menu and the experience will be rewarding.

餐廳位於一幢最近成功轉型的唐樓地下，成為入夜後最時尚的選擇。可試試坐在最後的房間用餐，老香港的影像全都投射在牆上。時尚的內部裝潢與食物非常配合，帶有強烈的四川和上海風格。跟從菜牌上的「規矩」而得來的用餐體驗，將令你非常滿足。

■ ADDRESS/地址
TEL.2527 6088
66 Johnston Road, Wan Chai
灣仔莊士敦道66號
www.ovologue.com.hk

■ OPENING HOURS, LAST ORDER
營業時間，最後點菜時間
Lunch/午膳 11:30-14:30 (L.O.)
Dinner/晚膳 18:30-22:45 (L.O.)

■ PRICE/價錢
Lunch/午膳　à la carte/點菜 $200-500
Dinner/晚膳　à la carte/點菜 $500-700

Oyster & Wine Bar

This cosmopolitan wine bar and seafood restaurant ensures that great harbour views are not the only draw. The extensive array of crustacea on display at the seafood counter is a feast for the eyes; oysters are a speciality and over 20 different varieties are offered – they come from the Brittany cliffs to Australian reefs. Along with the dextrous ecailler, expect sommeliers to recommend the perfect white wine to complement your chosen dish.

走時尚都會風格的酒吧兼海鮮餐廳並非只靠醉人景觀擄獲食客的心。海鮮吧台滿佈甲殼類海鮮，賞心悅目；這裡的蠔特別出色，提供多達二十種不同選擇——產地從法國布列塔尼懸崖到澳洲珊瑚礁，應有盡有。開生蠔的師傅技巧純熟，調酒師更會為你推介合適餐酒，搭配你所選擇的主菜。

■ ADDRESS/地址

TEL.2369 1111

19F, Sheraton Hotel, 20 Nathan Road, Tsim Sha Tsui, Kowloon
九龍尖沙咀彌敦道20號喜來登酒店19樓
www.sheraton.com/hongkong

■ OPENING HOURS, LAST ORDER
營業時間，最後點菜時間
Dinner/晚膳 18:30-23:00 (L.O.)

■ PRICE/價錢
Dinner/晚膳 à la carte/點菜 $ 550-1,450

Paul's Kitchen

The eponymous Paul is the owner-chef, whose time studying in England has given him a passion for British puddings; classics like apple crumble and bread and butter pudding are his speciality. A broader brush on starters and main courses means the menu touches most areas of Europe, delivering simple, fresh and good value dishes. This little place is not as stark as it first appears, thanks in part to the friendly service and homely feel.

著名店主兼主廚Paul在英國唸書的日子讓他愛上英式布丁；經典甜品如金寶蘋果批及牛油麵包布丁都是他的拿手好戲。前菜及主菜的豐富變化代表餐廳已涵蓋大部分歐洲國家的菜式，簡單，新鮮而物超所值。小小的餐廳其實不如第一印象般侷促，這得歸功於親切的服務態度和一種「家」的感覺。

■ ADDRESS/地址
TEL.2815 8003
24 Grough Street, Central
中環歌賦街24號
www.pauls-kitchen.com

■ OPENING HOURS, LAST ORDER
　營業時間，最後點菜時間
Lunch/午膳　12:00-14:30 L.O. 14:00
Dinner/晚膳　19:00-23:00 L.O. 22:00

■ PRICE/價錢
Lunch/午膳　set/套餐　　　$108-168
Dinner/晚膳　set/套餐　　　$260-380

Peking Garden (Admiralty)
北京樓 (金鍾)

✖✖

🍱10 🕐🍴

Belonging to the Maxim Empire and sitting pretty in Pacific Place, this restaurant offers a stylish, metropolitan atmosphere; the library room is a particularly attractive space for private parties. The menu offers classic Pekingese cuisine: barbequed Peking duck being the best seller, along with deep-fried yellow croaker fish with sweet and sour sauce and, of course, dim sum served here at both lunch and dinner.

這家隸屬美心王國的酒樓位處太古廣場，氣氛具都會時尚特色。一組組的小房間特別適合私人團體使用。提供傳統北京菜：北京填鴨和糖醋黃花魚固然最受歡迎，午市和晚市亦提供點心可供選擇。

■ ADDRESS/地址
TEL.2845 8452
Shop 005, LG, Pacific Place, 88 Queensway, Admiralty
金鐘金鐘道88號太古廣場地庫1樓5號舖
www.maxims.com.hk

■ OPENING HOURS, LAST ORDER
營業時間，最後點菜時間
Lunch/午膳 11:30-16:00 (L.O.)
Dinner/晚膳 17:30-23:00 (L.O.)
■ PRICE/價錢
Lunch/午膳 à la carte/點菜 $220-700
Dinner/晚膳 à la carte/點菜 $220-700

Peking Garden (Central)
北京樓 (中環)

At the end of a corridor, you'll find two massive wooden doors, each leading into a brightly lit dining room where the tables are neatly arranged and you're looked after by a team of chicly dressed hostesses. The signature item on the menu is the Peking duck, prepared with great precision at the table by the chef. Be sure to try the deep fried prawns in chilli sauce too. Beware when ordering as portions come in generous sizes.

走廊盡頭有兩道巨型的木門，每道門都能將你帶到一間明亮的餐室；裡面的餐桌排列整齊，侍應穿著時尚的制服，服務更是十分周到。招牌菜有北京填鴨，由廚師在餐桌旁為食客細心準備。宮爆蝦仁亦值得一試。因為食物份量豐富，點菜時要小心衡量。

■ ADDRESS/地址
TEL.2526 6456
GF, Alexandra House, 7-15 Des Voeux
Road Central, Central
中環德輔道中7-15號歷山大廈地下
www.maxims.com.hk

■ OPENING HOURS, LAST ORDER
營業時間，最後點菜時間
Lunch/午膳 11:30-15:00 (L.O.)
Dinner/晚膳 18:00-23:30 (L.O.)

■ PRICE/價錢
Lunch/午膳 à la carte/點菜 $260-600
Dinner/晚膳 à la carte/點菜 $260-600

Peking Garden (Kowloon)
北京樓 (九龍)

Lit by faux-crystal chandeliers, this is a huge, boisterous Peking restaurant with eight rooms and 500 seats. In the most spacious room (200 seats) diners are lucky indeed to get a table with a view onto the ferry pier. The well-structured staff are either supervising with calm deliberation, or pushing trolleys and serving. The hallmark is the barbecued Peking duck with pancake, or braised sliced perch with minced pork and salted cabbage.

人造水晶吊燈，燃亮著這家龐大熱鬧的北京餐廳。這裡共有8間餐室及500個座位，最大的餐室有200個座位，食客可在此觀賞碼頭海景。員工分工合作，或沉靜地監督著，或推餐車奉上食物。招牌菜是北京烤鴨配烙餅，或炆切片鱸魚配豬肉泡菜。

■ ADDRESS/地址

TEL.2735 8211

3F, Star House, 3 Salisbury Road, Tsim Sha Tsui, Kowloon

九龍尖沙咀梳士巴利道3號星光行3樓

www.maxims.com.hk

■ OPENING HOURS, LAST ORDER
   營業時間，最後點菜時間

Lunch/午膳 11:00-15:00 L.O. 14:30
Dinner/晚膳 14:30-22:30 L.O. 22:00

■ PRICE/價錢

Lunch/午膳	set/套餐	$105
	à la carte/點菜	$300-1,200
Dinner/晚膳	set/套餐	$200-300
	à la carte/點菜	$300-1,200

Peking Garden (Tai Koo Shing)
北京樓 (太古城)

Head for the City Plaza's indoor ice rink to find this ultra-smart restaurant. The interior hits the gold standard, its glitter an ornately ubiquitous statement - just what's required to draw in all those shoppers. The accomplished cuisine is mostly Peking, and the hallmark dish is Peking duck, but spice is nice here too: tuck in to fried prawns with chilli sauce. Sichuan and Shanghai elements are also on the menu, though dim sum is low key.

向太古城溜冰場的方向走，便會找到這家超時尚的餐廳。餐廳的內部實在金璧輝煌：發出閃閃生輝、無所不在的光芒，如此華麗的氣派正正吸引了購物者到此用餐。餐廳的菜式大部分是北京菜，招牌菜是北京填鴨，而這裡的香料亦頗美味：不仿試試京爆明蝦球。有些菜式含四川和上海元素，但點心則較少。

■ ADDRESS/地址

TEL.2884 4131
2F, Cityplaza II, Tai Koo Shing
太古城太古城中心第2期2樓
www.maxims.com.hk

■ OPENING HOURS, LAST ORDER
營業時間，最後點菜時間
Lunch/午膳 11:30-15:00 L.O. 14:30
Dinner/晚膳 18:00-23:30 L.O. 23:00

■ PRICE/價錢
Lunch/午膳   à la carte/點菜 $ 135-290
Dinner/晚膳   à la carte/點菜 $ 135-290

Petrus
珀翠

Perched on the 56th floor with dramatic views, this is firmly in the classical European style with moulded ceilings, chandeliers, elegantly draped curtains and refined table settings. The professional service blends in perfectly and demonstrates great attention to detail. All this is matched by very proficient French cooking that relies on a roll-call of wonderfully fresh ingredients. Exceptional wine list; live piano music at night.

餐廳座落於酒店56樓，可飽覽海港美景，設計別出心裁：雕有線條的天花、高雅的窗簾、吊燈及排列優雅的餐桌，盡顯經典歐洲格調。服務十分專業，細心周到。餐廳的法國菜廚藝一流，與絕對新鮮食材，相得益彰。出色的美酒清單，晚上更有現場鋼琴演奏。

■ ADDRESS/地址
TEL.2820 8590
56F, Island Shangri-La Hotel, Pacific Place, Supreme Court Road, Admiralty
中區法院道太古廣場港島香格里拉酒店56樓
www.shangri-la.com

■ OPENING HOURS, LAST ORDER
營業時間，最後點菜時間
Lunch/午膳　12:00-14:30 (L.O.)
Dinner/晚膳　18:30-22:30 (L.O.)

■ PRICE/價錢

Lunch/午膳	set/套餐	$428
	à la carte/點菜	$850-1,500
Dinner/晚膳	set/套餐	$1,380
	à la carte/點菜	$850-1,500

Pierre

Stylish restaurant, opened by celebrated French chef Pierre Gagnaire, with a rarefied air to match the Mandarin Oriental's highest floor. Picture windows frame large views of the harbour; the room itself has a contemporary flair, much like the menus on offer, which are complex but sober; the ambience is enhanced with soft lighting. High quality produce comes directly from France: Bigorre pork, Aubrac beef, Allaiton lamb, Bresse chicken.

由著名法國廚師Pierre Gagnaire開辦的時尚餐廳，位處文華東方頂層，居高臨下，氣勢不凡。透過窗戶可盡覽外面的大海景，餐廳本身散發著當代的氣息，就像這裡的菜單一樣，既複雜又沉實；加上柔和的燈光，氣氛十足。高質產品直接由法國進口：Bigorre省份的豬肉、Aubrac省份的牛肉、Allaiton省份的羊肉、Bresse省份的雞肉等等。

■ ADDRESS/地址

TEL.2825 4001

25F, Mandarin Oriental Hotel, 5
Connaught Road, Central
中環干諾道中5號文華東方酒店25樓
www.mandarinoriental.com/hongkong

■ ANNUAL AND WEEKLY CLOSING
　休息日期

Closed Saturday lunch, Sunday and
Public Holidays
週六午膳、週日及公眾假期休息

■ OPENING HOURS, LAST ORDER
　營業時間，最後點菜時間
Lunch/午膳 12:00-14:30 (L.O.)
Dinner/晚膳 19:00-22:30 (L.O.)

■ PRICE/價錢

Lunch/午膳	set/套餐	$440-1,488
	à la carte/點菜	$950-1,500
Dinner/晚膳	set/套餐	$1,488
	à la carte/點菜	$950-1,500

Prince
王子飯店

The artistically presented cuisine in Prince goes nicely with the elegant surroundings – One Peking is a smart building, and views from the 11th floor to the harbour are equally impressive. The self-proclaimed 'Imperial cuisine' is in fact a modern approach to Chinese food with specialities like braised grouper with ginger and spring onion, or dry braised shark fin soup with crab meat. Stylish service complements a smoothly comfortable ambience.

王子飯店環境優雅，與其雅緻的菜餚一脈相承。北京道一號是一幢時尚的建築物，從11樓看出去的海景同樣令人印象深刻。餐廳稱為「御膳」的其實是現代中國菜，包括砂鍋干迫海斑和生拆蟹 扒乾燒鮑翅。時尚的服務與舒適的氣氛配合得天衣無縫。

■ ADDRESS/地址
TEL.2366 1308
11F, One Peking Road, Tsim Sha Tsui, Kowloon
九龍尖沙咀北京道1號11樓
www.prince-catering.com

■ OPENING HOURS, LAST ORDER
  營業時間，最後點菜時間
Lunch/午膳 11:00-16:30 L.O. 16:00
Dinner/晚膳 18:00-24:00 L.O. 23:00

■ PRICE/價錢
Lunch/午膳   set/套餐 $138-398
             à la carte/點菜 $480-2,000
Dinner/晚膳 set/套餐 $480-1,380
             à la carte/點菜 $600-2,000

Queen's Palace
帝后殿

This late 2008 addition to Wan Chai's dining scene specialises in Shanghainese cooking and their menu helpfully includes photos of the specialities and an indication of their relative heat. Those specialities include smoked dishes and the crispy eel Wu Xi style; dim sum is also served at dinner. The restaurant features an impressive illuminated mirrored ceiling and caters well for larger tables. Service is friendly and prices sensible.

帝后殿於二零零八年底成為灣仔區食肆一員，主打上海菜，菜單上附有推介菜式照片，並標示辣度。名菜包括燻香菜式、無錫脆鱔，晚餐時分亦提供點心。餐廳以亮燈鏡面天花裝潢，亦提供大圓桌。服務親切，價錢合理。

■ ADDRESS/地址
TEL.2591 6338
27F, QRE Plaza, 202 Queen's Road East, Wan Chai
灣仔皇后大道東202號QRE Plaza 27樓
www.queenspalace.com.hk

■ OPENING HOURS, LAST ORDER
營業時間，最後點菜時間
10:00-22:30 (L.O.)

■ PRICE/價錢
Lunch/午膳　à la carte/點菜 $130-300
Dinner/晚膳　à la carte/點菜 $130-300

Regal Palace
富豪金殿

This elegant and imposing restaurant is on the third floor of the Regal Hotel and provides a sophisticated backdrop for fine cookery that mixes new culinary concepts with established traditions: no wonder the menu is labelled as "Innovation meets Nostalgia". The basis for many of the dishes is Cantonese but this has been overlaid with finely judged imagination and sharp technique to create a very contemporary dining experience.

位於富豪酒店三樓的富豪金殿裝潢瑰麗，精雕細琢的烹調手法獨具特色，融合最新餐飲概念和多年傳統；難怪餐牌題名為「創新中的懷舊」。不少菜式都以粵菜為基調，配合無窮創意，經過精心考慮和高巧技法渾成時尚的餐飲體驗。

■ ADDRESS/地址
TEL.2837 1773
3F, Regal Hotel, 88 Yee Wo Street, Causeway Bay
銅鑼灣怡和街88號富豪酒店3樓
www.regalhotel.com

■ OPENING HOURS, LAST ORDER
營業時間，最後點菜時間
Lunch/午膳 12:00-15:00 (L.O.)
Dinner/晚膳 18:00-23:00 (L.O.)

■ PRICE/價錢
Lunch/午膳　à la carte/點菜 $250-420
Dinner/晚膳　à la carte/點菜 $250-420

Ren Bai
任白

Two famous Chinese opera singers, Ren Jianhui and Bai Xuexian, inspired the name of this restaurant, hidden beneath the Mid-levels escalator. It's all very simple and cosy inside, with the sepia pictures, portraits and drawings contrasting with European 19C-style chairs. The Chinese cuisine is carefully prepared; popular dishes include marinated chicken in Hua Diao sauce, steamed fish Hangzhou style and deep-fried lamb steak Beijing style.

藏在半山手扶電梯後的餐廳，取名自兩位粵劇名伶──任劍輝和白雪仙。餐廳內陳設簡單溫暖，配有泛黃照片、肖像、以及圖畫，與歐洲十九世紀風格的椅子相映成趣。精心烹調的中菜，包括受歡迎的醉雞、西湖醋魚及京蔥爆羊肉。

■ ADDRESS/地址
TEL.2523 2872
BF, 59 Caine Road, Mid-level, Soho, Central
中環中半山堅道59號地下底層

■ OPENING HOURS, LAST ORDER
營業時間，最後點菜時間
Lunch/午膳 12:00-14:30 (L.O.)
Dinner/晚膳 18:00-22:30 (L.O.)

■ PRICE/價錢
Lunch/午膳　set/套餐　　　$68-330
　　　　　à la carte/點菜 $200-320
Dinner/晚膳　à la carte/點菜 $200-320

Roka

The Hong Kong outpost for this small but growing group of restaurants offering contemporary Japanese Robatayaki cuisine, has an appealing minimalist interior featuring wood, earth, iron and rice paper. The charcoal robata grill is used to great effect to cook fresh seafood, which arrives daily from Japan, and meat, mostly from Australia. Sashimi and tempura are also offered. If you want to watch the action, sit as the counter.

正在成長的Roka飲食集團在香港開設的分店提供現代日式爐端燒美食，內部裝潢簡潔吸引，以木、泥、鐵及米紙為主。炭燒爐端燒是炮製每天從日本運到的新鮮海鮮、或是澳洲運抵的鮮肉的上佳方法。店內亦提供刺身及天婦羅。如有興趣觀賞烹製過程，請坐在櫃檯位置。

■ ADDRESS/地址
TEL.3960 5988
Shop 002, LG1, Pacific Place, 88 Queensway, Admiralty
金鐘金鐘道88號太古廣場地庫1樓2號舖
www.rokarestaurant.com

■ OPENING HOURS, LAST ORDER
營業時間，最後點菜時間
11:30-22:30 (L.O.)

■ PRICE/價錢
Lunch/午膳	set/套餐	$140-428
	à la carte/點菜	$220-780
Dinner/晚膳	à la carte/點菜	$220-780

Sabatini

The original Sabatini is in Rome, so this version enjoys a fine pedigree and ticks all the right boxes. A comfy lounge bar sets you up nicely before your meal. The main dining room is large with a real trattoria décor comprising a wooden beam ceiling, a shiny floor made with old tiles, rustic furniture and yellow walls embellished with Italian style frescoes. The menu runs the gamut from antipasti to soup, pasta, fish, meat and dessert trolley.

首家Sabatini始創於羅馬，可見帝苑酒店的Sabatini來頭不小，美食正宗，佳釀一流。舒適的雅座酒吧是享用正餐的完美前奏。主餐室地方寬敞，天花由木橫樑組成，光滑的地板以舊磚鋪成，黃色牆壁掛著意式壁畫，加上質樸的傢具，構成真正的意大利餐廳格局。餐廳的菜單非常全面，涵蓋各種意式前菜、湯類、意大利麵食、魚類、肉類，以至甜品車。

■ ADDRESS/地址
TEL.2733 2000
3F, The Royal Garden Hotel, 69 Mody Road, East Tsim Sha Tsui, Kowloon
九龍尖東麼地道69號帝苑酒店3樓
www.sabatini.rghk.com.hk

■ OPENING HOURS, LAST ORDER
營業時間，最後點菜時間
Lunch/午膳　12:00-14:30 (L.O.)
Dinner/晚膳　18:00-23:00 (L.O.)

■ PRICE/價錢

Lunch/午膳	set/套餐	$198-348
	à la carte/點菜	$600-900
Dinner/晚膳	set/套餐	$680-980
	à la carte/點菜	$600-900

Sang Kee
生記

Having thrived for over 30 years in Wan Chai, it was inevitable that larger premises would have to be found for this family business. None of the philosophies have been forgotten in the move, such as regular trips to market trips for the best ingredients, particularly seafood. Steamed crab with preserved plums and garlic sauce and fried fresh squid in salt are of note. It's all overseen by Vicky and Dicken Wong and their dedicated team.

生記在灣仔已立足三十多年，這檔家族生意無可避免地必須擴充其面積，但其宗旨始終如一。如堅持定期前往街市尋找最佳材料，海鮮尤甚。梅子雙蒜蒸蟹和椒鹽鮮魷就值得一提。餐廳由黃氏家族及其盡忠職守的工作團隊主理。

■ ADDRESS/地址

TEL.2575 2236

1-2F, Hip Sang Building, 107-115
Hennessy Road, Wan Chai
灣仔軒尼詩道107-115號　生大廈1-2樓
www.sangkee.com.hk

■ ANNUAL AND WEEKLY CLOSING
　休息日期

Closed first Monday except Public
Holidays and Sunday lunch
週日午膳及第一個週一(公眾假期除外)休息

■ OPENING HOURS, LAST ORDER
　營業時間，最後點菜時間
Lunch/午膳 11:30-14:15 (L.O.)
Dinner/晚膳 18:00-22:15 (L.O.)

■ PRICE/價錢
Lunch/午膳　à la carte/點菜 $150-400
Dinner/晚膳　à la carte/點菜 $150-400

Senzuru
千鶴

This simple and straightforward restaurant focuses tightly on two styles of Japanese preparation: teppanyaki and sushi/sashimi. The first style has two counters where you can watch fish or meat being cooked directly in front of you. The second, smaller one is dedicated purely to the deft slicing of raw fish, much of which arrives daily from Japan. There's a list of over 40 different sakes to accompany the food.

這家簡樸的餐廳主力供應兩種日本菜式：天婦羅和壽司/刺身。前者設有兩張櫃檯，可面對面看廚師直接烹調魚或肉類菜式；後者則可看到廚師巧手將魚生切片，而大部分魚生均是從日本每天新鮮運抵。此外，餐廳亦供應超過40種不同的燒酒佐膳。

■ ADDRESS/地址
TEL.3160 6898
8F, Harbour Plaza Metropolis Hotel, 7 Metropolis Drive, Hung Hom, Kowloon
九龍紅磡都會道7號都會海逸酒店8樓
http://fnb.hpme.harbour-plaza.com

■ OPENING HOURS, LAST ORDER
營業時間，最後點菜時間
Lunch/午膳 12:00-14:30 (L.O.)
Dinner/晚膳 18:00-22:30 (L.O.)

■ PRICE/價錢
Lunch/午膳	set/套餐	$ 128
	à la carte/點菜	$ 220-800
Dinner/晚膳	set/套餐	$ 420-480
	à la carte/點菜	$ 220-800

Ser Wong Fun
蛇王芬

Established 70 years ago, and now under the stewardship of the fourth generation, it is little wonder there has been a book celebrating the family history and their cherished recipes. Regulars flock here for the snake soup and snake banquets in winter. No less than 15 varieties of double-boiled soups and a vast array of seasonal pot dishes are also offered; add to that barbecue and assorted seafood. Service is efficient, if a little brusque.

七十年前開店的蛇王芬如今由第四代傳人主理，更有出版書籍介紹家族歷史及其著名菜式。熟客經常來此品嚐蛇羹，冬天甚至品嚐蛇宴。超過十五種老火燉湯任君選擇，亦提供一系列煲仔飯；此外更提供燒烤雜錦海鮮。服務效率高，有時服務生會較為直率。

■ ADDRESS/地址
TEL.2543 1032
30 Cochrane Street, Central
中環閣麟街30號

■ ANNUAL AND WEEKLY CLOSING
　休息日期
Closed 4 days Lunar New Year
農曆新年休息4天

■ OPENING HOURS, LAST ORDER
　營業時間，最後點菜時間
11:00-22:30 (L.O.)

■ PRICE/價錢
Lunch/午膳　à la carte/點菜 $70-100
Dinner/晚膳　à la carte/點菜 $100-150

Se Wong Yee
蛇王二

Their signature snake soup has long been renowned and is served until midnight in winter; regulars are quick to occupy one of the few tables for this memorable experience and it is of little surprise to learn that the recipe has remained unchanged for many years. But now those regulars come also for the famed barbecued meats and speciality sausages with rice; the roast goose is especially good. Asked to wait outside for a seat? It's worth it.

此著名蛇羹集團一向聞名四方，冬天更營業至深夜零時。熟客急不及待佔駐其中一張桌，享受美味享受一貫的美味而不曾失望，基於製法多年來從未改變。如今，熟客對其著名叉燒臘腸飯亦趨之若鶩，燒鵝更具水準。要先在外面等等才有座位？你的等待將是有意義的。

■ ADDRESS/地址
TEL.2831 0163
24 Percival Street, Causeway Bay
銅鑼灣波斯富街24號

■ ANNUAL AND WEEKLY CLOSING
   休息日期
Closed 3 days Lunar New Year
農曆新年休息3天

■ OPENING HOURS, LAST ORDER
   營業時間，最後點菜時間
11:30-23:00 (L.O.)

■ PRICE/價錢
Lunch/午膳   à la carte/點菜 $50-80
Dinner/晚膳   à la carte/點菜 $50-80

Shanghai Garden
紫玉蘭

✕✕✕

🍱120 ◑🍴

Known for its range of classic dishes from the provinces of Shanghai, Sichuan and Beijing and hugely popular with local office staff at lunchtimes; the décor in the two large dining rooms may not be particularly noteworthy but it is the cuisine that's the attraction here. Specialities include deep-fried yellow croaker fish with sweet and sour sauce and sautéed freshwater shrimp; Beggar's chicken is worth ordering in advance.

紫玉蘭午市的經典上海、四川、北京菜在本地白領間早已聞名；相較兩個大型中菜廳，這裡的菜餚似乎更吸引。著名美食包括北京大紅袍松鼠黃魚及上海清炒河蝦仁。富貴雞應提早預訂──絕不會令你失望。

■ ADDRESS/地址
TEL.2524 8181
1F, Hutchison House, 10 Harcourt Road, Central
中環夏慤道10號和記大廈1樓
www.maxims.com.hk

■ OPENING HOURS, LAST ORDER
   營業時間，最後點菜時間
Lunch/午膳 11:30-14:30 (L.O.)
Dinner/晚膳 17:30-23:00 (L.O.)

■ PRICE/價錢
Lunch/午膳   à la carte/點菜 $180-550
Dinner/晚膳 à la carte/點菜 $180-550

Shanghainese/上海菜 MAP/地圖 21/B-2

Shanghai Lu Yang Cun
上海綠楊邨

Found in the World Trade Centre, with great views, and booths for added intimacy. The cuisine should tantalise all areas of the taste buds, from sweet and sour to salty and spicy: it's all covered in the Shanghainese menu with Sichuan and Hangzhou influences. Dry-braised Sichuan prawns and "Lu Yang" clove-flavoured chicken are signatures. It's part of a group established over 80 years ago, although this is the only one in Hong Kong.

餐廳位於世貿中心，景致醉人，更設有較親密的卡座。餐單方面絕對能刺激不同部分的味蕾，甜酸鹹辣通通激發：從吸收了四川、杭州影響的上海菜單可見一斑。馳名菜式包括乾燒大明蝦及綠楊丁香雞。餐廳所屬集團已於香港立足超過八十年，但這仍是香港唯一的分店。

■ ADDRESS/地址
TEL.2881 6669
11F, World Trade Centre, 280
Gloucester Road, Causeway Bay
銅鑼灣告士打道280號世貿中心商場11樓

■ OPENING HOURS, LAST ORDER
營業時間，最後點菜時間
Lunch/午膳 11:30-14:45 (L.O.)
Dinner/晚膳 17:30-23:00 (L.O.)

■ PRICE/價錢
Lunch/午膳　à la carte/點菜 $200-450
Dinner/晚膳　à la carte/點菜 $200-450

Shanghai Xiao Nan Guo (Kowloon Bay)
上海小南國 (九龍灣)

✗✗

&♿ 🅿 🍽20

A somewhat confusing array of escalators and lifts make this Shanghainese restaurant difficult to find. But once inside, you'll find yourself in a stylish, contemporary environment, with lots of wood, subtle orange lighting and an interesting collection of stone figures. It's also comfortable, with the best tables being those on the left. Classic dishes include drunken chicken in Shaoxing wine and braised pork trotter with Shanghai cabbage.

一連串的扶手電梯和升降機令這家店變得有點難找。但只要進入店內，你就會發現裝潢時尚現代，以大量木製、柔和橙色燈光及一系列有趣石雕妝點。餐廳環境亦非常舒適，尤其是左邊的桌子。經典菜式包括紹興花雕醉雞及元蹄伴棠菜。

■ ADDRESS/地址
TEL.2545 0880
Unit 2, Level 6, Megabox, 38 Wang Chiu Road, Kowloon Bay
九龍灣宏照道38號Megabox6樓2號舖

■ OPENING HOURS, LAST ORDER
營業時間，最後點菜時間
Lunch/午膳　11:30-15:00 L.O. 14:30
Dinner/晚膳　18:00-23:00 L.O. 22:30

■ PRICE/價錢
Lunch/午膳　à la carte/點菜 $153-530
Dinner/晚膳　à la carte/點菜 $153-530

Shanghai Xiao Nan Guo (TST)
上海小南國 (尖沙咀)

⛄ ⟨ 🍽40

Cantonese remains the most popular cuisine in Hong Kong but Shanghainese is probably the second favourite. This fact probably explains why so many locals head for the first floor of the Tsim Sha Tsui Centre. Of course, it could be for the harbour views but it's far more likely to be because of the authentic Shanghai dumplings, deep-fried yellow croaker fish with five spicy salt or 'Grandma's' braised pork belly, all of which are classics here.

粵菜作為本港最受歡迎的菜系，地位無庸置疑，但上海菜肯定緊隨其後，不遑多讓。這可能是吸引眾多人士來到尖沙咀中心一樓的原因。不排除有人是為了迷人海景而來，但更多人會為了其馳名正宗上海雲吞、椒鹽小黃魚及外婆紅燒肉而來。

■ ADDRESS/地址
TEL.2369 8899
UG2, TST Centre, 66 Mody Road, East Tsim Sha Tsui, Kowloon
九龍尖沙咀麼地道66號尖沙咀中心地面高層

■ OPENING HOURS, LAST ORDER
營業時間，最後點菜時間
Lunch/午膳 11:30-15:00 L.O. 14:45
Dinner/晚膳 18:00-23:00 L.O. 22:45

■ PRICE/價錢
Lunch/午膳 à la carte/點菜 $176-362
Dinner/晚膳 à la carte/點菜 $176-362

Shang Palace
香宮

Four golden statues by the entrance welcome you to this sumptuous room that vividly evokes the grandeur of the Sung Dynasty. Red lacquered walls, antique paintings and classic lanterns only add to the authentic atmosphere. The same care has been lavished on the Cantonese menu which includes well chosen vegetarian items. The cooking here is finely judged and the speciality Shang Palace three-layer basket includes abalone, scallops and aubergine.

大門的4個金色塑像歡迎你來到這家豪華的餐廳，宋朝的顯赫氣派活靈活現。紅色漆牆、古董國畫，以及傳統燈籠交織出古色古香的氣氛。這裡的粵菜亦同樣精巧，更提供不錯的素食菜式。烹調技巧出色，特色美色包括三元及第：金龍鮑、帶子及蒸茄子。

■ ADDRESS/地址
TEL.2733 8754
Lower level, Kowloon Shangri-La Hotel, 64 Mody Road, East Tsim Sha Tsui, Kowloon
九龍尖東麼地道64號九龍香格里拉酒店地庫1樓
www.shangri-la.com

■ OPENING HOURS, LAST ORDER
營業時間，最後點菜時間
Lunch/午膳 12:00-15:00 (L.O.)
Dinner/晚膳 18:00-23:00 (L.O.)

■ PRICE/價錢

Lunch/午膳	set/套餐	$238-788
	à la carte/點菜	$510-1,200
Dinner/晚膳	set/套餐	$680-788
	à la carte/點菜	$510-1,200

Sha Tin 18
沙田18

🕭 🏠 🅿 🍽14 🛋

The modern design of this stylish and relaxed restaurant takes second place to the unique concept of its three open-plan kitchens. Chefs toil away in one of three display areas; so you can watch the barbecue, be impressed by the fresh noodles being handmade for every order that comes in or be transfixed by the spontaneity of the wok chefs. A mix of Pekingese, Shanghainese and Cantonese dishes are all freshly made – just see for yourself.

餐廳設計風格時尚悠閒，精采程度僅次於其三個開放式廚房的設計。廚師在三個展示區域忙個不停；你可以觀察燒肉過程，讚嘆即叫即做的新鮮麵條，立刻由廚師以中式鑊炮製。混合京、滬、粵菜全都是新鮮炮製——有待你的親自驗證。

■ ADDRESS/地址
TEL.3723 1234
3F, Hyatt Regency Sha Tin, 18 Chak Cheung Street, University, Sha Tin, New Territories
新界沙田大學站澤祥街18號沙田凱悅酒店3樓
www.hongkong.shatin.hyatt.com

■ OPENING HOURS, LAST ORDER
營業時間，最後點菜時間
Lunch/午膳 11:30-14:30 (L.O.)
Dinner/晚膳 17:30-22:30 (L.O.)

■ PRICE/價錢
Lunch/午膳 à la carte/點菜 $160-500
Dinner/晚膳 à la carte/點菜 $250-600

Shui Hu Ju
水滸居

✗✗

🚌30 📞🍴

Arriving at this discreet location has been likened to the journey undertaken to reach the mystical mountain from where this establishment takes its name. Pushing open the heavy wooden doors reveals a set of carefully recreated interiors of old China with a limited number of seats. The cuisine is a combination of Sichuan, Shanghainese and Northern Chinese cooking with some subtle modern touches; braised meats are a speciality.

踏進這別出心裁的世外之地,有如登上水滸傳的傳奇梁山。推開一道道厚重木門後,舉目盡是古色古香的精心裝潢。座位數目不多,菜式方面融合了川菜,上海菜和北方風味,帶點現代修飾。燜肉尤其馳名。

■ ADDRESS/地址
TEL.2869 6927
68 Peel Street, Soho, Central
中環卑利街68號

■ OPENING HOURS, LAST ORDER
營業時間, 最後點菜時間
Dinner/晚膳 18:00-22:30 (L.O.)

■ PRICE/價錢
Dinner/晚膳 à la carte/點菜 $300-500

Siu Shun Village Cuisine
肇順名匯河鮮專門店

This elegant Shun Tak cuisine restaurant is situated in one of the newer shopping malls. Popular with locals, it is a restaurant with seating for 500 so is ideal for family gatherings, working lunches or a relaxing break with friends after a day of shopping. It's filled with bamboos and lamp shades styled like birdcages. The freshwater fish is an obvious highlight but their clay hot pots are also very popular.

這家優雅的餐廳位於新興商場內，廣受本地食客歡迎。餐廳可容納500人，適合家族聚會，商務飯局或與朋友逛街一整天後的小休。竹枝與燈影造成鳥籠般的效果，淡水魚是重點菜式，煲仔菜亦同樣吸引。

■ ADDRESS/地址
TEL.2798 9738
7F, MegaBox, 38 Wang Chiu Road, Kowloon Bay, Kowloon
九龍灣宏照道38號MegaBox7樓

■ OPENING HOURS, LAST ORDER
營業時間，最後點菜時間
Lunch/午膳 09:00-16:30 (L.O.)
Dinner/晚膳 18:00-23:30 (L.O.)
■ PRICE/價錢
Lunch/午膳 à la carte/點菜 $ 50-300
Dinner/晚膳 à la carte/點菜 $ 150-300

Snow Garden (Causeway Bay)
雪園 (銅鑼灣)

Established in 1992 at this sleek business address and known for its carefully prepared, traditional Shanghainese cuisine, this contemporary styled restaurant operates like clockwork. Staff all share the same enthusiasm which is immediately evident in the warm welcome. The long-standing chef's specialities are steamed herring and deep-fried chicken skin with four spices. Dishes arrive thoughtfully assembled and bursting with flavour.

餐廳於1992年創辦於此商業區熱點，其賣點在於精心烹調的上海菜，人流絡繹不絕。聲聲溫暖的歡迎字句反應所有員工的熱忱。四寶片皮雞是歷久不衰的廚師精選。菜式上碟經過精心編排，香味四溢。

■ ADDRESS/地址
TEL.2881 6837
2F, Ming An Plaza, 8 Sunning Road, Causeway Bay
銅鑼灣新寧道民安廣場2樓
www.snow-garden.com

■ ANNUAL AND WEEKLY CLOSING
　休息日期
Closed 3 days Lunar New Year
農曆新年休息3天

■ OPENING HOURS, LAST ORDER
　營業時間，最後點菜時間
Lunch/午膳 11:30-14:45 (L.O.)
Dinner/晚膳 18:00-22:45 (L.O.)

■ PRICE/價錢
Lunch/午膳　set/套餐　　　$120
　　　　　à la carte/點菜 $250-650
Dinner/晚膳　set/套餐　　　$488
　　　　　à la carte/點菜 $250-650

Spasso

Right on Ocean Centre's top floor, this has great views, particularly from the outdoor terrace. The interior is stylish with both the wine cellar and pizza oven fully open to view. Many artisanal products are specially imported from Italy for use in such signature dishes as spaghetti with fresh sardines, pine nuts and tomato and lamb chops with sausage and Norcia black truffles. The excellent wine list includes well over 50 choices by the glass.

座落於海洋中心頂樓，Spasso坐擁壯麗景觀，露天雅座的景色特別迷人。餐廳設計時尚，設有開放式的酒櫃和意大利薄餅焗爐，食客可直擊製作過程。店內很多工藝品特地由意大利入口，用以奉上招牌菜，包括蕃茄松子鮮沙甸意粉、肉腸羊扒配諾爾察黑松露菌。餐廳更提供超過50種上等葡萄酒。

■ ADDRESS/地址
TEL.2730 8027
Shop 403, 4F, Ocean Centre, Harbour City, 17 Canton Road, Tsim Sha Tsui, Kowloon
九龍尖沙咀廣東道17號海港城海洋中心4樓403號舖
www.spassoristorante-bar.com.hk

■ OPENING HOURS, LAST ORDER
營業時間，最後點菜時間
Lunch/午膳　12:00-15:30　L.O. 15:00
Dinner/晚膳　18:00-23:30　L.O. 23:00

■ PRICE/價錢
Lunch/午膳	set/套餐	$ 148-208
	à la carte/點菜	$ 320-850
Dinner/晚膳	set/套餐	$ 498
	à la carte/點菜	$ 320-850

Spoon by Alain Ducasse

Great views, stylish seating and a ceiling lined with spoons – characteristics of this fashionable outpost of the Alain Ducasse empire. The cooking is divided into two sections: Original is home to dishes including spit-roast saddle of lamb with honey jus semolina and dried fruits and nuts, whilst the Classic section is just that and features items such as chicken and crayfish with marbled sauce and potato gnocchi with girolles.

優美景觀、時尚雅座、排列著匙羹的天花板一打造成名廚艾倫杜卡斯(Alain Ducasse)美食王國的香港分部，實為潮流時尚之選。菜餚分為兩部分：「原 創」菜式包括燒羊柳伴法式炒中東米，而「經 典」菜式顧名思義，較為典型，特色美食包括雙色醬雞肉小龍蝦併雞油菌薯仔麵團等。

■ ADDRESS/地址

TEL.2313 2256

GF, Intercontinental Hotel, 18 Salisbury Road, Tsim Sha Tsui, Kowloon

九龍尖沙咀梳士巴利道18號洲際酒店地下

www.hongkong-ic.intercontinental.com

■ OPENING HOURS, LAST ORDER

營業時間，最後點菜時間

Dinner/晚膳 18:00-23:00 (L.O.)

■ PRICE/價錢

Dinner/晚膳　set/套餐　　　$888-1,088

à la carte/點菜 $456-1,250

Spring Deer
鹿鳴春

The name comes from a restaurant in Shan Dong, in eastern China, where the owner worked before opening this place over 40 years ago. The food is a little lighter here, although you know you can't go wrong when there are two chefs whose sole task is the roasting of 100 Peking ducks a day. Other dishes include baked shad on a hot metal-plate, prawns in chilli sauce and the Peking style deep-fried mutton. Service is swift but doesn't lack warmth.

此店名來自中國山東省的餐廳，四十多年前，餐廳東主曾於該餐廳工作。這邊的菜式較清淡，但絕對不需擔心水準，因為兩位廚師的唯一工作就是每天負責烤製超過一百頭北京填鴨。其他菜式包括鐵板鰣魚、宮爆大蝦及京燒羊肉。服務爽快而不失親切。

■ ADDRESS/地址
TEL.2366 5839
1F, 42 Mody Road, Tsim Sha Tsui, Kowloon
九龍尖沙咀 地道42號2樓

■ ANNUAL AND WEEKLY CLOSING
休息日期
Closed 3 days Lunar New Year
農曆新年休息3天

■ OPENING HOURS, LAST ORDER
營業時間，最後點菜時間
Lunch/午膳 11:00-14:30 (L.O.)
Dinner/晚膳 18:00-22:30 (L.O.)

■ PRICE/價錢
Lunch/午膳 set/套餐 $ 50-100
à la carte/點菜 $ 30-350
Dinner/晚膳 à la carte/點菜 $ 50-350

Spring Moon
嘉麟樓

XXX

🖐 🚌36 ©🍴

An elegant and luxurious Cantonese restaurant very much at home at The Peninsula. You can admire the tropical hardwood or the bamboo flower arrangements while sipping tea at the tea bar. Dine in the restaurant or on the more intimate mezzanine floor. Refined service oversees authentic dishes loaded with flavour. Different soy sauces are proposed to bring out the flavour of specialities, which include shark fin or roasted pigeon with osmanthus.

嘉麟樓位於半島酒店內，是一家優雅豪華的粵菜餐廳，令人感覺舒適。食客可以邊在"茶檔"茗茶，邊欣賞餐廳內的熱帶硬木或竹花排列。你可以選擇在餐廳內或在較隱蔽的私家房內用餐，完善的服務配合味道濃郁的原味菜餚。建議使用不同種類的豉油帶出美食的味道，包括魚翅及桂花燒乳鴿。

■ ADDRESS/地址

TEL.2315 3160

1F, The Peninsula Hotel, Salisbury Road, Tsim Sha Tsui, Kowloon

九龍尖沙咀梳士巴利道半島酒店1樓

www.peninsula.com

■ OPENING HOURS, LAST ORDER

　營業時間，最後點菜時間

Lunch/午膳　11:30-14:30 (L.O.)

Dinner/晚膳　18:00-22:30 (L.O.)

■ PRICE/價錢

Lunch/午膳	set/套餐	$368-448
	à la carte/點菜	$500-3,000
Dinner/晚膳	set/套餐	$928-1,928
	à la carte/點菜	$500-3,000

Summary Palace

Summer Palace
夏宮

🚹 ☞ 📷14 📞🍴

They've created a charming environment here in this 5th floor room, with its crystal chandeliers, traditional Chinese screens and well-placed tables. The Cantonese menu features all the true classics and the kitchen uses carefully chosen ingredients prepared without fussiness or over-elaboration. To drink, there's a varied selection of wines by the glass, Chinese liquors and exquisite teas.

他們在這位於五樓的空間營造了迷人的環境，配上水晶吊燈、傳統中國屏風及精心佈置的餐桌。粵菜菜譜提供所有經典名菜，廚房精心挑選食材，烹調時井井有條，毫不過火。餐酒方面具杯裝西洋餐酒、中國酒和高級茗茶。

■ ADDRESS/地址
TEL.2820 8553
5F, Island Shangri-La Hotel, Pacific Place, Supreme Court Road, Admiralty
中區法院道太古廣場港島香格里拉大酒店
5樓
www.shangri-la.com

■ OPENING HOURS, LAST ORDER
營業時間，最後點菜時間
Lunch/午膳 11:30-14:30 (L.O.)
Dinner/晚膳 18:30-22:30 (L.O.)

■ PRICE/價錢
Lunch/午膳　à la carte/點菜 $270-1,100
Dinner/晚膳　à la carte/點菜 $270-1,100

Sushi Kato
加藤壽司

A friendly little eatery that's worth searching out - don't be put off because it's on the first floor of an apartment block. The cosy interior has hand-made wood panelling, and Mr Kato himself is at the sushi bar. Straightforward menus are served at simple tables: sashimi, salads, soups, bento boxes, noodles, and a selection of grilled, fried or steamed favourites. It's good value; all the dishes are fresh, carefully prepared and authentic.

這家親切的小壽司店，位於一幢公寓大樓的一樓，但不要因此而卻步，這店實在值得專程尋找。店裡很舒適，採用了手工製作的木質鑲板，而加藤先生就在壽司吧親自下廚。簡單的餐桌配合簡單的菜單，菜式包括魚生、沙律、湯類、便當、麵食，以及一系列的精選烤物、炸物或蒸物。菜式純正，採用新鮮食材，準備細心，是超值之選。

■ ADDRESS/地址
TEL.2807 3613
Shop 7-9, 1F, 20-36 Wharf Road,
North Point
北角和富道20-36號1樓7-9號舖

■ ANNUAL AND WEEKLY CLOSING
　休息日期
Closed Tuesday
週二休息

■ OPENING HOURS, LAST ORDER
　營業時間，最後點菜時間
Lunch/午膳 12:00-14:00 (L.O.)
Dinner/晚膳 18:00-22:00 (L.O.)

■ PRICE/價錢
Lunch/午膳 à la carte/點菜 $350-600
Dinner/晚膳 à la carte/點菜 $350-600

Sushi Kuu
壽司喰

🚋20 🍴 ☎️🍴

Casual and relaxed, Sushi Kuu is unlike the more formal style Japanese restaurant you might be used to. The bar features an impressive sake list, while the sushi counter is always popular with late-night revellers. You can also eat at tables by the bar, or window booths overlooking busy Wyndham Street. There's a good choice of Japanese specialities, including traditional sushi and sashimi arriving every day from Japan, tempura and noodles.

壽司喰洋溢著輕鬆隨意的氣氛，不像那些風格較為正式的日本餐廳。吧檯提供令人驚喜的清酒選擇，而壽司吧則永遠都受夜遊客歡迎。食客亦可以選擇在吧檯附近的餐桌用餐，或是靠窗的雅座，邊吃邊俯瞰繁忙的雲咸街。這裡有不錯的日本菜選擇，包括傳統壽司、魚生，每天由日本新鮮運到，更有天婦羅及麵食可供選擇。

■ ADDRESS/地址
TEL.2971 0180
1F, Wellington Place, 2-8 Wellington Street, Central
中環威靈頓街2-8號威靈頓廣場1樓

■ ANNUAL AND WEEKLY CLOSING
　　休息日期
Closed Lunar New Year
年初一休息

■ OPENING HOURS, LAST ORDER
　　營業時間，最後點菜時間
Lunch/午膳 12:00-15:00 (L.O.)
Dinner/晚膳 18:00-23:00 (L.O.)

■ PRICE/價錢
Lunch/午膳　set/套餐　　　　　$ 130-280
　　　　　　à la carte/點菜 $ 250-600
Dinner/晚膳　à la carte/點菜 $ 250-600

Sushi Shota
壽司翔太

Here you're guaranteed respite, away from the bustle of Lockhart Road; just take a seat at the counter and watch the master at work. Sushi, sashimi, maki and tempura are the specialities but fish is also steamed with impressive precision. Need some help on what to order? The chef is also only too willing to assist and help create the perfect combinations from his superb ingredients. A concise but well chosen sake list completes the picture.

在此，你肯定可獲得一絲寧靜，遠離駱克道的煩囂；坐在壽司吧前看看師傅的手藝吧。壽司、魚生、手卷、天婦羅是精選餐點，蒸魚的時間亦控制得非常準確。不知道該怎麼選擇？大廚非常願意以鮮美材料為你提供不同組合。日本酒的選擇不算多，卻五臟俱全。

■ ADDRESS/地址

TEL.2834 3031

8F, Kyoto Plaza, 491-499 Lockhart Road, Causeway Bay
銅鑼灣駱克道491-499號京都廣場8樓

■ OPENING HOURS, LAST ORDER
　營業時間，最後點菜時間
Lunch/午膳 11:45-14:30 (L.O.)
Dinner/晚膳 18:00-22:30 (L.O.)

■ PRICE/價錢
Lunch/午膳　set/套餐　　　　$250-280
　　　　　　à la carte/點菜 $250-650
Dinner/晚膳　set/套餐　　　　$480-800
　　　　　　à la carte/點菜 $250-650

Tai Ping Koon (Causeway Bay)
太平館 (銅鑼灣)

The group was founded in Guangzhou in 1860 and locals have been making the pilgrimage to Tai Ping Koon for as long as anyone can remember. Expect booths, photos of the restaurant from when it opened and long-standing waiters serving Chinese interpretations of Western cuisines. The famous Chicken wings in a 'Swiss sauce' are really in a 'sweet soy sauce': the translation just got a little lost in the 30s. Try their house special, baked soufflé.

集團於1860年創立於廣州，太平館更是深受當地人寵愛。在櫃檯，你會看見餐廳當年開幕的照片，排成長列的服務生呈上西式餐飲的中式演釋。著名的太平館 "瑞士 (Swiss)" 雞翼配有 "甜醬油醬汁 (sweet soy)"，來自於三十年代翻譯的一個小偏差。嚐嚐他們的特製太平館式焗梳乎厘。

■ ADDRESS/地址
TEL.2576 9161
6 Pak Sha Road, Causeway Bay
銅鑼灣白沙道6號
www.taipingkoon.com

■ ANNUAL AND WEEKLY CLOSING
　　休息日期
Closed 3 days Lunar New Year
農曆新年休息3天

■ OPENING HOURS, LAST ORDER
　　營業時間, 最後點菜時間
11:00-24:00 L.O. 23:20

■ PRICE/價錢

Lunch/午膳	set/套餐	$125-198
	à la carte/點菜	$70-250
Dinner/晚膳	set/套餐	$125-198
	à la carte/點菜	$70-250

Tai Wing Wah
大榮華

Most people travelling all the way to Yuen Long (in the North of New Territories) are doing so for one reason: to visit this restaurant. Tai Wing Wah is found above its cake shop, which specialises in moon cakes and Chinese sausages. Serving dim sum throughout the day, 'Walled village' cuisine is offered along with classic Cantonese dishes. They come for the chicken in five spices, baked fish roe with eggs and, above all, the steamed egg cake.

很多人長途跋涉來到元朗(新界北部),只有一個原因:為了來大榮華。大榮華位於其餅店樓上,餅店專門售賣月餅和臘腸。除了全日提供的點心外,還提供圍村菜及經典粵菜。五味雞、魚春蒸蛋之外,當然少不了奶黃馬拉糕。

■ ADDRESS/地址

TEL.2476 9888
2F, 2-6 On Ning Road, Yuen Long,
New Territories
新界元朗安寧路2-6號2樓

■ OPENING HOURS, LAST ORDER
   營業時間,最後點菜時間
06:30-23:30 (L.O.)

■ PRICE/價錢
Lunch/午膳   à la carte/點菜 $80-250
Dinner/晚膳   à la carte/點菜 $80-250

Tai Woo (Causeway Bay)
太湖海鮮城 (銅鑼灣)

In a dense, busy street, this is easy to spot from the series of aquaria displayed on the outside. Inside, the staircase lined with culinary awards leads to some fairly modest but busy dining rooms where the freshest of seafood is brought both live and cooked up to a never-ending stream of regulars. Prawns in salted egg yolk and baked lobster with supreme sauce are perennial favourites. Most tables opt for the signature crispy juicy stewed beef.

即使在人來人往的繁華街道上，太湖海鮮城亦容易被找到，皆因外面展示著一系列的魚缸。餐廳的樓梯羅列著眾多的美食獎項，帶來並不奢華卻擠滿捧場客的進餐區。這裡的海鮮極其新鮮，大量生猛海鮮以供選購，故此捧場客絡繹不絕。西施伴霸王及上湯焗龍蝦等菜式長期大受歡迎。大部分食客都會點上一味馳名三弄回味牛肉。

■ ADDRESS/地址
TEL.2893 0822
27 Percival Street, Causeway Bay
銅鑼灣波斯富街27號
www.taiwoorestaurant.com

■ OPENING HOURS, LAST ORDER
營業時間，最後點菜時間
10:30-03:00 L.O. 02:15

■ PRICE/價錢
Lunch/午膳　à la carte/點菜　$ 200-300
Dinner/晚膳　set/套餐　　　$ 248
　　　　　à la carte/點菜　$ 200-300

Tai Woo (Tsim Sha Tsui)
太湖海鮮城 (尖沙咀)

Having the biggest neon sign on Hillwood Road means it's hard to miss this long-established Cantonese restaurant. The pavement side 'aquarium' of fish tanks will also grab your attention. As expected, it's brightly lit and vibrant on both floors, and always busy with diners using the pictures on the menu to choose dishes, many of which stand out, such as the crispy beef brisket with spring onion and sesame chicken baked in salt.

擁有山林道最大的霓虹燈牌,你不可能錯過這歷史悠久的中式餐廳。路旁的魚缸定會引起你的注意。一如所料,兩層均燈火通明,長期坐滿了絡繹不絕的食客,以餐牌上的照片選擇菜餚,有特別出色的,如　蔥脆腩片及芝麻鹽焗雞。

■ ADDRESS/地址

TEL.2739 8813
14-16 Hillwood Road, Tsim Sha Tsui, Kowloon
九龍尖沙咀山林道14-16號

■ OPENING HOURS, LAST ORDER
　營業時間,最後點菜時間
11:00-02:00 L.O. 01:30

■ PRICE/價錢

Lunch/午膳	set/套餐	$240-380
	à la carte/點菜	$150-250
Dinner/晚膳	set/套餐	$240-380
	à la carte/點菜	$150-250

Tak Lung
得龍

Originally a sidewalk stall, Tak Long moved to its current San Po Kong location over 40 years ago and is still going strong. This family business constantly strives to provide good quality traditional and original dishes. It's well worth pre-ordering the crystallised coin-shaped chicken. Lean pork is marinated in sugar and rose wine for a week then roasted in a skewer with barbecue pork and chicken liver: a classic dish which is now hard to find.

本為大排檔的得龍於四十多年前遷至位於新蒲崗的現址，依然極受歡迎。這樁家族生意一直致力為客人提供高品質的傳統及自創菜式。金錢雞隻需預訂。提早一星期前以砂糖及玫瑰露酒醃好的瘦肉與叉燒及雞肝同串燒烤：經典菜式，如今已非常罕見。

■ ADDRESS/地址
TEL.2320 7020
25-29 Hong Keung Street, San Po Kong, Kowloon
九龍新蒲崗康強街25號
www.taklung.com.hk

■ ANNUAL AND WEEKLY CLOSING
休息日期
Closed 3 days Lunar New Year
農曆新年休息3天

■ OPENING HOURS, LAST ORDER
營業時間，最後點菜時間
06:00-23:00 (L.O.)

■ PRICE/價錢
Lunch/午膳   à la carte/點菜 $80-300
Dinner/晚膳   à la carte/點菜 $150-300

Tam Chai Yunnan Noodles (Jordan Road)
譚仔雲南米線 (佐敦道)

You can't miss the bright yellow and green sign, even if you wanted to! This is one of a chain of eateries popular for its Sichuan-style spicy rice noodles. You simply pick one of three soup bases (clear soup, sour & spicy and super spicy); decide on the level of heat and then choose your own toppings to go with it. There are also three types of delicious chicken wings to add as a side dish. Just be prepared to do some queuing.

你絕不可能錯過這明亮的黃綠色招牌！這四川風味麻辣米線店極受歡迎，可從三種湯底（清湯、酸辣、麻辣）挑選，再選擇辣度和你喜歡的配料。另外，更有三款美味雞翼可作為小菜。做好排隊的心理準備吧。

■ ADDRESS/地址
TEL.2302 0982
36 Jordan Road, Jordan, Kowloon
九龍佐敦佐敦道36號

■ OPENING HOURS, LAST ORDER
營業時間，最後點菜時間
11:00-23:00 (L.O.)

■ PRICE/價錢

Lunch/午膳	set/套餐	$21-25
	à la carte/點菜	$21-80
Dinner/晚膳	set/套餐	$21-25
	à la carte/點菜	$21-80

Tandoor

🔲30 📞🍴

A traditional but charming looking Indian restaurant this may be, but it's the cuisine here which sets it apart. Different spices are delicately blended to produce exquisite flavours. Chef's special is lamb chops marinated in ginger and garlic, but his tikka massala and makhani sauces also add a tasty dimension to seafood and chicken. There are bargain lunches, dinner buffets (weekends only) and live music during dinner (except on Sundays).

傳統而迷人的一家印度餐廳，最吸引人的卻是其地道菜餚。不同的香料巧妙地混合起來，形成細膩的味道。廚師推介包括薑蒜汁羊扒，而tikka massala及makhani醬亦令海鮮及雞肉的滋味更上一層樓。提供特惠午餐、晚市自助餐（限週末）及晚餐時分現場奏樂（週日除外）。

■ ADDRESS/地址
TEL.2845 2262
1F, Lyndhurst Tower, 1 Lyndhurst Terrace, Central
中環擺花街1號中環大廈1樓
www.hktandoor.com

■ OPENING HOURS, LAST ORDER
營業時間，最後點菜時間
Lunch/午膳 12:00-14:45 (L.O.)
Dinner/晚膳 18:00-22:45 (L.O.)

■ PRICE/價錢
Lunch/午膳　set/套餐　　　$ 118
　　　　　　à la carte/點菜 $ 200-450
Dinner/晚膳　set/套餐　　　$ 198
　　　　　　à la carte/點菜 $ 200-450

T'ang Court
唐閣

Rich silks and contemporary art line the walls of the lavishly furnished main dining room, on the first floor above the hotel's grand lobby. There's also a dramatic staircase leading up to a second floor of tables and the exclusive private dining rooms named after famous Tang Dynasty poets. The cooking displays considerable skill, with particular emphasis on seafood. The service is also well structured and polished.

豐厚的絲緞配合富當代氣息的牆身，裝潢豪華的主菜廳位於酒店大堂樓上。一道極盡奢華的樓梯連上二樓各餐桌，更設有以唐代著名詩人命名的貴賓廳。菜餚極具功夫，海鮮更是當中首推菜式。服務經過精心編排。

■ ADDRESS/地址

TEL.2375 1133
1F, The Langham Hotel, 8 Peking Road, Tsim Sha Tsui, Kowloon
九龍尖沙咀北京道8號朗廷酒店1樓
www.hongkong.langhamhotels.com

■ OPENING HOURS, LAST ORDER
營業時間，最後點菜時間
Lunch/午膳　12:00-15:00 L.O. 14:30
Dinner/晚膳　18:00-23:00 L.O. 22:30

■ PRICE/價錢

Lunch/午膳	set/套餐	$248-450
	à la carte/點菜	$360-2,000
Dinner/晚膳	set/套餐	$450-650
	à la carte/點菜	$360-2,000

Tanyoto Hotpot (Wan Chai)
譚魚頭火鍋 (灣仔)

Want to cook but can't be bothered to shop before or clean up afterwards? Then head for Tanyoto Hotpot, where the team will assist you in creating a Sichuan hotpot meal to remember, using their secret ingredient – the unique soup base of peppers and tomatoes, grown on their own plot. They'll guide you to the best produce; try the fish head or Japanese style pork bone. Or you can go for breakfast, as they open for dim sum from 7am.

想煮食卻不願買菜洗盤子？到譚魚頭火鍋吧。服務團隊將以祕製材料助你炮製難忘的四川火鍋宴——加入獨家培植的胡椒番茄。他們更樂意為你介紹最佳材料，試試魚頭或日本豬骨吧。你或可在早餐時段前往——他們在早上七時開始提供點心。

■ ADDRESS/地址

TEL. 2893 9268
1-3F, 129-135 Johnston Road, Wan Chai
灣仔莊士敦道129-135號1-3樓
www.tanyotou.com.hk

■ OPENING HOURS, LAST ORDER
營業時間，最後點菜時間
07:00-01:00 (L.O.)

■ PRICE/價錢
Lunch/午膳   à la carte/點菜 $ 300-500
Dinner/晚膳   à la carte/點菜 $ 300-500

Tasty (Happy Valley)
正斗粥麵專家 (跑馬地)

It's worth taking the time to get here, because this is more than the average noodle dining experience. There's a sophisticated air, with polished wood enhancing a feeling of exclusivity. Waitresses wear colourful uniforms, and many customers call them over for the legendary won ton noodles. The range of congee toppings is comprehensive, while chef's special dim sum includes braised goose webs with abalone sauce and pomelo skin with shrimp roe.

這裡值得你花時間走一趟，因為此店有超乎一般的水準。這裡氣氛濃厚，拋光的木飾更添一種獨享感覺。服務員制服色彩繽紛，許多客人被口碑載道的雲吞麵深深吸引。粥的配菜種類很全面，同樣是廚師的點心特別推介包括鮑汁鵝掌及蝦子柚子皮。

■ ADDRESS/地址

TEL.2838 3922
21 King Kwong Street, Happy Valley
跑馬地景光街21號

■ OPENING HOURS, LAST ORDER
營業時間，最後點菜時間
11:30-24:00 (L.O.)

■ PRICE/價錢
Lunch/午膳 à la carte/點菜 $ 35-65
Dinner/晚膳 à la carte/點菜 $ 40-120

Tasty (Hung Hom)
正斗粥麵專家 (紅磡)

It's quite modest and simple inside, with dark wood walls and Chinese decorations but it's all enlivened by friendly and efficient waitresses. You can't reserve here and it's often so busy you're forced to queue. But it's worth it for the quality of the noodles, soup, congee and dim sum. Try dishes like salted lean pork and preserved egg congee or stir-fried rice noodle with beef. You won't be disappointed: you won't pay a lot either!

餐廳裝潢樸實簡單，深木色的牆身和中國傳統擺設。友善而高效率的女侍應更增加餐廳活力。這裡食客眾多，但沒有訂座服務，因此經常需要排隊輪候。不過，這裡的麵、湯、粥和點心都是優質美食，實在值得排隊等候。推介菜式包括皮蛋瘦肉粥或乾炒牛河。此外，這裡的菜式價錢相宜，絕對不會令你失望！

■ ADDRESS/地址
TEL.3152 2328
Shop 111, 1F, Whampoa Plaza, Site 8, Hung Hom, Kowloon
九龍紅磡黃埔花園第8期1樓111號舖

■ OPENING HOURS, LAST ORDER
營業時間，最後點菜時間
11:30-23:30 (L.O.)
■ PRICE/價錢
Lunch/午膳   à la carte/點菜 $75-150
Dinner/晚膳   à la carte/點菜 $75-150

Tasty (IFC)
正斗粥麵專家 (國際金融中心)

Sleek mall surroundings enhance Tasty's strikingly elaborate façade of ornate wood and coloured glass. Inside it's just as vivid: walls covered with 30,000 chopsticks, handmade chairs with intricate floral patterns, and eye-catching metal pots. You'll probably be asked to share a table before tucking into the hallmark shrimp won ton or the much-loved beef and rice noodle stir fry. Also recommended from the vast choice is congee with prawns.

豪華的商場環境突顯了正斗的木飾和彩色玻璃外觀。餐廳裡同樣有生氣：牆壁佈滿一萬五千雙筷子，手工椅子上有複雜精細的花卉圖案，還有引人注目的金屬壺。你可能需與人搭枱，不過能享用美食便值回票價。熱門菜包括招牌鮮蝦雲吞麵，或備受喜愛的干炒牛河。此外，在芸芸選擇中，我們特別推介生猛大蝦粥。

■ ADDRESS/地址

TEL.2295 0101

Shop 3016, Podium Level 3, IFC Mall, 1 Harbour View Street, Central
中環港景街1號國際金融中心商場第2期3樓3016號舖

■ OPENING HOURS, LAST ORDER
營業時間，最後點菜時間
11:30-22:45 (L.O.)

■ PRICE/價錢
Lunch/午膳　à la carte/點菜 $75-150
Dinner/晚膳　à la carte/點菜 $75-150

Thai Basil

Shoppers in Pacific Place mall can seek sustenance here, from a wide ranging menu of straightforward dishes which include the likes of soft shell crab tempura to king prawns in yellow curry. Don't miss the sticky banana pudding with honey ice cream to boost those energy levels. The simple wooden furniture and friendly young team of servers help create a relaxed atmosphere in this large dining room, open all day.

於太古廣場購物的人士可在此一解飢腸,餐單提供林林總總的選擇,從較簡單的菜式一如軟殼蟹米紙卷,或是大虎蝦黃咖喱,任君選擇。別錯過讓你精神百倍的雪糕香蕉布甸。簡約的木製家具和友善年輕的服務生在此偌大的餐廳營造悠閒氣氛,全日開放。

■ ADDRESS/地址
TEL.2537 4682
Shop 001, LG, Pacific Place, 88 Queensway, Admiralty
金鐘金鐘道88號太古廣場地庫1樓1號舖

■ OPENING HOURS, LAST ORDER
營業時間,最後點菜時間
11:30-22:30 (L.O.)

■ PRICE/價錢
Lunch/午膳　à la carte/點菜 $220-320
Dinner/晚膳　à la carte/點菜 $220-320

The Drawing Room

🍴🍴

📐12 🕐🍴 🔗

Opened in April 2009, the Drawing Room is a warm and stylish restaurant on the first floor of the chic JIA boutique hotel. The striking and original metal art pieces from local creators are quite a feature and the bar sets the mood: this is the place of the moment. Choose from the two daily-changing set menus created with the best available ingredients. Italian is the most prominent influence on both the cooking and the wine list.

餐廳於2009年4月開幕，位於時尚酒店JIA的一樓，溫暖而具流行風格。本地藝術家創作了讓人一見難忘的原創金屬藝術品，甚具特色，酒吧更洋溢情調：此時此刻，就在此地。可從兩款每日更替的菜單中選擇，全由當日最佳新鮮食材炮製。不論煮食方法或是名酒清單都極具義大利特色。

■ ADDRESS/地址

TEL.2915 6628
1F, 1-5 Irving Street, Causeway Bay
銅鑼灣伊榮街1-5 號1樓
www.thedrawingroom.com.hk

■ ANNUAL AND WEEKLY CLOSING
    休息日期
Closed Sunday
週日休息

■ OPENING HOURS, LAST ORDER
    營業時間，最後點菜時間
Dinner/晚膳 18:00-23:00 (L.O.)

■ PRICE/價錢
Dinner/晚膳 set/套餐 $580-880

The Lounge

Nestling in the lobby corner of the Four Seasons hotel is this all-day dining restaurant. Its contemporary décor, great harbour views and live music (piano or jazz trio) create a perfect blend of informal elegance. The cuisine blends East and West: Scottish salmon with smoked caviar served with yuzu cream, Niçoise salad, squid ink linguine pasta and roasted pigeon on Savoy cabbage are just some examples. Afternoon tea is also popular.

位於四季酒店大堂一隅，餐廳全日提供服務。當代裝潢，醉人海景及現場音樂演奏（鋼琴或爵士三重奏）締造輕鬆而不失優雅的氣氛。餐單方面包括東西方精選：蘇格蘭三文魚伴煙燻魚子醬及柚子忌廉、尼斯沙律、墨魚汁幼麵烤乳鴿配皺葉捲心菜。下午茶亦甚受歡迎。

■ ADDRESS/地址
TEL.3196 8820
1F, Four Seasons Hotel, 8 Finance Street, Central
中環金融街8號四季酒店1樓
www.fourseasons.com/hongkong

■ OPENING HOURS, LAST ORDER
營業時間，最後點菜時間
Lunch/午膳 11:00-15:00 (L.O.)
Dinner/晚膳 17:30-23:30 (L.O.)

■ PRICE/價錢
Lunch/午膳 à la carte/點菜 $350-750
Dinner/晚膳 à la carte/點菜 $350-750

The Pawn

This former pawn shop, dating from 1888, enjoyed a new lease of life 120 years later when it became a modern British dining room. The first floor is for the likes of sausage and mash, washed down with a beer; but the main event is on the second. Here you'll find robust British dishes such as fish and chips or braised lamb shank, followed by classic desserts like Eton Mess or lemon posset. Roasts on Sundays; bookings are a must.

餐廳前身是1888年開始經營的大押，120年後重新當舖活化成型格英倫餐廳。一樓是香腸及薯蓉愛好者的必到之處，加上啤酒更為完滿；但好戲在二樓。二樓供應炸魚薯條、焗羊膝等，配上經典甜品如英式奶油草莓布丁及英式檸檬布丁。星期天更設有烤肉，必須預訂。

■ ADDRESS/地址

TEL.2866 3444

2F, 62 Johnston Road, Wan Chai
灣仔莊士敦道62號2樓
www.thepawn.com.hk

■ OPENING HOURS, LAST ORDER
   營業時間，最後點菜時間
Lunch/午膳 12:00-14:30 (L.O.)
Dinner/晚膳 18:30-22:30 (L.O.)

■ PRICE/價錢
Lunch/午膳   set/套餐 $190
              à la carte/點菜 $350-500
Dinner/晚膳 à la carte/點菜 $350-500

The Press Room

A local newspaper once occupied these premises but it's now home to a typically French brasserie that offers a pleasant, relaxed atmosphere. The panelling and high ceiling is enlivened by some interesting contemporary Chinese art. There's plenty to read, from a large menu of classics that covers everything from soups and salads to grills and seafood. The extensive range of cheeses and wines by the glass are certainly newsworthy.

這物業範圍曾是某本地報社的所在位置,但如今已變身為法式小菜館,氣氛舒適宜人。隔板及高天花以有趣的現代中國藝術裝飾。餐牌提供眾多選擇,從餐湯、沙律、烤肉、海鮮,應有盡有。餐廳提供的芝士和餐酒,更是絕不能錯過。

■ ADDRESS/地址
TEL.2525 3444
108 Hollywood Road, Central
中環荷里活道108號
www.thepressroom.com.hk

■ OPENING HOURS, LAST ORDER
　營業時間,最後點菜時間
12:00-23:00 (L.O.)

■ PRICE/價錢
Lunch/午膳　à la carte/點菜 $300-600
Dinner/晚膳　set/套餐　　　$250
　　　　　　à la carte/點菜 $300-600

227

The Royal Garden
帝苑軒

 80

Cross a small bridge in the basement to get to this sleek, panelled restaurant, which, on closer inspection, is modelled on a Chinese official's formal water garden of yesteryear. Home-cooked, seasonal Cantonese cuisine and daily fresh seafood are served here, with lunchtime dim sum a big favourite. Specials include pig's lung soup with assorted meat, pak choy and almond juice, or steamed red crab with 'Hua Teow' wine.

在地庫層橫過一道小橋，便可到達這家雅致的中式餐廳。餐廳牆上嵌著飾板，仔細一看，原來餐廳是摹仿昔日中國古色的園林而設計。這裡的四季風味粵菜全是自家烹調，天天採用新鮮的海鮮，而午餐點心更是一大熱門。特色美食包括杏汁白菜膽燉豬肺湯、雞油花雕蒸大紅花蟹等。

■ ADDRESS/地址

TEL.2724 2666

B2F, The Royal Garden Hotel, 69 Mody Road, East Tsim Sha Tsui, Kowloon
九龍尖東麼地道69號帝苑酒店地庫2樓
www.rghk.com.hk

■ OPENING HOURS, LAST ORDER
營業時間，最後點菜時間
Lunch/午膳　11:30-14:30 (L.O.)
Dinner/晚膳　18:00-22:30 (L.O.)

■ PRICE/價錢
Lunch/午膳　à la carte/點菜 $250-1,000
Dinner/晚膳　set/套餐　　　$1,988
　　　　　　à la carte/點菜 $250-1,000

The Square
翠玉軒

⊡12 🕐🍴

This first dining room is an elegant affair with a number of display cabinets dotted around and filled with pieces of porcelain; when making reservations, make sure you get seated here, as the two other dining rooms are simpler. The menu offers a very diligently prepared selection of Cantonese dishes, including such specialities as vegetable purée with conpoy and tofu, golden crispy tangerine prawns.

第一中菜廳極為高雅,配有一系列展示櫃,內有珍藏瓷器;預約時謹記安排坐在此處,因為另外兩個中菜廳佈置較簡單。餐廳的粵菜菜式烹調甚見巧思,美食包括瑤柱豆腐菜茸羹及柑橘脆蝦球。

■ ADDRESS/地址
TEL.2525 1163
4F, Two Exchange Square, 8
Connaught Place, Central
中環康樂廣場8號交易廣場第2期4樓
www.maxims.com.hk

■ OPENING HOURS, LAST ORDER
營業時間,最後點菜時間
Lunch/午膳 11:00-15:00 (L.O.)
Dinner/晚膳 18:00-23:00 (L.O.)

■ PRICE/價錢

Lunch/午膳	set/套餐	$218-868
	à la carte/點菜	$170-600
Dinner/晚膳	set/套餐	$868
	à la carte/點菜	$170-600

The Steak House

Possibly one of the most sophisticated grill rooms in town, this area has its own dramatic wine bar with a spectacular wine list – particularly the selection of reds! Service is both professional and friendly and the products used here are top quality. Beef sourced from Australia, the U.S., Japan and Argentina is supplemented by seafood and simple desserts. The cooking is sensibly straightforward.

The Steak House可能是城中功力最到家的扒房之一，更擁有一流的酒吧，提供獨特的葡萄酒，而對紅酒的選擇尤其出色！服務專業友善，美酒佳餚全屬優質。牛肉由澳洲、美國、日本和阿根廷入口，亦有提供海鮮和簡單的甜品。菜式毫不花巧，簡單直接。

■ ADDRESS/地址
TEL.2313 2405
LF, Intercontinental Hotel, 18 Salisbury Road, Tsim Sha Tsui, Kowloon
九龍尖沙咀梳士巴利道18號洲際酒店地庫1樓

■ OPENING HOURS, LAST ORDER
營業時間，最後點菜時間
Dinner/晚膳 18:00-23:00 (L.O.)

■ PRICE/價錢
Dinner/晚膳　set/套餐　　　　$810-1,880
　　　　　　à la carte/點菜　$540-2,500

Tim Ho Wan
添好運

It would not be an exaggeration to say that this little dim sum shop has brought life into this quite street in Mong Kok. In March '09, two chefs joined forces and opened here; it has been a success ever since, hence the queue outside. There's no doubt about their ingredients; special mention can be given to the steamed dumpling 'chiu chow style', the steamed egg cake and, most definitely, the baked bun with barbecued pork. The wait is worth it.

説這家小小的點心店為旺角較為靜寂的街角增添了生氣，這個説法並不為過。2009年3月，兩位師傅聯手創辦此店。值得留意的有潮洲蒸粉果、香滑馬拉糕，酥皮焗叉燒包更是絕對不能錯過。你會發現，這裡的點心絕對不負期待。

■ ADDRESS/地址
TEL.9332 2896
8 Kwong Wa Street, Mong Kok, Kowloon
九龍旺角廣華街8號

■ OPENING HOURS, LAST ORDER
營業時間，最後點菜時間
10:00-21:15 (L.O.)

■ PRICE/價錢
Lunch/午膳   à la carte/點菜 $30-50
Dinner/晚膳   à la carte/點菜 $30-50

Tim's Kitchen
桃花源小廚

No doubt about it...this is a hidden gem. Don't be put off by the fact it's in a somewhat shabby spot, and has only seven tables, plastic seats and a bring-your-own-wine policy. Sweet, endearing service soon wins you round, but it's the exquisite Cantonese cooking that's the real eye-opener – owner Tim has remarkable respect for his ingredients. The menu is much simpler at lunch; food lovers might prefer to make reservations for dinner time.

毫無疑問，這是顆隱蔽的寶石。餐廳位於一條頗為簡陋的街道，裡面只有七張餐桌，座椅更是塑膠造的，餐廳鼓勵客人自攜餐酒。但不要因此而卻步，親切友善的服務很快便可贏得你的歡心。真正令人大開眼界的是這裡別緻的粵菜。東主黎先生對食材的要求十分嚴謹。午市餐牌選擇不多，嗜食者應考慮選擇晚市時段。

■ ADDRESS/地址
TEL.2543 5919
93 Jervois Street, Sheung Wan
上環蘇杭街93號

■ ANNUAL AND WEEKLY CLOSING
　休息日期
Closed Sunday and Public Holidays
週日及公眾假期休息

■ OPENING HOURS, LAST ORDER
　營業時間，最後點菜時間
Lunch/午膳 12:00-14:30 (L.O.)
Dinner/晚膳 18:30-22:00 (L.O.)

■ PRICE/價錢
Lunch/午膳　à la carte/點菜 $ 100-180
Dinner/晚膳　à la carte/點菜 $ 150-900

Tokoro

Based around the robatayaki concept of the Japanese barbecue, many raw ingredients are on display here for you to select. Once that's done, you take your seat either at a counter or in one of three bird cages which swivel to face either the kitchen or not. Interaction between guests and chefs makes for a lively atmosphere and there's plenty of sake on hand to lubricate things further. There are also elegant private rooms and a tiny sushi bar.

這家以爐端燒為主題的餐廳，用很多原材料展示出來以供食客挑選。選料後食客可隨意選擇座位，既可以坐在櫃檯用餐，亦可選擇三個鳥籠的其中一個，旋轉致面向廚房或背向廚房位置。食客和廚師之間的交流令這裡充滿生氣。餐廳更有提供多種燒酒，並設有典雅的私人餐室和小型壽司吧。

■ ADDRESS/地址

TEL.3552 3330
3F, Langham Place Hotel, 555
Shanghai Street, Mong Kok, Kowloon
九龍旺角上海街555號朗豪酒店3樓
www.tokoro.com.hk

■ OPENING HOURS, LAST ORDER
營業時間，最後點菜時間
Lunch/午膳 12:00-14:30 (L.O.)
Dinner/晚膳 18:30-22:30 (L.O.)

■ PRICE/價錢
Lunch/午膳　set/套餐　　　$127-237
　　　　　　à la carte/點菜 $300-500
Dinner/晚膳 set/套餐　　　$400-950
　　　　　　à la carte/點菜 $300-500

Tsim Chai Kee (Queen's Road)
沾仔記 (皇后大道中)

Formerly of Connaught Road, Tsim Chai Kee moved here in late 2008. The simple, but neat and clean, basement room is hidden away somewhat, with steps leading down to its narrow entrance. However, it's the good value, straightforward cooking that people come for. The concise menu lists dishes such as king prawn wonton noodle, fresh minced fish ball or fresh sliced beef noodle; choose between yellow or flat white noodles or vermicelli.

以往位於干諾道的沾仔記於2008年底遷至此處。簡約清潔的地下室有樓梯連至其窄小入口。人們前來只為一嚐其物有所值、直接了當的菜式。餐牌雖然選擇不多，但五臟俱全，列出招牌雲吞麵、鮮鯪魚球、鮮牛肉麵；從麵、河、米粉中選出一種吧。

■ ADDRESS/地址
TEL.2581 3369
153 Queen's Road Central, Central
中環皇后大道中153號

■ OPENING HOURS, LAST ORDER
　營業時間，最後點菜時間
09:00-22:00 (L.O.)

■ PRICE/價錢
Lunch/午膳　à la carte/點菜 $ 16-24
Dinner/晚膳　à la carte/點菜 $ 16-24

Tsim Chai Kee (Wellington Street)
沾仔記 (威靈頓街)

This highly regarded, simple noodle shop may be here since 1998 but it's still looking good. The staff are as bright as their aprons; the popular side booths are quickly snapped up and the regulars know to eat outside peak times when the pace is less frenetic. The attraction is the handmade fish balls, the generously filled wontons and the fresh beef served with the noodles. It's easy to spot –just look for the lunchtime queues.

享負盛名的沾仔記於一九九八年開業,裝修簡單,但依然整潔舒適。侍應制服明亮潔淨。卡位非常受歡迎,經常滿座;熟客會在非繁忙時間光顧,氣氛則較為輕鬆。著名菜式包括自製的鮮鯪魚球、餡料豐富的招牌雲吞,以及鮮牛肉麵。餐廳容易尋找,午市時段外面大排長龍的那家就是了!

■ ADDRESS/地址
TEL.2850 6471
98 Wellington Street, Central
中環威靈頓街98號

■ ANNUAL AND WEEKLY CLOSING
　　休息日期
Closed 4 days Lunar New Year
農曆新年休息4天

■ OPENING HOURS, LAST ORDER
　　營業時間,最後點菜時間
09:00-22:00 (L.O.)

■ PRICE/價錢
Lunch/午膳　à la carte/點菜 $ 16-24
Dinner/晚膳　à la carte/點菜 $ 16-24

Tuscany by H

🍴16 ☎🍴 🍇

The name doesn't give the whole picture as this soberly dressed, modern restaurant looks to all parts of Italy for its influences, not just Tuscany. Expect a wide range of classics, all exuding a certain rustic style of cooking that is all about the flavours. The 36 month aged Parma ham, the beef cheek ravioli and the veal chop are some of the dishes to pair with a choice of over 200 bottles from the wine list.

餐廳名字不足以表達其全貌;這家經過精心裝潢、富現代感的餐廳受到義大利不同地區的影響,不只是塔斯卡尼。餐廳提供一系列經典,全都表現出濃厚意式鄉土風味,注重調味。三十六個月的風乾巴拿馬火腿,牛頰肉意式雲吞和小牛排是其中一些精選擇,配上酒牌上超過二百種餐酒可供選擇。

■ ADDRESS/地址

TEL.2522 9798
58-62 D'Aguilar Street, Lan Kwai Fong, Central
中環蘭桂芳德己立街58-62號
www.tuscany-by-h.com

■ ANNUAL AND WEEKLY CLOSING
    休息日期
Closed Sunday lunch and Public Holidays lunch
週日午膳及公眾假期午膳休息

■ OPENING HOURS, LAST ORDER
    營業時間,最後點菜時間
Lunch/午膳 12:00-15:00 (L.O.)
Dinner/晚膳 18:00-23:00 (L.O.)

■ PRICE/價錢
Lunch/午膳   set/套餐 $218
              à la carte/點菜 $300-800
Dinner/晚膳   set/套餐 $488-880
              à la carte/點菜 $300-800

Va Bene

This smart Italian establishment offers a little corner of Tuscany when you walk into the endlessly long dining room. But the whole of Italy is featured on the menu where the gastronomic highlight is Casoncelli alla Bergamasca e tartufo nero – their signature dish. What marks this out is the constant presence of the long-standing manager and his highly attentive team. Make room for a little Grappa at the end of the meal.

這家時尚的長形意大利餐廳，提供極具情懷的塔斯卡尼美食體驗。不過，食客可在餐牌上找到意大利全國各地的佳餚，招牌菜是 Casoncelli alla Bergamasca e tartufo nero，堪稱其美食之冠。在此工作多年的經理和服務周到的員工，是餐廳另一特別之處。用膳過後，別忘了品嘗一杯格拉巴酒。

■ ADDRESS/地址
TEL.2845 5577
17-22 Lan Kwai Fong, Central
中環蘭桂坊17-22
www.vabeneristorante.com

■ ANNUAL AND WEEKLY CLOSING
休息日期
Closed Sunday lunch and Public Holidays lunch
週日午膳及公眾假期午膳 休息

■ OPENING HOURS, LAST ORDER
營業時間，最後點菜時間
Lunch/午膳 12:00-14:30 (L.O.)
Dinner/晚膳 18:30-23:30 (L.O.)

■ PRICE/價錢
Lunch/午膳 set/套餐 $198
            à la carte/點菜 $400-600
Dinner/晚膳 à la carte/點菜 $400-600

Union J

A Jason and a Johnson, fresh from Jean Georges in New York and Shanghai, are the union behind this attractive contemporary bistro offering 'new American cuisine'. Their short menu changes constantly to ensure the freshest ingredients, but expect to see plenty of beef in various forms from tartare to sirloin, along with hamachi and fresh crab. Their cheesecake is not to be missed. It's an affordable and relaxed place.

Jason和Johnson分別來自紐約和上海的Jean Georges餐廳，是這家時代餐廳的幕後功臣，提供"新派美國菜"。餐牌雖短，卻不斷更新，確保採用最新鮮食材，但你定可找到一系列牛肉的選擇，從他他牛到西冷牛不等，更有油甘魚及鮮蟹。其芝士蛋糕更不容錯過。在此用餐不算昂貴卻可享受輕鬆悠閒時光。

■ ADDRESS/地址
TEL.2537 2368
1F, California Tower, 30-32 D'Aguilar Street, Lan Kwai Fong, Central
中環蘭桂芳德己立街30-32號加州大廈1樓
www.elite-concepts.com

■ ANNUAL AND WEEKLY CLOSING
休息日期
Closed Saturday lunch and Sunday
週六午膳及週日休息

■ OPENING HOURS, LAST ORDER
營業時間，最後點菜時間
Lunch/午膳 12:00-15:00 (L.O.)
Dinner/晚膳 18:00-22:30 (L.O.)

■ PRICE/價錢
Lunch/午膳 set/套餐 $150-320
Dinner/晚膳 à la carte/點菜 $400-550

Unkai
雲海

Lots of small rooms emanating from a central bamboo provide a characteristic Japanese minimalist setting for Unkai. There's a tatami room for a taste of real Japan, private rooms for intimacy, or rooms where the chefs will prepare teppanyaki in front of your eyes. Not forgetting the ubiquitous sushi bar. Cuisine from the Osaka region is a speciality here, and sake lovers will raise a smile over the fact there are 62 varieties of it on offer!

由中央的竹，延伸至用來間隔小房間的到頂的木條，構成了雲海的日本極潔抽象風格。餐廳包括一個榻榻米房間、較有私隱的私人餐室，以及廚師即席在人前烹調鐵板燒的房間。此外，壽司吧亦無處不在。這裡的特色美食包括大阪菜式，而這裡有62種清酒之多，愛好清酒者真是口福不淺！

- **ADDRESS/地址**
TEL.2369 1111
3F, Sheraton Hotel, 20 Nathan Road, Tsim Sha Tsui, Kowloon
九龍尖沙咀彌敦道20號喜來登酒店3樓
www.sheraton.com/hongkong

- **OPENING HOURS, LAST ORDER**
營業時間，最後點菜時間
Lunch/午膳　12:00-14:30 (L.O.)
Dinner/晚膳　18:30-22:30 (L.O.)

- **PRICE/價錢**
Lunch/午膳　set/套餐　　　$180-420
　　　　　à la carte/點菜 $300-850
Dinner/晚膳 set/套餐　　　$350-795
　　　　　à la carte/點菜 $300-850

238

Uno Más

This energetic and contemporary first floor tapas bar opened in February 2009 in among the bright lights of Wan Chai. Sit back with friends and absorb the atmosphere, while the open kitchen prepares charcuteria, croquetas and tortillas; the speciality Fideuá seafood paella can be ordered in advance and no meal is complete without the addictive churros with chocolate and orange mousse. Two terraces look down over the bustling streets below.

這家充滿活力而富當代感的樓上西班牙風味小館於2009年2月在灣仔的燈幕下開張。與三五知己共聚，享受其獨特氣氛，等待廚房烹調西班牙香腸、炸肉球及玉米粉圓餅。馳名焗西班牙海鮮米粉／飯Paella，可作預訂，少不了西班牙甜甜圈伴朱古力和香橙慕絲。從兩個平台花園看下去，可望見樓下熙來攘往的街道。

- **ADDRESS/地址**
TEL.2527 9111
1F, 54-62 Lockhart Road, Wan Chai
灣仔駱克道54-62號1樓
www.arcanatables.com

- **OPENING HOURS, LAST ORDER**
營業時間，最後點菜時間
12:00-01:00(L.O.)

- **PRICE/價錢**
Lunch/午膳　set/套餐　　　$110-138
　　　　　à la carte/點菜 $200-400
Dinner/晚膳 à la carte/點菜 $200-400

239

Wagyu Kaiseki Den

Don't let the name confuse you - Wagyu beef is not the only ingredient. In fact, its just one of numerous imported items that appears on the daily-changing, no choice Kaiseki menu, where some modern touches sit alongside more traditional elements. Seasonality and freshness are fundamental to the passionate Japanese chef here; watch him and his team perform by reserving at the counter. The charming, detailed decoration enhances the experience.

別讓店名模糊了視線——和牛並非唯一食材。其實，和牛只是無數每天新鮮入口的不同食材的其中一種，由廚師決定的懷石菜單，傳統中帶有現代修飾。對充滿熱情的日籍廚師來說，時令及新鮮程度是基本要素。預訂櫃檯位置，看看他和團隊如何施展渾身解數吧。迷人精緻的裝潢，令用餐體驗更臻完美。

■ ADDRESS/地址

TEL.2851 2820

263 Hollywood Road, Sheung Wan
上環荷李活道263號

■ ANNUAL AND WEEKLY CLOSING
　　休息日期

Closed 3 days Lunar New Year
and Sunday
農曆新年3天及週日休息

■ OPENING HOURS, LAST ORDER
　　營業時間，最後點菜時間
Dinner/晚膳 18:30-23:00 (L.O.)

■ PRICE/價錢
Dinner/晚膳　set/套餐　　　＄1,680

Wasabisabi
山葵

🍽14 ☷ ◑🍴

This über-chic environment manages to blend together Japanese simplicity with something far more futuristic. As you step onto a subtly lit cat-walk passage, you'll find the brash red of the Lipstick Lounge on one side and the cooler tones of the main dining room on the other. Culinary styles too are thrown up in the air and incorporate everything from mustard beef tenderloin bento boxes to Japanese tiramisu. You have been warned!

餐廳裝潢融合了日本簡約風格和未來主義，走在時尚尖端。踏上燈光黯淡的catwalk大道，可見一邊是豔紅色的Lipstick Lounge，而另一邊的主餐室則以較深沉的色調為主。菜式風格實在是各式各樣，芥辣籽汁燒牛柳便當、綠茶芝士餅等，定會使你驚喜萬分！

■ ADDRESS/地址
TEL.2506 0009
Shop 1301, 13F, Food Forum, Times Square, 1 Matheson Street, Causeway Bay
銅鑼灣勿地臣街1號時代廣場食天13樓1301號舖
www.aqua.com.hk

■ OPENING HOURS, LAST ORDER
　營業時間，最後點菜時間
Lunch/午膳　12:00-15:00 (L.O.)
Dinner/晚膳　18:00-24:00 (L.O.)

■ PRICE/價錢
Lunch/午膳　set/套餐　　　$ 178-278
　　　　　　à la carte/點菜 $ 400-500
Dinner/晚膳　set/套餐　　　$ 548
　　　　　　à la carte/點菜 $ 400-500

Watermark

The views of Kowloon and the harbour from this large, glass-sided, contemporary restaurant on Pier 7 are superb but this is certainly not its only asset. USDA certified beef from Nebraska, as well as supremely fresh seafood, feature on a menu that delivers contemporary touches to classic dishes. Non-carnivores should try crispy fillet of red emperor with pinto beans. A great location to while away a Sunday brunch.

這家位於七號碼頭的餐廳其中一邊為落地玻璃，盡覽九龍方向及海港景色，但這並非唯一賣點。布拉斯加牛肉，極其新鮮的海鮮，出現在為傳統餐點帶來一絲現代氣息的餐牌上。不好肉類的食客可嚐嚐脆炸紅皇帝石斑伴斑豆。此處亦是星期天早午合餐的絕佳地點。

■ ADDRESS/地址

TEL.2167 7251

Level P, Central Pier 7, Star Ferry, Central
中環7號碼頭P樓
www.igors.com

■ OPENING HOURS, LAST ORDER
營業時間，最後點菜時間
Lunch/午膳 11:30-14:30 (L.O.)
Dinner/晚膳 18:00-22:30 (L.O.)

■ PRICE/價錢

Lunch/午膳	set/套餐	$230
Dinner/晚膳	set/套餐	$425

Wing Wah
永華雲吞麵家

This simple operation has been maintaining high standards for well over 50 years now. And the secret is that they do everything from scratch upstairs, making their noodles by hand using bamboo. So proud are they of their skills that there's a photographic display on the walls showing what they do. Finest offerings include shrimp wonton and barbecued pork noodle as well as a dessert of coconut milk with honeydew melon and sago.

這家簡單的餐廳營運至今逾50年，依然保持一貫的高水準，成功秘訣在於一手包辦所有工作，在樓上用竹昇手打麵便可見一斑。他們以自家技術深感自豪，牆上貼著製作過程的照片。招牌美食包括鮮蝦雲吞麵及炸醬麵，甜品方面首推蜜瓜椰汁西米露。

■ ADDRESS/地址
TEL.2527 7476
89 Hennessy Road, Wan Chai
灣仔軒尼詩道89號

■ ANNUAL AND WEEKLY CLOSING
休息日期
Closed Lunar New Year
年初一休息

■ OPENING HOURS, LAST ORDER
營業時間，最後點菜時間
12:00-04:00 (L.O.)
Sunday/週日 12:00-01:00 (L.O.)

■ PRICE/價錢
Lunch/午膳　à la carte/點菜 $50
Dinner/晚膳　à la carte/點菜 $50

Wu Kong Shanghai (Causeway Bay)
滬江 (銅鑼灣)

🍱 16 ☎️🍴

Whether you're a member of the local business community or just in need of a break from shopping, then head down to Wu Kong, established in the heart of Times Square since 1994. Authentic Shanghainese recipes are given due respect here in practiced classics; braised mandarin fish with sweet and sour sauce and the legendary drunken chicken are of note. In contrast, the room has a more modern feel; the young team provide well meaning service.

不管你是本地商界的一員，或是純粹在購物過後小歇一番，都可前往1994年起已座落於時代廣場中心部份的滬江。正宗上海菜完全尊重並按照傳統製法；松子桂花魚和上海醉雞值得一提。相對之下，貴賓房較富當代氣息；年輕團隊提供貼心服務。

■ ADDRESS/地址
TEL.2506 1018
Shop1303, 13F, Food Forum, Times Square, 1 Matheson Street, Causeway Bay
銅鑼灣勿地臣街1號時代廣場食通天13樓1303號舖
www.wukong.com.hk

■ ANNUAL AND WEEKLY CLOSING
　休息日期
Closed Lunar New Year
年初一休息

■ OPENING HOURS, LAST ORDER
　營業時間，最後點菜時間
Lunch/午膳 11:45-14:45 (L.O.)
Dinner/晚膳 17:45-22:45 (L.O.)

■ PRICE/價錢
Lunch/午膳　set/套餐　　　　　$ 100
　　　　　à la carte/點菜 $ 150-400
Dinner/晚膳　à la carte/點菜 $ 150-400

Xin Dan Ji
新斗記

🔑 ⛶50

Originally known for its 'street food', this restaurant, in the heart of Jordan, is better known these days for its pigeon, suckling pork and hotpot dishes – items for which its customers will travel some distance. Seafood is also a speciality and there are impressive numbers of live specimens in the tank from which to choose. Look out for the pictures of Old Kowloon in the large first floor dining room.

此位於佐敦中心位置的餐館，最著名的本是街頭小吃，如今卻以烤乳鴿、燒乳豬及火鍋作招徠，吸引遠道前來的顧客。海鮮亦是此處的拿手食材，包括魚缸內為數不少的鮮活海鮮可供選擇。可在偌大的一樓餐室找到九龍區的陳年舊照片。

■ ADDRESS/地址

TEL.2388 6020
18 Cheong Lok Street, Jordan, Kowloon
九龍佐敦長樂街18號

■ ANNUAL AND WEEKLY CLOSING
休息日期
Closed Lunar New Year
年初一休息

■ OPENING HOURS, LAST ORDER
營業時間，最後點菜時間
Dinner/晚膳 18:00-03:00 L.O. 02:00

■ PRICE/價錢
Dinner/晚膳 à la carte/點菜 $ 150-500

Xinjishi Shanghai
新吉士

⛶16 ☎🍴

Space is limited at this unpretentious second floor operation in the heart of a shopping and business centre. It may take a little while for your dishes to arrive but it's worth the wait: you can follow their progress as you watch the ingredients of many classic Shanghai dishes being assembled in the lively open kitchen. Try the unusual preserved crab in sweet prune.

新吉士位於二樓，座落於購物和商業地帶中心，面積雖稱不上寬闊，但格局實而不華。菜餚烹飪需時，但絕對值得等待，因為餐廳設有開放式廚房，讓食客觀看烹調過程，最後便可享用碟碟經典上海美食。記得品嚐獨特的話梅醉羔蟹。

■ ADDRESS/地址
TEL.2890 1122
Shop 201-203, 2F, Lee Gardens Two,
28 Yun Ping Road, Causeway Bay
銅鑼灣恩平道28號利園2期2樓201-203號舖

■ OPENING HOURS, LAST ORDER
　營業時間，最後點菜時間
12:00-22:30 (L.O.)

■ PRICE/價錢
Lunch/午膳　à la carte/點菜 $200-400
Dinner/晚膳　à la carte/點菜 $200-400

Xi Yan Sweets
囍宴 甜 · 藝

The well-thumbed menu is an indication of how popular this vibrant place has become. Created by interior designer/celebrity chef Jacky Yu, it makes quite a statement in its vivid red. The Zhenjiang spareribs are usually taken by every table, along with the Sichuan spicy chicken and fried soft shell crab in plum sauce. Desserts are renowned, with the lychee ice cream in osmanthus wine one highlight. Service is suitably snappy.

令人食指大動的餐牌顯示這家餐廳的受歡迎程度。由著名室內設計師兼星級廚師余健志打造的美食空間以鮮紅作宣言。幾乎每一桌都會點上一道秘製鎮江骨，金牌口水雞及梅子軒殼蟹。這裡的甜品亦非常著名，包括桂花酒釀荔枝雪糕。敏捷的服務來得恰到好處。

■ ADDRESS/地址
TEL.2833 6299
8 Wing Fung Street, Wan Chai
灣仔永豐街 8 號
www.xiyan.com.hk

■ OPENING HOURS, LAST ORDER
   營業時間，最後點菜時間
11:30-22:30 (L.O.)

■ PRICE/價錢

Lunch/午膳	set/套餐	$60-88
	à la carte/點菜	$140-250
Dinner/晚膳	à la carte/點菜	$140-250

Yan Toh Heen
欣圖軒

This elegant room with its lovely views is smartly detailed by using jade show plates, napkin rings and chopstick rests. The authentic Cantonese menu makes a speciality of shark's fin, abalone and dried seafood and there also several dishes requiring advance ordering such as Hangzhou beggar's fortune chicken which is wrapped in clay. Round things off with a double-boiled imperial bird's nest in whole coconut.

這家高雅的餐廳景致迷人，而墊碟、餐巾圈及筷子架均是玉製品，風格時尚。粵菜菜式原汁原味，特色美食包括魚翅、鮑魚及海味；需預訂的菜式包括杭州富貴雞，甜品則推介椰盅燉官燕。

■ ADDRESS/地址
TEL.2313 2243
GF, Intercontinental Hotel, 18 Salisbury Road, Tsim Sha Tsui, Kowloon
九龍尖沙咀梳士巴利道18號洲際酒店地下

■ OPENING HOURS, LAST ORDER
營業時間，最後點菜時間
Lunch/午膳 12:00-14:30 (L.O.)
Dinner/晚膳 18:00-23:00 (L.O.)

■ PRICE/價錢
Lunch/午膳　set/套餐　　　$430
　　　　　　à la carte/點菜 $290-8,000
Dinner/晚膳　set/套餐　　　$430
　　　　　　à la carte/點菜 $310-8,000

Yat Tung Heen (Jordan)
逸東軒 (佐敦)

⊟30

Considering its basement setting, this subtly lit restaurant is warm and atmospheric. A highly personable manager heads up a friendly and efficient team. The menu is strictly Cantonese with its emphasis on seafood, refined broths and bird's nests. Dim sum is served both at lunchtime and Sunday breakfast and includes such preparations as steamed mince mud carp fish dumplings and pan-fried turnip cake with conpoy.

逸東軒位於酒店地庫，燈光昏暗，洋溢著溫暖的氣氛。經理親切有禮，而侍應則態度友善，服務高效。餐廳提供純粹粵菜，主打包括海鮮、老火湯及燕窩。午市時段和週日早餐均有點心供應，菜式包括市橋鯪魚賣及瑤柱煎蘿蔔糕。

■ ADDRESS/地址

TEL.2710 1093
B2F, Eaton Hotel, 380 Nathan Road, Jordan, Kowloon
九龍佐敦彌敦道380號逸東酒店地庫2樓
www.hongkong.eatonhotels.com

■ OPENING HOURS, LAST ORDER
營業時間，最後點菜時間
Lunch/午膳 11:00-15:30 (L.O.)
Dinner/晚膳 18:00-22:30 (L.O.)

■ PRICE/價錢
Lunch/午膳　à la carte/點菜 $ 160-1,010
Dinner/晚膳　à la carte/點菜 $ 200-1,010

Yat Tung Heen (Wan Chai)
逸東軒（灣仔）

The business community who occupy the Great Eagle Centre can count themselves lucky to be sharing their building with this restaurant. The menu is firmly Cantonese; however, along with the classics such as abalone and shark's fin, as well as some good dim sum at lunch, there are some gems on the menu which shouldn't be ignored: smoked duck breast with citron honey and purple clay casserole dishes are well worth making an investment in.

租用了鷹君中心的商務客可暗自慶幸能與此餐廳共用同一大廈。餐單上的菜式貫徹粵菜風格，除了必備的鮑魚和魚翅外，還有午餐時分出色的點心，菜牌上有些菜式不容錯過：蜂蜜柚子煙鴨胸、紫砂鍋絕對值得投資。

■ ADDRESS/地址
TEL.2878 1212
2F, Great Eagle Centre, 23 Harbour Road, Wan Chai
灣仔港灣道23號鷹君中心2樓

■ OPENING HOURS, LAST ORDER
營業時間，最後點菜時間
Lunch/午膳 11:00-16:00 (L.O.)
Dinner/晚膳 18:00-24:00 (L.O.)

■ PRICE/價錢
Lunch/午膳   set/套餐 $ 100-850
            à la carte/點菜 $ 120-350
Dinner/晚膳 set/套餐 $ 290-850
            à la carte/點菜 $ 230-350

Yellow Door Kitchen
黃色門廚房

Take the elevator to this inconspicuous restaurant where the tightly set tables will have you practically sharing your neighbour's dinner! You'll feel instantly at home with the friendly service, and even more relaxed when you tuck into the tasty Sichuan and Shanghainese cooking, prepared by the all-female team. Don't be afraid to tackle the dinner tasting menu of eight starters, six main courses, dim sum and dessert: small, delicious portions.

程搭升降機來到這家不甚起眼的餐廳，裡面的餐枱緊緊排列在一起，使你幾乎可以分享鄰座的晚餐！親切的服務令你賓至如歸；嚐到美味四川和上海菜由全女班團隊炮製。放膽試試包含八道前菜、六道主菜、點心和甜品的推薦套餐，全部都是份量小而美味的菜式。

■ ADDRESS/地址
TEL.2858 6555
6F, 37 Cochrane Street, Central
中環閣麟街37號6樓
www.yellowdoorkitchen.com.hk

■ ANNUAL AND WEEKLY CLOSING
　　休息日期
Closed 3 days Lunar New Year, Sunday and Public Holidays
農曆新年3天、週日及公眾假期休息

■ OPENING HOURS, LAST ORDER
　　營業時間，最後點菜時間
Lunch/午膳　12:00-14:30 (L.O.)
Dinner/晚膳　18:30-22:30 (L.O.)

■ PRICE/價錢
Lunch/午膳　à la carte/點菜 $120-200
Dinner/晚膳　set/套餐　　　 $288

Yè Shanghai (Admiralty)
夜上海（金鐘）

Surrounded by watch and jewellery shops, and with a bijou chocolate shop at the entrance, this large dining room, with floor to ceiling windows, is elegantly decorated. Attentive staff will guide you through the intricacies of the menu which specialises not only in the cuisine of Shanghai but also its neighbouring provinces of Jiangsu and Zhejiang. Try the deep-fried sweet and sour yellow fish with pine nuts or the baked stuffed crab shell.

餐廳附近盡是鐘錶和珠寶店，入口處則設有一家小巧的巧克力店。餐廳佔地寬廣，設有落地玻璃，裝修優雅，侍應樂於為你介紹餐單上的繁複菜式；特色美食不但包括上海菜，更有江蘇及浙江菜。建議一試松子黃魚及蟹粉釀蟹蓋。

■ ADDRESS/地址
TEL.2918 9833
Shop 332, 3F, Pacific Place, 88 Queensway, Admiralty
金鐘金鐘道88號太古廣場3樓332號舖
www.elite-concepts.com

■ OPENING HOURS, LAST ORDER
營業時間，最後點菜時間
Lunch/午膳 11:30-14:30 (L.O.)
Dinner/晚膳 18:00-22:30 (L.O.)

■ PRICE/價錢
Lunch/午膳	set/套餐	$380
	à la carte/點菜	$200-600
Dinner/晚膳	set/套餐	$380
	à la carte/點菜	$200-600

Yè Shanghai (Kowloon)
夜上海 (九龍)

Expertly balanced, subtle cooking is provided here, drawing not only on Shanghai but also the neighbouring provinces of Jiangsu and Zhejiang. Specialities include braised Tianjin cabbage with ham and steamed pork belly wrapped in lotus leaves. Contemporary décor recalls echoes of 1930s Shanghai in its use of dark woods, subdued lighting and semi-private alcoves. A lively, sophisticated operation with very attentive service.

這裡的烹調水準專業，技術精湛，不但提供上海菜，更涵蓋江蘇及浙江菜。特色美食包括金華火腿津白及稻草扎肉。餐廳以當代風格設計，燈光昏暗，採用深色木材，設有半掩餐室，散發著三十年代上海的味道。餐廳充滿生氣，營運順暢，服務非常周到。

■ ADDRESS/地址

TEL.2376 3322

6F, Marco Polo Hotel, Harbour City,
Canton Road, Tsim Sha Tsui, Kowloon
九龍尖沙咀廣東道海運大廈馬哥孛羅酒店
6樓
www.elite-concepts.com

■ OPENING HOURS, LAST ORDER
    營業時間，最後點菜時間
Lunch/午膳 11:30-15:30 L.O. 15:00
Dinner/晚膳 18:00-24:00 L.O. 23:00

■ PRICE/價錢
Lunch/午膳   à la carte/點菜 $ 300-600
Dinner/晚膳   set/套餐 $ 380
                à la carte/點菜 $ 300-600

Yeung's Noodle
楊記麵家

Mr Yeung's done it again, this time in Wan Chai. There's a fresh and modern red and black interior, and the swift and efficient team keep a beady eye on the proceedings. The recipes are proven, and the prices very reasonable considering the quality. Fish balls, fresh beef and seasonal vegetables flood out of the small kitchen in steaming bowls of soup or upon a choice of noodles. The shrimp roe lao mian is definitely worth a try.

楊先生再展拳腳，今次選定灣仔，創立楊記麵家。餐廳內部採用了時尚的紅色和黑色設計，感覺煥然一新。高效的侍應有型有格，反應非常敏捷，隨時為食客提供服務。菜式水準有保證，相對下價錢確是十分合宜。侍應不斷從廚房捧出一碗碗的時菜、魚蛋和鮮牛肉湯或麵。這裡的蝦子撈麵絕對值得一試。

■ ADDRESS/地址
TEL.2511 1336
219 Hennessy Road, Wan Chai
灣仔軒尼詩道219號

■ ANNUAL AND WEEKLY CLOSING
　休息日期
Closed 4 days Lunar New Year
農曆新年休息4天

■ OPENING HOURS, LAST ORDER
　營業時間，最後點菜時間
11:00-22:00 (L.O.)

■ PRICE/價錢
Lunch/午膳　à la carte/點菜 $ 19-24
Dinner/晚膳　à la carte/點菜 $ 19-24

Yue Kee
裕記

It proves that people will travel any distance for a good roast goose. This may be a very popular second-generation family business but the owners are still very humble. Their geese are chosen from eight farms in Mainland China. For the healthy conscious, go in the summer for a goose with less fat and firmer meat. In winter, you can enjoy goose with crispier skin, more fat but more tender meat. Look for the charming goose chef logo in the shop.

這家餐廳證明了食客絕對願意長途跋涉，只為尋覓優質燒鵝。這是著名的家族生意第二代，但負責人依然十分謙虛。鵝隻是從中國大陸的八個農場挑選。注重健康的人士可在夏天覓得脂肪較少及更結實的燒鵝。在冬天，你可享受脆皮燒鵝，脂肪較多但肉質較鮮嫩。在店內找找可愛的燒鵝大廚標示吧。

■ ADDRESS/地址

TEL.2491 0105
9 Sham Hong Road, Sham Tseng,
New Territories
新界深井深康路9號
www.yuekeerest.biz.com.hk

■ ANNUAL AND WEEKLY CLOSING
　休息日期

Closed 3 days Lunar New Year
農曆新年休息3天

■ OPENING HOURS, LAST ORDER
　營業時間，最後點菜時間
11:00-23:15 (L.O.)

■ PRICE/價錢
Lunch/午膳　à la carte/點菜 $100-300
Dinner/晚膳　à la carte/點菜 $150-350

Yun Fu
雲府

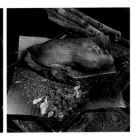

The presence of Lok Shan Buddha and eerie symbolic music lend a mystical tone to this discreet establishment once you get the other side of its ornate dark wooden front door. Warm lighting leads you past the private rooms to the minimal main dining room. Yun Fu also offers a few Mongolian recipes like roasted meats which may require ordering in advance. Try the steamed pork cheek wrapped in lotus leaves or the boneless lamb ribs.

甫踏入餐廳的華麗木門，你便會看到樂山大佛，聽到象徵性的詭異音樂，到處洋溢著一片神秘的氣氛。你可在柔和的燈光下，由私人餐室走到簡約的主餐室。雲府亦提供好幾種蒙古菜，如蒙古烤肉，其中一些需要預訂；特別推介跑三跑或京燒羊肉。

■ ADDRESS/地址
TEL.2116 8855
BF, 43-45 Wyndham Street, Central
中環雲咸街43-55號地庫
www.aqua.com.hk

■ ANNUAL AND WEEKLY CLOSING
休息日期
Closed Lunar New Year
年初一休息

■ OPENING HOURS, LAST ORDER
營業時間，最後點菜時間
Dinner/晚膳 18:00-24:00 (L.O.)

■ PRICE/價錢
Dinner/晚膳 à la carte/點菜 $260-600

Yung Kee (Central)
鏞記 (中環)

This can best be described as an institution as it seats over a 1,000 people at every mealtime and the higher the floor the better the food! Outside, the frontage is golden and inside, there's an army of waiters scurrying up and down 4 packed floors delivering a selection of largely Cantonese dishes involving much roasted goose and barbecued pork. If you fancy a fractionally less hectic experience, try to ask for a table on the VIP top floor.

鏞記在午市時段的食客超過一千人,可謂城中最大型的酒家之一,以食物亦一層此一層好!金色的正門內熙熙攘攘,侍應忙得不可開交,在四層樓之間穿插來往,奉上以粵菜為主的美食,包括燒鵝和叉燒。如要享受較為悠閒的美食體驗,建議預訂貴賓房。

■ ADDRESS/地址

TEL.2522 1624

32-40 Wellington Street, Central
中環威靈頓街32-40號
www.yungkee.com.hk

■ ANNUAL AND WEEKLY CLOSING
　　休息日期
Closed 3 days Lunar New Year
農曆新年休息3天

■ OPENING HOURS, LAST ORDER
　　營業時間,最後點菜時間
11:00-23:30 (L.O.)

■ PRICE/價錢
Lunch/午膳　à la carte/點菜 $220-600
Dinner/晚膳　à la carte/點菜 $220-600

Yung Kee Siu Choi Wong
容記小菜王

Despite being hidden behind a local market, this restaurant's fame is widely spread - just look around and you'll see the shop decked out with photos of the owner and all the famous celebrities who have visited. A must-try would be their crispy roasted pork and special Yung Kee dish (chives with dried prawns and squids) or the chicken with baked fish intestine. It's always busy, so be prepared to share your table with others.

雖然隱藏在本地街市後，你會發現這家餐廳遠近馳名，不容小覷——看看四周，你會看見店內滿佈店主和來訪著名藝人的合照。不能錯過其脆皮燒肉及小炒王（韭黃蝦乾炒鮮魷），或是鮮雞焗魚腸。餐廳經常滿座，要有和陌生人同檯的心理準備。

■ ADDRESS/地址
TEL.2387 1051
108 Fuk Wa Street, Sham Shui Po, Kowloon
九龍深水埗福華街108號

■ ANNUAL AND WEEKLY CLOSING
　休息日期
Closed 4 days Lunar New Year
農曆新年休息4天

■ OPENING HOURS, LAST ORDER
　營業時間，最後點菜時間
Dinner/晚膳　17:30-02:00 (L.O.)

■ PRICE/價錢
Dinner/晚膳　à la carte/點菜 $80-200

Yunyan
雲陽閣

A classic case of 'don't be put off by the appearance', Yunyan is located in an uninspiring mall, and its bright lights are hardly conducive to a romantic experience. But the quality of the food – and the pricing – sets it apart. Spicy Sichuan dishes are served: it's called 'Red Hot Cuisine', either as an enticement, or a warning! Specialities are pork and shrimp dumplings with chilli oil as dim sum, and sautéed prawns in garlic and chillies.

這是「不要因餐廳外觀而卻步」的典型例子，雲陽閣位於一間不太吸引的商場，餐廳明亮的燈光亦難以營造浪漫的用餐氣氛；不過，菜式的品質和價錢才是致勝之道。這裡供應辛辣的四川菜，又稱為「當紅川菜」，聽上去既像誘惑，又似警告！特色美食點心包括鐘水餃及魚香鮮蝦球。

■ ADDRESS/地址

TEL.2375 0800

4F, Miramar Shopping Centre, 132-134 Nathan Road, Tsim Sha Tsui, Kowloon

九龍尖沙咀彌敦道132-134號美麗華商場 4樓

■ OPENING HOURS, LAST ORDER
營業時間，最後點菜時間
Lunch/午膳 11:30-14:45 (L.O.)
Dinner/晚膳 17:30-22:45 (L.O.)

■ PRICE/價錢
Lunch/午膳   à la carte/點菜 $ 125-840
Dinner/晚膳 à la carte/點菜 $ 125-840

Zen
采蝶軒

♿ 24

Located in a luxurious shopping centre, this restaurant offers a refreshingly contemporary look. It consists of a capacious main room, and two private dining rooms. The tasty Cantonese cuisine is served by warm and welcoming staff. Fresh, seasonal ingredients abound in specialities including double-boiled shark's fin soup, steamed fresh shrimp dumplings, and deep-fried boneless chicken wings stuffed with glutinous rice.

這家餐廳位於一個豪華的購物中心內，時尚設計煥然一新。餐廳包括一個寬敞的主餐室，以及兩個私人用餐室。親切的服務員奉上粵式佳餚。撚手菜式採用的新鮮季節性食材比比皆是，包括燉魚翅，冬荀鮮蝦餃和釀雞翼。

■ ADDRESS/地址
TEL.2845 4555
Shop 003, LG, Pacific Place,
88 Queensway, Admiralty
金鐘金鐘道88號太古廣場地庫1樓3號舖

■ OPENING HOURS, LAST ORDER
營業時間，最後點菜時間
Lunch/午膳 11:30-15:30 (L.O.)
Dinner/晚膳 17:30-22:30 (L.O.)

■ PRICE/價錢
Lunch/午膳　set/套餐　　　$ 264
　　　　　à la carte/點菜 $ 220-900
Dinner/晚膳　set/套餐　　　$ 868
　　　　　à la carte/點菜 $ 220-900

Zuma

Currently caught in the zeitgeist of fashion and celebrity, this is spread across 2 floors with a cool Sake bar and lounge hovering above the main dining room and both linked by a dramatic spiral staircase. Dishes are prepared in three distinct areas: the open kitchen, the sushi bar and the robata grill allowing a mix of calm precision and dramatic flourish. Over 1,000 wines, 40 different types of sake and shochu are available. A DJ plays at weekends.

餐廳風格緊貼名人和時尚潮流,共分為兩層:主餐室樓上設有型格的燒酒吧及酒廊,以螺旋形樓梯連接,設計獨特。廚房包括三個部分:開放式廚房、壽司吧,以及爐端燒,廚藝精巧,味道一流。餐廳提供超過一千種葡萄酒及四十種不同的日本酒及燒酒,週末更有DJ在場打碟。

■ ADDRESS/地址
TEL.3657 6388
5-6F, The Landmark, 15 Queen's Road, Central
中環皇后大道中15號置地廣場5-6樓
www.zumarestaurant.com

■ OPENING HOURS, LAST ORDER
營業時間,最後點菜時間
Lunch/午膳 12:00-15:00 (L.O.)
Dinner/晚膳 18:00-23:00 (L.O.)

■ PRICE/價錢
Lunch/午膳   set/套餐 $ 255-445
            à la carte/點菜 $ 350-900
Dinner/晚膳   set/套餐 $ 870-1,086
            à la carte/點菜 $ 350-900

HOTELS
酒店

HOTELS BY ORDER OF COMFORT
酒店 — 以舒適程度分類

Four Seasons 四季	278	MAP/地圖 16/C-1
Mandarin Oriental 文華東方	312	MAP/地圖 16/D-3
The Peninsula 半島	340	MAP/地圖 11/B-3
Intercontinental 洲際	290	MAP/地圖 12/C-3

Conrad 港麗	268	MAP/地圖 18/B-2
Island Shangri-La 港島香格里拉	294	MAP/地圖 18/A-2

The Landmark Mandarin Oriental 置地文華東方	332	MAP/地圖 16/C-3

The Langham 朗廷	334	MAP/地圖 11/B-2
Langham Place 郎豪	302	MAP/地圖 9/B-2
Kowloon Shangri-La 九龍香格里拉	300	MAP/地圖 12/D-2
JW Marriott 萬豪	298	MAP/地圖 18/B-2
Grand Hyatt 君悅	280	MAP/地圖 19/B-1
Marco Polo 馬哥孛羅	314	MAP/地圖 11/A-3
Harbour Plaza Kowloon 海逸	282	MAP/地圖 10/D-3
Nikko 日航	318	MAP/地圖 12/D-2
Intercontinental Grand Stanford 海景嘉福	292	MAP/地圖 12/D-2
Sheraton 喜來登	328	MAP/地圖 12/C-3
The Park Lane 柏寧	338	MAP/地圖 22/C-2

Conrad
港麗

With its enviable location above the Pacific Place shopping and entertainment complex, this skilfully mixes the traditional and the modern. The vast oval lobby superbly showcases Chinese vases and bronze sculptures. Bedrooms are located between the 40th and 61st floors ensuring sweeping views; the suites are particularly spacious and have elegantly marbled bathrooms. An outdoor swimming pool offers an equally dramatic panorama of the city.

RESTAURANTS/ 餐廳

Recommended/推薦			Also/其他
Golden Leaf/金葉庭	✿	🍴🍴🍴	Brasserie on the Eight/
Nicholini's/意寧谷		🍴🍴🍴🍴	懷歐敘
			Garden Café/咖啡園
			Lobby Lounge/樂敘廊

酒店位處集購物娛樂於一身的太古廣場之上，巧妙地混合了傳統和現代元素。龐大的橢圓形大堂展示著中式花瓶及銅像，優雅而壯麗。寢室全在40至61樓之間，坐擁遼闊美景，而套房則特別寬敞，設有雲石浴室。室外游泳池同樣讓你飽覽香港全景。

■ ADDRESS/地址
TEL.2521 3838
FAX. 2521 3888
Pacific Place, 88 Queensway, Admiralty
金鐘金鐘道88號太古廣場
www.conradhotels.com

■ ROOMS AND SUITES/客房及套房
Rooms/客房 =467
Suites/套房 =46

■ PRICE/價錢

🛉	$ 4,400-5,800
🛉🛉	$ 4,400-5,800
Suites/套房	$ 7,000-38,000
☕	$ 280

Cosmo
麗悅

 ♿ ⍀

Conveniently located close to Times Square, this sister hotel to the Cosmopolitan offers travellers well-equipped, good value accommodation. Bedrooms are compact but are brightly colour-coded in orange, green and yellow, styled in a modern way with retro hints of the 1960s. Unusually, room numbers are displayed on floors, not doors. A chic bar, The Nooch, is one of the more fashionable places in which to drink in Wan Chai.

RESTAURANTS/ 餐廳

Recommended/推薦   Also/其他

鄰近時代廣場的麗悅酒店選址便利，是麗都的姐妹酒店，為旅行人士提供設備齊全，物有所值的住宿。睡房較為小巧，以鮮豔的橙、綠、黃為主色，富有現代風格之餘隱約流露六十年代懷舊色彩。房間號碼罕有地顯示在地板上，而非門牌。風格時尚的酒吧The Nooch更是灣仔區最入流的酒吧之一。

■ ADDRESS/地址

TEL.3552 8388

FAX. 3552 8399

375-377 Queen's Road East, Wan Chai

灣仔皇后大道東375-377號

www.cosmohotel.com.hk

■ ROOMS AND SUITES/客房及套房

Rooms/客房 ＝139

Suites/套房 ＝3

■ PRICE/價錢

🛉	$ 1,700-2,400
🛉🛉	$ 1,700-2,400
Suites/套房	$ 3,800-5,000
☕	$ 90

Cosmopolitan
麗都

This large operation sits on the site of the former Xin Hua News Agency Building, in effect, the old Chinese embassy before Hong Kong's handover. Today, it is the perfect choice for anyone wanting to attend the Happy Valley Racecourse: some rooms even offer a full view of the proceedings. Bedrooms are smart and unpretentious although some may be a little compact. A complimentary shuttle bus links the hotel to a number of local amenities.

RESTAURANTS/ 餐廳

Recommended/推薦	Also/其他
	La Maison de l'Orient/ 大宅門餐廳

這間大型酒店前身為新華社香港分社的所在地,實際上是香港回歸前的中國大使館。今天,對希望觀看跑馬地賽事的人來說,這間酒店是完美選擇,有些客房甚至讓你看到整場賽事的全貌。寢室設計既時尚又不造作,不過部分房間可能有點小巧。設有免費穿梭巴士,往返酒店及一些著名市區設施。

■ ADDRESS/地址
TEL.3552 1111
FAX. 3552 1122
387-97 Queen's Road East, Wan Chai
灣仔皇后大道東387-397號
www.cosmopolitanhotel.com.hk

■ ROOMS AND SUITES/客房及套房
Rooms/客房 ＝431
Suites/套房 ＝23

■ PRICE/價錢

👤	$ 1,800-3,200
👥	$ 1,800-3,200
Suites/套房	$ 4,200-4,500
☕	$ 128

Eaton
逸東

This is located near both the Jade Market and the Tin Hau temple, and in its 4th floor lobby there's a pleasant terrace with fishponds. Nearby, you'll find the colonial Planter's Bar and Metro Buffet & Grill. Bedrooms are compact but neatly kept: a sizeable number have recently been renovated and labelled as "deluxe". This friendly establishment is a firm favourite with marrying couples: they host over 700 wedding receptions each year!

RESTAURANTS/ 餐廳

Recommended/推薦	Also/其他
Yat Tung Heen (Jordan)/逸東軒 (佐敦) XX	Metro Buffet & Grill
	Yagura

酒店鄰近玉器市場和天后廟,四樓大堂更設有景致宜人的花園和魚池。富殖民地色彩的逸東吧和Metro Buffet & Grill自助烤肉餐廳亦近在咫尺。客房面積不大,但整潔舒適;不少房間最近更翻新為高級客房。這家設備完善的酒店廣受新婚人士歡迎,每年舉行超過七百次婚宴。

■ ADDRESS/地址
TEL.2782 1818
FAX. 2385 8132
380 Nathan Road, Kowloon
九龍彌敦道380號
www.hongkong.eatonhotels.com

■ ROOMS AND SUITES/客房及套房
Rooms/客房 ＝445
Suites/套房 ＝20

■ PRICE/價錢

🧍	$ 2,150-2,650
🧍🧍	$ 2,150-2,650
Suites/套房	$ 2,850-5,200
☕	$ 138

Empire (Tin Hau)
天后皇悅

Designed by the Japanese interior architect Koichiro Ikebu-chi and opened in May 2009. The minimalist lobby is instant-ly calming. In contrast, the uniformly shaped bedrooms are bright and modern with every essential amenity, including the latest 42inch LCD televisions. The higher up you stay the better the view. Bathrooms have a quirky magic glass fea-ture. Dining is an Asian-inspired, informal experience.

RESTAURANTS/ 餐廳

Recommended/推薦

Also/其他

Empire's Kitchen/皇悅廚房

由享負盛名的日藉室內設計師Koichiro Ikebuchi操刀，全新的天后皇悅酒店於
2009年五月開張。大堂設計簡約，令人瞬感安寧；形狀規則、明亮、富現代
感的客房設計則與大堂形成強烈對比。房間配備所有必須用品，包括最新型號
42吋液晶電視，樓層越高，景致就越迷人。浴室設有神奇玻璃，可隨意調節
透光度。輕鬆隨意的餐飲風格具亞洲特色。

■ ADDRESS/地址
TEL.3692 2333
FAX. 3692 2300
8 Wing Hing Street, Tin Hau
天后永興街8號
www.empirehotel-hongkong.com/
causewaybay

■ ROOMS AND SUITES/客房及套房
Rooms/客房 ＝276

■ PRICE/價錢

👤	$ 1,600-2,400
👤👤	$ 1,600-2,400
☕	$ 150

Four Seasons
四季

♿ ⟨ 🤚 🚗 🅿 ⫽ 🏃 ⤵ 🧖 🎎

Not only does the hotel boast a majestic setting over the harbour but it also offers some of the most spacious and stylish accommodation in Hong Kong. Many rooms have contemporary detailing; others are more oriental. The aptly named Blue Bar offers just that – a wide range of blue-hued cocktails – whilst the vast and impressive spa area has two infinity pools overlooking Victoria Harbour. Service is detailed and enthusiastic.

RESTAURANTS/ 餐廳

Recommended/推薦			Also/其他
Caprice	✿✿✿	✕✕✕✕✕	
Lung King Heen/龍景軒	✿✿✿	✕✕✕✕	
The Lounge		✕✕	

酒店不僅毗鄰海港，坐擁壯麗景色，而且提供一些香港最時尚及寬敞的客房。很多客房以當代風格裝飾，其他則較具東方特色.。Blue Bar名副其實，提供選擇繁多的藍色雞尾酒。至於龐大的水療區，設有兩個無邊際泳池(infinity pool)，可俯瞰維港景色。服務細心且熱誠。

■ ADDRESS/地址
TEL. 3196 8888
FAX. 3196 8899
8 Finance Street, Central
中環金融街8號
www.fourseasons.com/hongkong

■ ROOMS AND SUITES/客房及套房
Rooms/客房　＝399
Suites/套房　＝54

■ PRICE/價錢

👤	$ 4,200-5,300
👥	$ 4,200-5,300
Suites/套房	$ 8,000-50,000
☕	$ 220

Grand Hyatt
君悅

There's a classic 1930s feel to the lobby of this grand hotel, which has been a fixture in the Wan Chai area for over 20 years. Bedrooms, by contrast, are contemporary, being sleek and minimalist in their decoration, with deluxe rooms offering more space and views. Plenty of marble and granite have been used to create particularly opulent bathrooms. There are 14 Plateau rooms with a Japanese feel and direct access to the spa.

RESTAURANTS/ 餐廳

Recommended/推薦		Also/其他
Grissini	✗✗✗	JJ's
One Harbour Road/港灣壹號	✗✗✗✗	Kaetsu/鹿悅
		Thai & Grill Restaurant
		Tiffin/茶園

酒店紮根於灣仔區二十年以上而大堂極具三十年代的經典風格。相比之下，客房設計更具現代特色，裝潢流暢簡潔，豪華房間提供更大空間，更寬廣觀景。奢華浴室用大量大理石及花崗岩打造而成。酒店設有十四間靜水沁園日式房間，直接通往水療設施。

■ ADDRESS/地址

TEL.2588 1234
FAX. 2802 0677
1 Harbour Road, Wan Chai
灣仔港灣道1號
www.hongkong.grand.hyatt.com

■ ROOMS AND SUITES/客房及套房
Rooms/客房 ＝536
Suites/套房 ＝13

■ PRICE/價錢

👤	$ 5,000-7,200
👥	$ 5,200-7,600
Suites/套房	$ 8,500-55,000
☕	$ 260

Harbour Plaza Kowloon
海逸

First impressions do not disappoint here. This shimmering glass structure is right on the waterfront, offering superb views across Victoria Harbour, and there's a spectacular lobby with an impressive white marble staircase. The bedrooms are bright, comfortable and well-equipped, if sober by comparison to other areas. Make the most of the dramatic rooftop pool with its glass-sided walls, as well as the top floor fitness centre and steam bath.

RESTAURANTS/ 餐廳

Recommended/推薦

Harbour Grill	✗✗✗
Hoi Yat Heen/海逸軒	✗✗✗

Also/其他

Robatayaki/炉端燒
The Promenade
Waterfront Bar & Terrace/
水雲間

這裡的第一印象絕對不會令你失望。這座閃閃發亮的玻璃建築毗鄰維港，
金碧輝煌的大堂設有白色雲石階梯。房間開揚舒適，設備齊全，相比酒店其
他設施或較樸實。住客可盡情享受天台設有玻璃幕牆的游泳池、頂樓健身中
心和蒸氣浴。

■ ADDRESS/地址
TEL.2621 3188
FAX. 2621 3311
20 Tak Fung Street, Whampoa
Garden, Hung Hom, Kowloon
九龍紅磡黃埔花園德豐街20號
www.harbour-plaza.com/hphk

■ ROOMS AND SUITES/客房及套房
Rooms/客房 ＝468
Suites/套房 ＝38

■ PRICE/價錢

👤	$ 2,500-2,900
👥	$ 2,700-3,100
Suites/套房	$ 4,800-32,000
☕	$ 185

Harbour Plaza Metropolis
都會海逸

This large establishment with its distinctive zigzag frontage is well placed for the Hong Kong Coliseum. Its marble lobby is vast, with great floor-to-ceiling windows and a sweeping staircase. The bedrooms aren't large but are crisply contemporary and many have excellent harbour-front views. Some even have small balcony gardens. An outdoor swimming pool and fitness room offer the chance to get away from it all.

RESTAURANTS/ 餐廳

Recommended/推薦		Also/其他
Senzuru/千鶴	✂	Promenade
		The Metropolis Harbour
		View/景逸軒

酒店佔地寬廣，曲線形設計的正門獨具特色，鄰近紅磡香港體育館，佔盡地利。雲石大堂建築宏偉，主樓梯和落地玻璃格外壯觀。客房面積不大，但風格時尚，而且大部分都能飽覽海港醉人景色，部分房間甚至設有小型露台花園。室外游泳池和健身室設備一應俱全，讓你忘卻日常煩憂。

■ ADDRESS/地址

TEL. 3160 6888

FAX. 3160 6999

7 Metropolis Drive, Hung Hom, Kowloon

九龍紅磡都會道7號

www.harbour-plaza.com/hpme

■ ROOMS AND SUITES/客房及套房

Rooms/客房 = 456

Suites/套房 = 285

■ PRICE/價錢

🜊	$ 2,100-3,150
🜊🜊	$ 2,200-3,350
Suites/套房	$ 3,300-30,000
☕	$ 185

Harbour Plaza North Point
北角海逸

For the moment, this has the longest outdoor swimming pool on Hong Kong Island (at 25 metres) as well as a smartly equipped fitness centre. Spread over 32 floors, everything is very contemporary, right from the moment you enter the lobby with its unusual water feature. Bedrooms here are good sized and quiet - most only have a shower so if you require a bath ask when booking. There are 200 serviced suites designed for long-stay clients.

RESTAURANTS/ 餐廳

Recommended/推薦

Also/其他

Green/綠怡廳
Hoi Yat Heen/海逸軒

樓高32層的北角海逸酒店擁有目前港島最大型的戶外游泳池（25米），以及
設施齊全的健身中心。酒店的裝飾極富時代感，從大堂的水池即可見一斑。
客房寬敞而寧靜：大部分房間只有淋浴設備，如需浸浴，緊記在預訂房時事
先詢問。酒店另設有200間為長期住客而設的服務式套房。

■ ADDRESS/地址

TEL.2187 8888

FAX. 2187 8899
665 King's Road, North Point
北角英皇道665號
www.harbour-plaza.com

■ ROOMS AND SUITES/客房及套房
Rooms/客房 ＝469
Suites/套房 ＝200

■ PRICE/價錢

👤	$ 1,950-2,050
👥	$ 2,150-2,650
Suites/套房	$ 3,650-6,450
☕	$ 135

Hyatt Regency Sha Tin
沙田凱悅

Opened in February 2009, this hotel is within a five minute walk from University station (adjacent to the Chinese University). It is styled in a contemporary way, making clever use of neutral colours and natural materials like stones and wood to create a soothing ambience. The 26-floor building includes multiples terraces and balconies and is also well equipped with many facilities, including a private spa and fitness centre.

RESTAURANTS/ 餐廳

Recommended/推薦		Also/其他
Sha Tin 18/沙田18	✕✕	Café/咖啡廳

沙田凱悅於2009年2月開幕，從大學港鐵站（毗鄰香港中文大學）前往僅需步行五分鐘。酒店設計現代，巧妙運用中性色彩及天然物料如石材及木材製造柔和融諧的感覺。樓高26層的酒店擁有多個平臺花園及露臺，更配備完善設施，包括私人水療設備及健身中心。

- ■ ADDRESS/地址
TEL.3723 1234
FAX. 3723 1235
18 Chak Cheung Street, University,
Sha Tin, New Territories
新界沙田大學站澤祥街18號
www.hongkong.shatin.hyatt.com

- ■ ROOMS AND SUITES/客房及套房
Rooms/客房 ＝467
Suites/套房 ＝100
- ■ PRICE/價錢

👤	$ 2,500-4,500
👥	$ 2,500-4,500
Suites/套房	$ 3,100-12,500
☕	$ 188

Intercontinental
洲際

Deceptively unremarkable from the outside, but it is decidedly impressive once you're in the grand lobby with its magnificent harbour views. All bedrooms are spacious and well appointed in quiet neutral tones: they have large marble bathrooms. Relax in either the lovely swimming pool or the infinity spa pool or take a massage in an outside cabana. Options for dining are particularly good (see separate entries) and the service is meticulous.

RESTAURANTS/ 餐廳

Recommended/推薦			Also/其他
Nobu		✕✕	Harbourside
Spoon by Alain Ducasse		✕✕	
The Steak House		✕✕✕	
Yan Toh Heen/欣圖軒	✿	✕✕✕	

酒店平凡的外表也許會讓人認為不外如是，但踏入富麗堂皇的酒店大堂，望著一流海景，絕對會令你留下深刻印象。所有客房都非常寬敞，淺色調的裝潢亦讓人感覺寧靜，更設有寬闊的大理石浴室。你可以在漂亮的游泳池或無邊際水療池鬆弛身心，或在戶外的池邊小室享受一下按摩服務。酒店內的餐飲服務非常出色（請參照其他有關的介紹），而且服務水準一流。

■ ADDRESS/地址
TEL.2721 1211
FAX. 2739 4546
18 Salisbury Road, Tsim Sha Tsui, Kowloon
九龍尖沙咀梳士巴利道18號
www.intercontinental.com

■ ROOMS AND SUITES/客房及套房
Rooms/客房 ＝370
Suites/套房 ＝25

■ PRICE/價錢

👤	$ 2,890-3,690
👥	$ 2,890-3,690
Suites/套房	$ 7,500-78,000
☕	$ 280

Intercontinental Grand Stanford
海景嘉福

Although originally built in 1981, this sizeable 18-storey waterfront property has been drastically upgraded over the last few years but still retains its unusual zigzag frontage. The best bedrooms benefit from excellent views over Victoria Harbour and Hong Kong Island and have charming French "Empire" style furniture. A fitness centre and outdoor heated swimming pool are both perched on the roof of the building.

RESTAURANTS/ 餐廳

Recommended/推薦	Also/其他
	Hoi King Heen/海景軒
	The Mistral/海風餐廳

雖然這幢18層的龐大臨海建築物建於1981年，但在過去幾年已大幅升級，並
保留了獨特的曲折正門。酒店內最佳的寢室坐擁維港及港島美景，並採用了迷
人的法國帝王式傢具。酒店頂層設有健身室及戶外溫水泳池。

■ ADDRESS/地址
TEL.2721 5161
FAX. 2732 2233
70 Mody Road, East Tsim Sha Tsui,
Kowloon
九龍尖東麼地道70號
www.hongkong.intercontinental.com

■ ROOMS AND SUITES/客房及套房
Rooms/客房 ＝556
Suites/套房 ＝23
■ PRICE/價錢

👤	$ 3,100-4,100
👥	$ 3,100-4,100
Suites/套房	$ 5,200-9,000
☕	$ 185

Island Shangri-La
港島香格里拉

The intricate beauty of possibly the world's largest Chinese silk painting towers over the glamorous atrium and rises up all of 16 storeys. More sparkle is provided by the dazzling array of chandeliers placed round the hotel. Up above, the accommodation is classic and sumptuously appointed, especially those on the executive floors (52nd to 55th). The Island Shangri-La feels somewhat like a father-figure of the Hong Kong hotel scene.

RESTAURANTS/ 餐廳

Recommended/推薦			Also/其他
Lobster Bar and Grill/龍蝦吧		✗✗	Café TOO
Petrus/珀翠	✿✿	✗✗✗✗	Nadaman/灘萬
Summer Palace/夏宮	✿	✗✗✗	

屹立在迷人的中庭，高高越過酒店的16層：這幅可能是世上最大的中國絲綢畫，散發著複雜精細的美。酒店四處掛著的吊燈燈光，五光十色，令人眼花撩亂。樓上是奢華典雅的客房，尤其是52至55樓商務樓層的房間，十分豪華。港島香格里拉給人的感覺，就像香港酒店業的前輩一樣。

■ ADDRESS/地址
TEL.2877 3838
FAX. 2521 8742
Pacific Place, Supreme Court Road, Admiralty
中區法院道太古廣場
www.shangri-la.com

■ ROOMS AND SUITES/客房及套房
Rooms/客房 ＝531
Suites/套房 ＝34

■ PRICE/價錢

🧍	$ 4,200-5,600
🧍🧍	$ 4,500-6,900
Suites/套房	$ 7,500-34,000
☕	$ 268

JIA

Jia means 'home' but the idea of having a Philippe Starck designed home is not within most people's reach, so staying at this hip hotel is the next best thing. The interior is as modern as you expect, with bold contemporary pieces contrasting with a white palette. It's located in a fairly vibrant area so asking for a bedroom on an upper floor is a good idea. Continental breakfast, afternoon tea and evening wine are all included in the rate.

RESTAURANTS/ 餐廳

Recommended/推薦	Also/其他

Jia代表「家」，但對大多數人來說，擁有由知名創意設計大師Philippe Starck（菲利浦史塔克）設計的家是遙不可及的； 在這家潮流精品酒店住宿，大概是最好的次選了。內部裝潢一如所想，極富現代特色，強烈的當代作品與純白的調色板相映成趣。酒店位於繁華地段，因此選擇較高樓層的房間會是個好主意。房間價錢已包括歐陸早餐、下午茶及黃昏美酒。

■ ADDRESS/地址

TEL.3196 9000
FAX. 3196 9001
1-5 Irving Street, Causeway Bay
銅鑼灣伊榮街1-5 號
www.jiaboutiquehotels.com

■ ROOMS AND SUITES/客房及套房
Rooms/客房 ＝26
Suites/套房 ＝28
■ PRICE/價錢

🧍	$ 2,500
🧍🧍	$ 2,500
Suites/套房	$ 3,500-6,000

JW Marriott
萬豪

This business-oriented hotel boasts 602 rooms spread over 35 storeys with, at the pinnacle, a series of executive floors with their own discreet lounge and meeting rooms. A major renovation in during 2009 has made the bedrooms more contemporary and functional. Pleasant outdoor swimming pool and well-equipped fitness centre; large choice of different cuisines, from Cantonese to Californian, seafood to wine bar and a tea room.

RESTAURANTS/ 餐廳

Recommended/推薦		Also/其他
Man Ho/萬豪殿	XX	Fish Bar/魚吧
		JW's California/JW's 加州
		Marriott Café/萬豪咖啡室
		The Lounge

以商務住客為主的萬豪酒店樓高三十五層，客房數量達602間。位於頂樓的一列行政套房，更附有設計素雅的休息室和會議室供住客專用。2009年的主要更新是將房間改造得更富現代感、更實用。設有環境宜人的戶外游泳池及設備齊全的健身中心，各地餐飲任君選擇，廣東菜到加州菜應有盡有，海鮮、酒吧、茶室悉隨尊便。

■ ADDRESS/地址

TEL.2810 8366
FAX. 2845 0737
Pacific Place, 88 Queensway,
Admiralty
金鐘金鐘道88號太古廣場
www.jwmarriotthongkong.com

■ ROOMS AND SUITES/客房及套房

Rooms/客房 =577
Suites/套房 =25

■ PRICE/價錢

🚹	$4,100-5,500
🚹🚹	$4,100-5,500
Suites/套房	$8,800-40,000
☕	$250

Kowloon Shangri-La
九龍香格里拉

Built in the early 1980's, this large business-orientated hotel impresses with the proportions of its breathtaking lobby: the sheer wealth of marble, sparkling chandeliers, even a tiered water fountain. It's the perfect location for a traditional afternoon tea. Heading upstairs, the colour of the carpet in the lifts might seem different: it changes on a daily basis! The Horizon Club floors offer the best bedrooms and their own exclusive lounge.

RESTAURANTS/ 餐廳

Recommended/推薦			Also/其他
Angelini		❌❌❌	Café Kool
Shang Palace/香宮	✿✿	❌❌❌	Nadaman (Kowloon)/
			灘萬 (九龍)

這間以商務為主的大型酒店建於80年代初，大堂很多部分都十分壯麗：多不勝數的大理石，波光粼粼的吊燈，甚至有個分層的噴水池！這裡是享用傳統下午茶的完美地點。你在上樓時可能發覺電梯的地毯很特別，那是因為每天都會更換顏色！豪華閣的樓層提供最佳寢室及其專用休息室。

■ ADDRESS/地址
TEL.2721 2111
FAX. 2723 8686
64 Mody Road, East Tsim Sha Tsui,
Kowloon
九龍尖東麼地道64號
www.shangri-la.com

■ ROOMS AND SUITES/客房及套房
Rooms/客房 ＝670
Suites/套房 ＝30

■ PRICE/價錢
👤	$ 3,250-4,800
👥	$ 3,250-4,800
Suites/套房	$ 4,980-18,500
☕	$ 218

Langham Place
郎豪

Not only is this 42-storey glass tower filled with every gadget a technophile could ever want, it also functions as a wonderful showcase for Chinese modern art. Over 1,500 paintings, sculptures and installations are spread impressively around the building. Bedrooms are crisply contemporary in their style and offer a range from 'vital' through to 'prime'. The pool is even equipped with an underwater audio system!

RESTAURANTS/ 餐廳

Recommended/推薦			Also/其他
Ming Court/明閣	✿✿	✗✗✗	The Place
Tokoro		✗✗	

玻璃塔般的大樓樓高42層,不僅有每個科技發燒友夢寐以求的電子產品,亦是個空間廣闊的中國現代美術展覽場。超過1,500 幅畫作、雕塑與裝置藝術品分佈於整棟大樓之內。客房的設計極富現代感,從「基 本」到「全 盛」系列,應有盡有。泳池甚至設有水底音響系統。

■ ADDRESS/地址
TEL.3552 3388
FAX. 3552 3322
555 Shanghai Street, Mong Kok,
Kowloon
九龍旺角上海街555號
www.hongkong.langhamplacehotels.
com

■ ROOMS AND SUITES/客房及套房
Rooms/客房 =625
Suites/套房 =40

■ PRICE/價錢

♦	$ 2,600-3,550
♦♦	$ 2,600-3,550
Suites/套房	$ 4,300-15,000
☕	$ 178

Lan Kwai Fong
蘭桂坊

It may not have the harbour views but you can always enjoy the light show from the surrounding towers. A stylish mix of Chinese and contemporary furniture, neutral tones and dark wood veneers has been used to create a calming environment. Try to secure one of the corner bedrooms or a suite with a balcony if you need a little more space. Celebrity Cuisine offers a Cantonese menu at both lunch and dinner.

RESTAURANTS/ 餐廳

Recommended/推薦	Also/其他
Celebrity Cuisine/名人坊　❀　🍴🍴	

這裡未必能欣賞維港景觀，但附近大樓的璀璨燈光也絕不遜色。融合了中國傳統與現代家俱，中性色調及深色木質薄板，打造舒適環境。如果你需要更寬敞空間，建議預訂轉角位置的房間或附露臺的套房。名人坊於午餐及晚餐時段提供美味的廣東菜。

■ ADDRESS/地址
TEL.3650 0000
FAX. 3650 0088
3 Kau U Fong, Central
中環九如坊3號
www.lankwaifonghotel.com.hk

■ ROOMS AND SUITES/客房及套房
Rooms/客房 ＝157
Suites/套房 ＝5

■ PRICE/價錢

🧍	$ 1,200-3,400
🧍🧍	$ 1,200-3,400
Suites/套房	$ 3,800-6,800
☕	$ 140

Lanson Place

An elegant European style façade marks Lanson Place out as a stylish boutique hotel, dovetailing effortlessly with its chic location. Classical and contemporary designs interweave to create a calm exclusivity. There's a serene patio, and the interior artwork creates a feel of warmth and tranquillity. The spacious rooms include a small kitchen for long-stay guests, and many look out to HK Stadium. A cool, calm lounge fits the bill perfectly.

RESTAURANTS/ 餐廳

Recommended/推薦

Also/其他

Lanson Place擁有歐洲風格的優雅外觀，是時尚的精品酒店，與時尚的地理位置一脈相承。古典和當代設計交織成這裡的專屬氣派。寧靜的露台配合室內的藝術作品，營造溫暖寧靜的感覺。寬敞客房內的小廚房，專為長期逗留的客人而設。另一方面，很多人都會觀望外面的香港大球場。寧靜安逸的酒廊可說是完全值回票價。

■ ADDRESS/地址

TEL.3477 6888

FAX. 3477 6999

133 Leighton Road, Causeway Bay

銅鑼灣禮頓道133號

www.lansonplace.com

■ ROOMS AND SUITES/客房及套房

Rooms/客房 =173

Suites/套房 =21

■ PRICE/價錢

🚹	$2,500-3,800
🚹🚹	$2,500-3,800
Suites/套房	$4,800-10,500

Le Méridien Cyberport
數碼港艾美

This design-led, über-stylish corporate hotel is an ultra-chic place to stay with a spectacular sea-front setting. The slinky lobby, with its eye-catching fabric cylinders that stretch to the ceiling, makes its own statement. Up-to-the-minute business facilities, attractive outside pool, and hip bedrooms with rain shower bathrooms, all enhance the wow factor. Choose from three restaurants, with Japanese, Cantonese or international menus.

RESTAURANTS/ 餐廳

Recommended/推薦	Also/其他
	Nam Fong/南方
	Prompt/提示
	Umami

這間設計新穎的公司酒店極度時尚，同時更坐擁壯麗的海景，是高尚的住宿地點。閃爍的大堂內，布質圓柱伸延至天花板，十分矚目。酒店提供分秒更新的商業設施、吸引的室外泳池，以及設有陣雨浴室的時尚寢室，全都令人驚嘆不已。酒店內有三間餐廳選擇，分別是日式、粵式和國際菜式。

■ ADDRESS/地址
TEL.2980 7788
FAX. 2980 7850
100 Cyberport Road
數碼港道100號
www.lemeridien.com/hongkong

■ ROOMS AND SUITES/客房及套房
Rooms/客房 = 167
Suites/套房 = 3

■ PRICE/價錢
👤	$3,200
👥	$3,700
Suites/套房	$7,800
☕	$238

LKF
蘭桂坊

Smaller than most hotels in Central, LKF naturally styles it-self in the 'boutique' class. Its hub centres round the higher floors. Slash, on the 29th, is a modern and intimate lounge bar. Up the staircase on floor 30 Azure is a cool restaurant offering eye-popping city views. Spacious and contemporary bedrooms have espresso machines to give you a high, and pristine beds with sumptuous goose down pillows to bring you back down.

RESTAURANTS/ 餐廳

Recommended/推薦	Also/其他
	Azure

LKF 比中環大部分酒店細，自然歸入「精品」級酒店。其樞紐中心位處較高樓層：
29樓的Slash是舒適的現代酒廊；30樓的Azure是一家風格不凡的餐廳，客人可將
迷人的景觀盡收眼底。寬敞及時尚的客房設有特濃咖啡機讓你提提神，而純樸的
床放置了豪華的鵝絨枕頭，讓你好好休息。

■ ADDRESS/地址
TEL.3518 9688
FAX. 3518 9699
33 Wyndham Street, Lan Kwai Fong, Central
中環蘭桂坊雲咸街33號
www.hotel-LKF.com.hk

■ ROOMS AND SUITES/客房及套房
Rooms/客房 ＝86
Suites/套房 ＝9

■ PRICE/價錢

🧍	$3,500-4,800
🧍🧍	$3,500-4,800
Suites/套房	$6,000-7,000
☕	$170

Mandarin Oriental
文華東方

Opened in 1963, this luxury hotel defines the term and recent renovations has made it even more special. Tai Pan style
(wood and brown colours) or Veranda style (brighter, with
harbour views) bedrooms are superb. The Spa is a spiritual
haven, perhaps the best in Asia. The presidential Mandarin
Suite has its own private treatment room. Service is exem-
plary. Dining options are many and varied; raise a glass to it
all in the legendary Captain's Bar!

RESTAURANTS/ 餐廳

Recommended/推薦			Also/其他

Recommended/推薦

Mandarin Grill + Bar/
文華扒房+酒吧 ❀ 🍴🍴🍴

Man Wah/文華廳 🍴🍴

Pierre ❀ 🍴🍴🍴

Also/其他

Café Causette

Chinnery/千日里

Clipper Lounge/快船廊

The Krug Room

文華東方於1963年開業，完全可以闡釋「豪華酒店」的定意，近期的裝修也令酒店變得更特別。臥房分為大班樣式（木色及棕色）或外廊樣式（較明亮及附海景），兩者同樣出色。被評為亞洲最佳的水療設施，是心靈的避難所。而Mandarin Suite(總統套房)更是眼見為實：有自己的私人治療室。服務質素一向稱著，餐飲選擇林林總總；讓我們向享負盛名的Captain's Bar敬一杯！

■ ADDRESS/地址
TEL.2522 0111
FAX. 2810 6190
5 Connaught Road, Central
中環干諾道中5號
www.mandarinoriental.com/hongkong

■ ROOMS AND SUITES/客房及套房
Rooms/客房 ＝436
Suites/套房 ＝65

■ PRICE/價錢

👤	$ 4,500-5,800
👥	$ 4,500-5,800
Suites/套房	$ 6,500-45,000
☕	$ 248

Marco Polo
馬哥孛羅

First opened in 1969, this waterfront operation is well placed for transport links plus plentiful shopping opportunities. The modern stylish Lobby Lounge is well laid out, whilst Café Marco offers a broad range of international dishes. Bedrooms are less contemporary in feel but the best accommodation is on the 17th and 18th Club Continental floors with a dedicated private lounge. A fitness centre is located in the shopping mall next door.

RESTAURANTS/ 餐廳

Recommended/推薦

Cucina　　　　　　　　　　　　　🍴🍴
Yè Shanghai (Kowloon)/
夜上海（九龍）　　　　🏵　🍴🍴🍴

Also/其他

Café Marco/馬哥孛羅咖啡廳
Nishimura/西村

馬可孛羅酒店於1969年創辦，毗鄰維港，座落於海港城，交通和購物都極為便利。
餐廳方面，「大堂雅座」設計時尚現代，佈局精巧；「馬可孛羅咖啡廳」
則提供形形色色的國際美食。客房的設計風格較為普通，而最佳的客房位於
17及18樓的貴賓樓層，可尊享私人休息室；至於健身中心則位於海港城內。

■ ADDRESS/地址
TEL.2113 0088
FAX. 2113 0011
Harbour City, Canton Road, Tsim Sha
Tsui, Kowloon
九龍尖沙咀廣東道海港城
www.marcopolohotels.com

■ ROOMS AND SUITES/客房及套房
Rooms/客房 ＝615
Suites/套房 ＝49

■ PRICE/價錢
🧍	$ 2,500-4,500
🧍🧍	$ 2,800-4,800
Suites/套房	$ 5,000-12,000
💻	$ 175

Metropark (Causeway Bay)
銅鑼灣維景

Near to Victoria Park, this 31-storey tower offers very good comforts and facilities for business travellers. Most bedrooms have excellent harbour views and all have bathrooms lined with marble. The roof-top swimming pool is extremely well laid out with its glass walls and underwater music. The Café du Parc offers all-day buffet dining and blends French and Japanese cooking plus other international favourites.

RESTAURANTS/ 餐廳

Recommended/推薦

Also/其他

Café Du Parc/繽紛維苑餐廳

酒店大樓樓高三十一層，鄰近維多利亞公園，為商務旅客提供舒適環境及設施。大部分客房都坐擁無敵海景及設有大理石浴室。天台游泳池經過精心設計，玻璃幕牆和水底音樂都別出心裁。繽紛維苑餐廳 （Café du Parc）提供全日自助餐，搜羅法國、日本及其他國際美食。

■ ADDRESS/地址
TEL.2600 1000
FAX. 2600 1111
148 Tung Lo Wan Road, Causeway Bay
銅鑼灣道148號
www.metroparkhotel.com

■ ROOMS AND SUITES/客房及套房
Rooms/客房 ＝243
Suites/套房 ＝23

■ PRICE/價錢

🛉	$ 900-3,000
🛉🛉	$ 1,700-3,000
Suites/套房	$ 5,500
☕	$ 120

Nikko
日航

Just over 20 years old, this hotel is well placed for shopping
and business links and provides a free shuttle-bus service
for its guests. Large, comfortable rooms are stylishly decorated using a palette of earthy tones; the top 4 floors house
executive rooms with their own private lounge. The roof-
top swimming pool offers an away-from-it-all atmosphere. It
has unparalleled views during the day, and so does the Sky
Lounge at night.

RESTAURANTS/ 餐廳

Recommended/推薦

Also/其他

Les Célébrités/名仕餐廳
Sagano/嵯峨野
Toh Lee/桃李

簇新的日航酒店營運僅20年，鄰近購物和商務中心，更為住客提供免費穿梭巴士服務。客房寬敞舒適，以土系色調為主，設計時尚；位於最高四層的商務樓層客房更設有私人休憩中心。天台泳池氣氛悠然，仿如世外桃源，日間更坐擁無敵景致。晚上則可於星月廊欣賞醉人夜景。

■ ADDRESS/地址
TEL.2739 1111
FAX. 2311 3122
72 Mody Road, East Tsim Sha Tsui, Kowloon
九龍尖東麼地道72號
www.hotelnikko.com.hk

■ ROOMS AND SUITES/客房及套房
Rooms/客房 ＝445
Suites/套房 ＝18

■ PRICE/價錢

👤	$ 2,400-3,400
👥	$ 2,400-3,400
Suites/套房	$ 6,000-14,000
☕	$ 190

Novotel Century
諾富特世紀

Business travellers and tourists alike will find this property convenient as it's located close to the Hong Kong Convention and Exhibition Centre. It was refurbished at the end of 2007 and features modern, well-equipped bedrooms in a uniform style, with light wood furniture and quite small bathrooms. Superior rooms are more spacious and have the harbour views. An international buffet is offered at Le Café; Italian food at Pepino.

RESTAURANTS/ 餐廳

Recommended/推薦

Also/其他

Le Café
Pepino

商務客及需求相若的旅客會發覺這家酒店位置方便，毗鄰近香港會議展覽中心。酒店於2007年底裝修，客房風格統一為富有現代感、設備完善的設計，輕木傢俱和小巧的浴室。豪華房間則更寬敞，並可觀賞維多利亞港景色。Le Café 提供多國自助餐，Pepino則提供義大利餐點。

■ ADDRESS/地址

TEL.2598 8888
FAX. 2598 8866
238 Jaffe Road, Wan Chai
灣仔謝斐道238號
www.novotel.com/asia

■ ROOMS AND SUITES/客房及套房

Rooms/客房 =491
Suites/套房 =20

■ PRICE/價錢

👤	$1,600-2,000
👤👤	$1,600-2,000
Suites/套房	$4,000-5,000
☕	$130

Panorama
麗景

This relative newcomer offers the latest in contemporary design with its 324 rooms slotting into 3 different bedroom types: silver, gold and platinum. The higher you go, the better the view but the best rooms are on corner sites where you can even enjoy the stunning harbour vista relaxing in the bath tub. On the 38th floor is the Santa Lucia restaurant that offers a broad range of international dishes in an exhilarating modern setting.

RESTAURANTS/ 餐廳

Recommended/推薦   Also/其他

這家酒店簇新落成，324間客房均以當代最新穎的款式，設計出三種不同的房間類型，包括銀賓客房、黃金客房和白金客房。要從更佳位置俯瞰景色，便要更上一層樓；而酒店的最佳客房則位於角位，客人更可以一邊享受浸浴，一邊欣賞迷人的維港景致。位於38樓的樂醉西餐廳佈置時尚，教人心動，各式各樣的各國佳餚正待君細嚐。

■ ADDRESS/地址
TEL. 3550 0388
FAX. 3550 0288
8A Hart Avenue, Tsim Sha Tsui, Kowloon
九龍尖沙咀赫德道8A號
www.hotelpanorama.com

■ ROOMS AND SUITES/客房及套房
Rooms/客房 ＝312
Suites/套房 ＝12

■ PRICE/價錢
♂   ＄2,400-3,900
♂♀   ＄2,400-3,900
Suites/套房   ＄5,800

Renaissance Kowloon
九龍萬麗

Built in 1978 but now possibly lacking the gloss of some of its more cutting-edge neighbours and competitors, this is nonetheless a well-placed, comfortable hotel - next to the New World Centre and the harbour-front promenade. Whilst the compact bedrooms don't always benefit from expansive views, they are well maintained. The 4th floor Panorama restaurant is a popular focal point for its buffet Sunday brunch.

RESTAURANTS/ 餐廳

Recommended/推薦	Also/其他
Dynasty (Tsim Sha Tsui)/滿福樓 (尖沙咀) ✕✕	Panorama/港畔

於1978年落成的九龍萬麗酒店,在鄰近的新興競爭對手比較下,至今可能略
為失色;不過,酒店毗鄰新世界中心和星光大道,依然坐享位置之便利,亦不
失為一家舒適的酒店。客房並非全都坐擁廣闊景致,空間亦不算大,但是設備
齊全。港畔餐廳位於酒店四樓,這裡的周日海景早午自助餐十分受歡迎。

■ ADDRESS/地址
TEL.2369 4111
FAX. 2369 9387
22 Salisbury Road, Tsim Sha Tsui,
Kowloon
九龍尖沙咀梳士巴利道22號
www.renaissancehotels.com/HKGNW

■ ROOMS AND SUITES/客房及套房
Rooms/客房 ＝492
Suites/套房 ＝53

■ PRICE/價錢

👤	$2,300-4,600
👥	$2,300-4,600
Suites/套房	$5,600-8,600
☕	$175

Royal Plaza
帝京

The Royal Plaza's impressive marble lobby creates a rather grand ambience for arriving guests. Bedrooms are designed in a range of styles: from sober, classic elegance, via early 19th century French Empire, to the contemporary 'Executive Club' on the top two floors. Whatever the choice, all have great views. There's an outdoor pool with an unexpected Roman décor complete with columns; the solarium area boasts a particularly relaxing atmosphere.

RESTAURANTS/ 餐廳

Recommended/推薦

Also/其他

La Scala/花月庭
Royal Plaza/帝京軒

帝京酒店的雲石大堂格調相當華麗，造成一種堂皇的格調迎接來賓。客房的風格琳琳總總，包括十九世紀法國帝國的沉實古雅設計、最高兩層「行政樓層」的當代設計等，各適其式，所有客房更坐擁醉人美景。酒店的露天羅馬式泳池以圓柱作裝飾，設計風格令人驚喜；而日光浴地區的氣氛則特別輕鬆惬意。

■ ADDRESS/地址
TEL.2928 8822
FAX. 2928 8822
193 Prince Edward Road West,
Kowloon
九龍太子道西193號
www.royalplaza.com.hk

■ ROOMS AND SUITES/客房及套房
Rooms/客房 ＝659
Suites/套房 ＝34

■ PRICE/價錢

🛉	$ 1,800-3,200
🛉🛉	$ 2,000-3,400
Suites/套房	$ 4,900-23,800
☕	$ 195

Sheraton
喜來登

One of Hong Kong's biggest hotels, it's located on the main-land but is a short walk from the Star Ferry Pier. All of which adds up to great views of Victoria Harbour. These can be best appreciated from the Health Club's roof-top pool, over a plate of oysters in the wine bar, or from a swish sea-facing executive room on the 16th and 17th floors. More down-to-earth but thoroughly pleasant are a cigar room, a wine shop and an international café.

RESTAURANTS/ 餐廳

Recommended/推薦			Also/其他
Celestial Court/天寶閣		✗✗	The Café
Morton's of Chicago	✿	✗✗	
Oyster & Wine Bar		✗✗	
Unkai/雲海		✗✗	

這是香港最大的酒店之一，位於九龍半島，只需短短的步行距離便到天星碼頭。客人可盡覽維多利亞港的壯麗景色，最佳位置包括Health Club的天台游泳池、16樓及17樓的高級面海行政室，在蠔酒吧吃蠔時亦可享受美景。較為沉實但完全舒適的有雪茄廊、酒舖和國際咖啡廳。

■ ADDRESS/地址
TEL.2369 1111
FAX. 2739 8707
20 Nathan Road, Tsim Sha Tsui,
Kowloon
九龍尖沙咀彌敦道20號
www.sheraton.com/hongkong

■ ROOMS AND SUITES/客房及套房
Rooms/客房 ＝750
Suites/套房 ＝91

■ PRICE/價錢

🧍	$ 3,000-4,600
🧍🧍	$ 3,100-4,800
Suites/套房	$ 5,700-13,500
☕	$ 215

The Emperor
英皇駿景

Staying on business but still want to try your luck at the races? Then consider Happy Valley. This is a well-established, traditional hotel, whose neatly kept rooms are identical and fine for a short stay. All are well-equipped and the bathrooms sparkle sufficiently. Breakfast is an American buffet-style and is served in the coffee shop on the fourth floor. Their Golden Valley restaurant offers traditional Cantonese and Sichuan cuisine.

RESTAURANTS/ 餐廳

Recommended/推薦	Also/其他
Golden Valley/駿景軒　　⚅　ⅩⅩ	

想於商務旅程中偷閒一試綠茵場上的手氣？跑馬地是你的不二之選。這家傳統完善的酒店，房間統一整潔，適合短期居住。所有房間設備齊全，浴室乾淨得發亮。四樓的咖啡廳提供美式自助風格早餐。駿景軒供應傳統粵菜及四川菜。

■ ADDRESS/地址
TEL.2893 3693
FAX. 2834 6700
1 Wang Tak Street, Happy Valley
跑馬地宏德街1號
www.emperorhotel.com.hk

■ ROOMS AND SUITES/客房及套房
Rooms/客房 ＝149
Suites/套房 ＝1

■ PRICE/價錢

🧍	$ 1,700-2,100
🧍🧍	$ 1,700-2,100
Suites/套房	$ 4,500-5,500
☕	$ 80

The Landmark Mandarin Oriental
置地文華東方

♿ ☞ ⚥ 🏃 🖼 💆 🛏

No less exclusive than its larger sibling, this luxury boutique-style hotel is the destination of choice for visiting glitte-rati. Spa choices are endless and include the signature Time Ritual treatment. Rooms are big on luxury and in size (450 or 600m²); the bathrooms are especially impressive in the larger ones and you can luxuriate while enjoying surround-sound TV or your iPod system. MO Bar offers comfort food for beautiful people.

RESTAURANTS/ 餐廳

Recommended/推薦			Also/其他
Amber	✿✿	✗✗✗	MO Bar

一點都不比文華東方遜色的置地文華東方是一間精品風格的豪華酒店，更是
訪港社會名流的最佳落腳點。在這裡你可盡享水療設施，包括招牌服務Time
Ritual。客房盡極奢華，並十分寬敞，備有四百五十及六百平方米客房以供
選擇。大型客房的浴室尤其出色，可一邊享受沐浴，一邊聽著立體聲電視或
自己的iPod選曲系統。MO Bar為俊男美女提供輕巧美食。

■ ADDRESS/地址
TEL. 2132 0188
FAX. 2132 0199
15 Queen's Road, Central
中環皇后大道中15號
www.mandarinoriental.com/landmark

■ ROOMS AND SUITES/客房及套房
Rooms/客房 ＝100
Suites/套房 ＝13

■ PRICE/價錢

🜊	$ 5,200-6,800
🜊🜊	$ 5,200-6,800
Suites/套房	$ 9,300-45,000
⛾	$ 218

The Langham
朗廷

The clamour of Peking Road is left behind as you enter the hushed surroundings of this elegant establishment. Its impressive lobby, furnished in a classical European style, is luxurious and features some impressive contemporary art and sculptures. Bedrooms are a mix of classic luxury and more attractive contemporary Chinese styling in the Grand rooms. All this charm is underpinned by modern facilities and attentive service.

RESTAURANTS/ 餐廳

Recommended/推薦			Also/其他

T'ang Court/唐閣 ❀❀ ✕✕✕

L'Eclipse
Main St. Deli
The Bostonian/美岸海鮮廳

進入這棟優雅建築物,讓你立刻忘卻北京道熙來攘往的煩囂。設計奪目的大堂
以傳統歐洲風格裝潢,極盡奢華,更以出色當代藝術品及雕塑點綴。豪華客房
融合經典奢華風格及相當吸引的當代中國裝潢。一切迷人之處,更見於現代設
施及細心服務。

■ ADDRESS/地址
TEL.2375 1133
FAX. 2375 1133
8 Peking Road, Tsim Sha Tsui,
Kowloon
九龍尖沙咀北京道8號
www.hongkong.langhamhotels.com

■ ROOMS AND SUITES/客房及套房
Rooms/客房 ＝469
Suites/套房 ＝26

■ PRICE/價錢

👤	$ 2,800-3,500
👥	$ 2,800-3,500
Suites/套房	$ 4,800-8,000
☕	$ 210

The Luxe Manor
帝樂文娜公館

Leaving the outside world behind, you enter a stylish jewel-box that somehow manages to jumble up oriental influences with Surrealist furnishings creating plenty of quirky charm. The dramatically lit red and black lobby flings together gilt-edged thrones, scallop-shaped banquettes and Baroque armchairs upholstered in cartoon characters. Most bedrooms are small, apart from the studio rooms and six individually themed suites on the 12th floor.

RESTAURANTS/ 餐廳

Recommended/推薦	Also/其他
Aspasia 🍴🍴🍴	

踏入珠寶盒般的時尚酒店，仿如置身世外桃源。帝樂文娜揉合了東方元素和超現實設計，營造迷人的虛幻氣氛。紅黑色的大堂燈光璀璨，照亮鍍金邊的寶座、印有扇貝圖案的走廊，以及裝上卡通人物坐墊的巴洛克風格扶手椅。除了12樓的尊尚客房及六間獨立主題套房外，大部分客房的空間不算大。

■ ADDRESS/地址

TEL.3763 8888

FAX. 3763 8899

39 Kimberley Road, Tsim Sha Tsui, Kowloon

九龍尖沙咀金巴利道39號

www.theluxemanor.com

■ ROOMS AND SUITES/客房及套房

Rooms/客房 ＝153

Suites/套房 ＝6

■ PRICE/價錢

👤	$ 2,200-2,800
👥	$ 2,200-2,800
Suites/套房	$ 10,000

The Park Lane
柏寧

Within easy walking distance of Times Square, this tall block directly faces Victoria Park with its jogging routes and tennis courts. Many of the rooms offer superb views of the park's lush greenery. Accommodation is stylish and understated with the Premier Club rooms proving especially spacious and well equipped. Of all the food outlets, Riva (on the top floor) provides European based menus and fantastic view, with a buffet at lunch.

RESTAURANTS/ 餐廳

Recommended/推薦	Also/其他
	Riva

柏寧酒店高聳而立，座落於銅鑼灣區，距離時代廣場僅咫尺之遙，面向維多利亞公園的緩跑徑和網球場。酒店大部分客房均坐擁綠樹林蔭的維園美景。客房設計時尚，與商務樓層(Premier Club)的房間實為完美配搭，地方特別寬敞，設備亦更齊全。位於頂層的Riva法國餐廳冠絕全酒店的食肆，配上歐陸餐點及絕佳景觀，午市更提供自助餐。

■ ADDRESS/地址
TEL.2293 8888
FAX. 2576 7853
310 Gloucester Road, Causeway bay
銅鑼灣告士打道310號
www.parklane.com.hk

■ ROOMS AND SUITES/客房及套房
Rooms/客房 ＝771
Suites/套房 ＝39

■ PRICE/價錢

👤	$ 2,500-5,500
👥	$ 2,500-5,500
Suites/套房	$ 6,500-18,000
☕	$ 170

The Peninsula
半島

Celebrating 82 years of operation, this is the grandee of Hong Kong hotels. Testimony to its niche position is the fleet of Rolls-Royce and unique helipad. The iconic lobby is the place for afternoon tea, though its proximity to exclusive shops on both sides makes it something of a thoroughfare. Superb spa boasts Roman styled pool and swish terrace. Rooms blend Victorian English and delicate Asian touch; corner suites make most of harbour vista.

RESTAURANTS/ 餐廳

Recommended/推薦		Also/其他
Chesa/瑞樵閣	✗✗	Felix
Gaddi's/吉地士	✗✗✗✗	Imasa/今佐
Spring Moon/嘉麟樓	✗✗✗	Verandah/露台餐廳

開幕至今已有八十二年歷史的半島酒店是本港酒店業老大哥，一列列的勞斯萊斯和獨有的直昇機坪，印證其特殊地位。大堂一如酒店標誌，極適合享用下午茶，只要你不介意兩旁的名店讓它看來仿似馬路。一流的水療設施包括羅馬式游泳池和時尚陽台。客房揉合了英國維多利亞風格及雅緻的亞洲風味，角位套房可將廣闊海景盡收眼底。

■ ADDRESS/地址
TEL. 2920 2888
FAX. 2722 4170
Salisbury Road, Tsim Sha Tsui,
Kowloon
九龍尖沙咀梳士巴利道
www.peninsula.com

■ ROOMS AND SUITES/客房及套房
Rooms/客房　＝246
Suites/套房　＝54

■ PRICE/價錢

👤	$ 4,200-5,800
👥	$ 4,200-5,800
Suites/套房	$ 6,800-68,000
☕	$ 250

The Royal Garden
帝苑

In a prized position close to Victoria Harbour, the Royal Garden exudes cool class. Its prized possession is a 110 foot atrium that brims with daylight. Its foliage-strewn presence is ubiquitous, as guestrooms are accessible through corridors overlooking it. Some of the rooms boast an enviable harbour view, all of them have relaxing tones: they're more functional than trendy. On the roof is a welcoming surprise: a very pleasant swimming pool.

RESTAURANTS/ 餐廳

Recommended/推薦		Also/其他
Dong Lai Shun/東來順	✕✕	
Inagiku (Kowloon)/稻菊 (九龍)	✕✕	
Le Soleil 🍴	✕✕	
Sabatini	✕✕✕	
The Royal Garden/帝苑軒	✕✕	

帝苑酒店毗鄰維多利亞港，地理位置優越，別樹一格。110呎高的中庭陽光普照，氣派不同凡響；又以葉飾作為點綴，從通往客房的走廊望去舉目皆是。部份客房更坐擁怡人海景，所有客房均採用了休閒放鬆的格調，重實用多於潮流。此外，頂層設有一個非常舒適的露天泳池，為住客帶來意想不到的驚喜。

■ ADDRESS/地址
TEL.2721 5215
FAX. 2369 9976
69 Mody Road, East Tsim Sha Tsui, Kowloon
九龍尖東麼地道69號
www.rghk.com.hk

■ ROOMS AND SUITES/客房及套房
Rooms/客房 ＝371
Suites/套房 ＝48

■ PRICE/價錢

🧍	＄2,900-3,900
🧍🧍	＄3,100-4,100
Suites/套房	＄4,800-15,800
☕	＄220

The Royal Pacific
皇家太平洋

Situated very near the China and Macao Ferry terminal, this sizeable operation is made up of two buildings: the Hotel wing and the Tower wing. Most bedrooms in the Hotel have been recently renovated and offer sharp modern comforts with minimalist styling. In the Tower, things are more traditional but equally well-maintained. The business traveller is well catered for with a good communications centre and meeting facilities.

RESTAURANTS/餐廳

Recommended/推薦	Also/其他
	Café on the Park/柏景餐廳
	Pierside/堤岸
	Satay Inn/沙嗲軒

酒店位置優越，港澳碼頭近在咫尺，共分為兩部分：園景翼和海景翼。園景翼的大部分客房最近經過裝修，風格簡單時尚，十分舒適。至於海景翼，裝潢則較為傳統，但同樣舒適。商務客人更可享用先進的視聽通訊設備和會議設施。

■ ADDRESS/地址
TEL. 2736 1188
FAX. 2736 1212
33 Canton Road, China Hong Kong
City, Tsim Sha Tsui, Kowloon
九龍尖沙咀中港城廣東道33號
www.royalpacific.com.hk

■ ROOMS AND SUITES/客房及套房
Rooms/客房 ＝629
Suites/套房 ＝34

■ PRICE/價錢

🧍	$ 1,400-2,300
🧍🧍	$ 1,400-2,300
Suites/套房	$ 4,800-13,800
☕	$ 130

W

With room categories like 'Wonderful' and 'Extreme Wow' one can probably guess that the W hotel is a little unconventional. On top of Elements shopping mall, it offers stylish, modern design at every turn, from the bathroom's rainforest showers to the surround sound in every bedroom. It has one of the worlds highest outdoor pools on the 76th floor: the 'wet', along with a gym 'sweat' and a spa 'bliss'. Perhaps 'fab far east' sums it up.

RESTAURANTS/ 餐廳

Recommended/推薦	Also/其他
	Fire
	Kitchen

從「奇妙客房」到「頂級驚喜客房」等客房分類，已可感受到W酒店與別不同。W位於圓方購物商場，從浴室的熱帶雨林花灑以致每間臥房的環迴立體聲，每個角落均設計得時尚而現代。它擁有全球最高樓層的室外泳池- --76樓：'wet'、健身室'sweat'及水療設備'bliss'。也許'fab far east'是最為貼切的形容方式。

■ ADDRESS/地址
TEL.3717 2222
FAX. 3717 2888
1 Austin Road West, Kowloon Station, Kowloon
九龍柯士甸道西1號九龍站
www.whotels.com/hongkong

■ ROOMS AND SUITES/客房及套房
Rooms/客房 ＝351
Suites/套房 ＝42

■ PRICE/價錢

👤	$3,200-3,700
👥	$3,200-3,700
Suites/套房	$8,000-10,000
☕	$250

MACAU
澳門

RESTAURANTS
餐廳

STARRED RESTAURANTS

Within this selection, we have highlighted a number of restaurants for their particularly good cooking. When awarding one, two or three Michelin Stars there are a number of factors we consider: the quality and compatibility of the ingredients, the technical skill and flair that goes into their preparation, the clarity and combination of flavours, the value for money and above all, the taste. Equally important is the ability to produce excellent cooking not once but time and time again. Our inspectors make as many visits as necessary, so that you can be sure of the quality and consistency.

A two or three star restaurant has to offer something very special that separates it from the rest. Three stars – our highest award – are given to the very best.

Cuisines in any style of restaurant and of any nationality are eligible for a star. The decoration, service and comfort levels have no bearing on the award.

星級餐廳

在這系列的選擇裡，我們特意指出菜式上佳的餐廳。
給予一、二或三粒米芝蓮星時，我們考慮到以下因
素：材料的質素和相容性、烹調技巧和特色、氣味
濃度和組合、價錢是否相宜，以及味道。同樣重要
的是能夠持續提供美食。我們的評審員會因應需要
而多次到訪，所以讀者可肯定食物品質和一致性。
二或三星餐廳必有獨特之處，比其他餐廳更出眾。
最高評級-三星-只會給予最好的餐廳。
不論餐廳的風格如何，供應哪個國家的菜式，都可獲
星級。餐廳陳設、服務及舒適程度亦不會影響評級。

Exceptional cuisine, worth a special journey.
出類拔萃的菜餚，值得專程到訪。

One always eats here extremely well, sometimes superbly. Distinctive dishes are precisely executed, using superlative ingredients.

食客可在這裡享用美味的菜餚，有時令人更讚不絕口。獨特的菜式以最高級的材料精密地烹調。

Robuchon a Galera 法國餐廳	XxX	388	MAP/地圖 31/B-3

Excellent cuisine, worth a detour.
傑出美食，值得繞道前往。

Skilfully and carefully crafted dishes of outstanding quality.

有技巧地精心烹調菜餚，品質優秀。

Zi Yat Heen 紫逸軒	XxX	399	MAP/地圖 34/C-3

A very good restaurant in its category.
同類別中出眾的餐廳。

A place offering cuisine prepared to a consistently high standard.

持續高水準菜式的地方。

Aurora 奧羅拉	XxX	364	MAP/地圖 33/B-1
Jade Garden 蘇浙匯	XX	374	MAP/地圖 32/C-3
Lei Garden 利苑酒家	XX	378	MAP/地圖 34/C-3
The Eight 8餐廳	XxX	392	MAP/地圖 31/B-3
Tim's Kitchen 桃花源小廚	XX	394	MAP/地圖 31/B-3
Tung Yee Heen 東怡軒	XxX	396	MAP/地圖 32/D-2
Wing Lei 永利軒	XxX	397	MAP/地圖 31/B-3

BIB GOURMAND

This symbol indicates our inspector's favourites for good value. Restaurants offering good quality cooking for $ 300 or less (price of a 3 course meal excluding drinks).

這標誌表示評審員認為價錢合理而美味的餐廳。300 元或以下便可享用優質美食（三道菜式的價錢，不包括飲料）。

Laurel 丹桂軒	XX	377	MAP/地圖 32/C-3
Lung Wah Tea House 龍華茶樓	🥢	380	MAP/地圖 29/B-2
Noodle & Congee Corner 粥麵莊	🥢	384	MAP/地圖 31/B-3
Oja Sopa De Fita Cheong Kei 祥記	🥢	385	MAP/地圖 29/A-3
Square Eight 食・八方	X	390	MAP/地圖 32/C-1

RESTAURANTS BY AREA
餐廳 — 以地區分類

Coloane/路環

Macau/澳門

RESTAURANTS BY CUISINE TYPE
餐廳 — 以菜式分類

Cantonese/粵菜

Canton 喜粵			✗✗✗	368	MAP/地圖 34/C-3
Imperial Court 金殿堂			✗✗✗	372	MAP/地圖 32/C-1
Kwun Hoi Heen 觀海軒			✗✗✗	375	MAP/地圖 36/C-2
Laurel 丹桂軒	⊕		✗✗	377	MAP/地圖 32/C-3
Lei Garden 利苑酒家			✗✗	378	MAP/地圖 34/C-3
Lung Wah Tea House 龍華茶樓	⊕	ᕮ		380	MAP/地圖 29/B-2
The Eight 8餐廳	✿		✗✗✗	392	MAP/地圖 31/B-3
Tim's Kitchen 桃花源小廚	✿		✗✗	394	MAP/地圖 31/B-3
Tou Tou Koi 陶陶居			✗	395	MAP/地圖 29/A-3
Tung Yee Heen 東怡軒	✿		✗✗✗	396	MAP/地圖 32/D-2
Wing Lei 永利軒	✿		✗✗✗	397	MAP/地圖 31/B-3
Ying 帝影樓			✗✗✗	398	MAP/地圖 33/B-1
Zi Yat Heen 紫逸軒	✿✿		✗✗✗	399	MAP/地圖 34/C-3

Chinese/中式

Red 8 紅8			✗	387	MAP/地圖 31/B-3
Square Eight 食 · 八方	⊕		✗	390	MAP/地圖 32/C-1

French/法式

Aux Beaux Arts 寶雅座			✗✗	365	MAP/地圖 32/C-1

French contemporary/時尚法式

Robuchon a Galera 法國餐廳	✿✿✿		✗✗✗✗	388	MAP/地圖 31/B-3

International/國際菜

Belcanção 鳴詩			✗✗	367	MAP/地圖 34/C-3

Italian/意式

Aurora 奧羅拉	✿		✗✗✗	364	MAP/地圖 33/B-1

Don Alfonso 當奧豐素		✗✗✗	370	MAP/地圖 31/B-3
Il Teatro 帝雅廷		✗✗✗	371	MAP/地圖 31/B-3

Japanese/日式

Inagiku 稻菊		✗✗	373	MAP/地圖 32/C-3
New Furusato 新故鄉		✗✗	383	MAP/地圖 31/B-3
Okada 岡田		✗✗	386	MAP/地圖 31/B-3

Japanese Tempura/日式天婦羅

Tenmasa 天政		✗✗	391	MAP/地圖 33/B-1

Macanese/澳門菜

Litoral 海灣餐廳		✗	379	MAP/地圖 31/A-1

Mediterranean/地中海菜

Rossio 盛事		✗✗	389	MAP/地圖 32/C-1

Noodles and Congee/粥麵

Noodle & Congee Corner 粥麵莊	⊕	🍜	384	MAP/地圖 31/B-3
Oja Sopa De Fita Cheong Kei 祥記	⊕	🍜	385	MAP/地圖 29/A-3

Portuguese/葡式

Antonio 安東尼奧		✗✗	362	MAP/地圖 33/B-2
A Petisqueria 葡國美食天地		✗	363	MAP/地圖 33/B-2
Banza 百姓		✗	366	MAP/地圖 33/B-1
Clube Militar de Macau 澳門陸軍俱樂部		✗✗	369	MAP/地圖 31/B-3

Shanghainese/上海菜

Jade Garden 蘇浙匯	✿	✗✗	374	MAP/地圖 32/C-3

Spanish/西班牙菜

La Paloma 芭朗瑪		✗✗	376	MAP/地圖 31/A-2

Steakhouse/扒房

Morton's of Chicago		✗✗✗	381	MAP/地圖 34/C-3
The Kitchen 大廚		✗✗	393	MAP/地圖 31/B-3

Thai/泰式

Naam 藍		✗✗	382	MAP/地圖 32/D-2

RESTAURANTS PARTICULARLY PLEASANT
上佳的餐廳

Aurora 奧羅拉		✿	XxX	364	MAP/地圖 33/B-1
Aux Beaux Arts 寶雅座			XX	365	MAP/地圖 32/C-1
Belcanção 鳴詩			XX	367	MAP/地圖 34/C-3
Canton 喜粵			XxX	368	MAP/地圖 34/C-3
Don Alfonso 當奧豐素			XxxX	370	MAP/地圖 31/B-3
Il Teatro 帝雅廷			XxX	371	MAP/地圖 31/B-3
Imperial Court 金殿堂			XxX	372	MAP/地圖 32/C-1
Robuchon a Galera 法國餐廳	✿✿✿		XxxX	388	MAP/地圖 31/B-3
Rossio 盛事			XX	389	MAP/地圖 32/C-1
Tenmasa 天政			XX	391	MAP/地圖 33/B-1
The Eight 8餐廳		✿	XxX	392	MAP/地圖 31/B-3
The Kitchen 大廚			XX	393	MAP/地圖 31/B-3
Wing Lei 永利軒		✿	XxX	397	MAP/地圖 31/B-3
Ying 帝影樓			XxX	398	MAP/地圖 33/B-1
Zi Yat Heen 紫逸軒	✿✿		XxX	399	MAP/地圖 34/C-3

RESTAURANTS WITH A VIEW
有景觀的餐廳

Aurora 奧羅拉	✿	XxX	364	MAP/地圖 33/B-1
Il Teatro 帝雅廷		XxX	371	MAP/地圖 31/B-3
Kwun Hoi Heen 觀海軒		XxX	375	MAP/地圖 36/C-2
Tenmasa天政		XX	391	MAP/地圖 33/B-1
The Kitchen 大廚		XX	393	MAP/地圖 31/B-3
Ying 帝影樓		XxX	398	MAP/地圖 33/B-1

RESTAURANTS
WITH PRIVATE ROOMS
具備私人房間的餐廳

Aurora 奧羅拉	✿	XxX	364	MAP/地圖 33/B-1
Aux Beaux Arts 寶雅座		XX	365	MAP/地圖 32/C-1
Canton 喜粵		XxX	368	MAP/地圖 34/C-3
Clube Militar de Macau 澳門陸軍俱樂部		XX	369	MAP/地圖 31/B-3
Don Alfonso 當奧豐素		XxxX	370	MAP/地圖 31/B-3
Il Teatro 帝雅廷		XxX	371	MAP/地圖 31/B-3
Imperial Court 金殿堂		XxX	372	MAP/地圖 32/C-1
Inagiku 稻菊		XX	373	MAP/地圖 32/C-3
Jade Garden 蘇浙匯	✿	XX	374	MAP/地圖 32/C-3
Kwun Hoi Heen 觀海軒		XxX	375	MAP/地圖 36/C-2
La Paloma 芭朗瑪		XX	376	MAP/地圖 31/A-2
Laurel 丹桂軒	⊛	XX	377	MAP/地圖 32/C-3
Lei Garden 利苑酒家		XX	378	MAP/地圖 34/C-3
Litoral 海灣餐廳		X	379	MAP/地圖 31/A-1
Morton's of Chicago		XxX	381	MAP/地圖 34/C-3
New Furusato 新故鄉		XX	383	MAP/地圖 31/B-3
Okada 岡田		XX	386	MAP/地圖 31/B-3
Robuchon a Galera 法國餐廳	✿✿✿	XxxX	388	MAP/地圖 31/B-3
Rossio 盛事		XX	389	MAP/地圖 32/C-1
Tenmasa 天政		XX	391	MAP/地圖 33/B-1
The Eight 8餐廳	✿	XxX	392	MAP/地圖 31/B-3
The Kitchen 大廚		XX	393	MAP/地圖 31/B-3
Tim's Kitchen 桃花源小廚	✿	XX	394	MAP/地圖 31/B-3
Tou Tou Koi 陶陶居		X	395	MAP/地圖 29/A-3
Tung Yee Heen 東怡軒	✿	XxX	396	MAP/地圖 32/D-2
Wing Lei 永利軒	✿	XxX	397	MAP/地圖 31/B-3
Ying 帝影樓		XxX	398	MAP/地圖 33/B-1
Zi Yat Heen 紫逸軒	✿✿	XxX	399	MAP/地圖 34/C-3

Antonio
安東尼奧

You really feel you're in Portugal when you're in cosy little Antonio's, with its dark wood floor, Portuguese inspired paintings and crisp blue and white tiles. Ask Antonio for his menu recommendations: not only will he tell you his specials, which include gratinated goat cheese with honey and olive oil as a starter, and monkfish, rice and prawns as a main course; he'll also happily give you the lowdown on how he got from Portugal to Macau.

置身於舒適的安東尼奧餐廳，感覺就像身處葡萄牙一樣：深色木地板、葡式油畫，以及典型的藍白色瓷磚，裝潢甚具風味。安東尼奧的推介相當不錯，他不但會向你推薦他的拿手菜式，包括蜜糖橄欖油烤山羊芝士作前菜，以及鮟鱇魚鮮蝦飯作主菜；同時亦很樂於細說他從葡萄牙來到澳門的故事。

■ ADDRESS/地址
TEL.2899 9998
3 Rua dos Negociantes, Taipa
氹仔客商街3號
www.antoniomacau.com

■ OPENING HOURS, LAST ORDER
　營業時間，最後點菜時間
Lunch/午膳 12:30-15:00 (L.O.)
Dinner/晚膳 18:30-23:00 (L.O.)

■ PRICE/價錢
Lunch/午膳　à la carte/點菜 MOP400-520
Dinner/晚膳　à la carte/點菜 MOP400-520

A Petisqueria
葡國美食天地

Don't be put off by the unattractive façade. Step through the door here and you could be in a cosy little restaurant in the Portuguese countryside. A tiny bar at the entrance leads you into a simple, rustic dining room with nothing fancy on the menu, just decent Portuguese cuisine served in a friendly, unpretentious atmosphere. Authentic dishes include bacalhau prepared in five different ways, fried clams, and six to seven specials of the day.

不要因餐廳外觀不吸引而卻步，踏入大門你便會感受到這裡舒適的葡國風情。餐廳入口設有小酒吧，而餐室本身設計簡樸，菜式亦毫不花巧，以親切友善的服務奉上不俗的葡國美食。正宗的菜式包括以五種不同方法烹調的馬介休、炒蜆，以及六至七款是日精選。

■ ADDRESS/地址
TEL.2882 5354
15 Rua S. Joao, Taipa
氹仔生央街15號

■ ANNUAL AND WEEKLY CLOSING
　　休息日期
Closed Monday
週一休息

■ OPENING HOURS, LAST ORDER
　　營業時間，最後點菜時間
Lunch/午膳 12:30-14:30 (L.O.)
Dinner/晚膳 19:00-22:00 (L.O.)

■ PRICE/價錢
Lunch/午膳　à la carte/點菜 MOP170-340
Dinner/晚膳　à la carte/點菜 MOP170-340

Aurora
奧羅拉

Diners are spoilt for choice at Aurora: there's the option of easy-going Gallic brasserie fare or a more upmarket gastronomic menu based on southern Italian cuisine. You have a choice of where to eat, too: the high tables for tapas, an elegant dining room, or the outside terrace with its great views over Macau. There's a remarkable 500-strong wine list and this is also a great place for cocktails or Sunday brunch. Try the chef's saffron risotto.

這裡菜式選擇之多令食客三心兩意,涵蓋高盧式簡樸餐館的菜式,及以南意大利美食為主的較高價菜式。食客亦可自選用餐的地方,包括無拘束的西班牙小點高桌、高雅餐室、以及坐擁澳門美景的露台。可供選擇的還有五百種烈酒,琳瑯滿目。適合舉行雞尾酒會或星期天早午併餐。試試大廚推介的帶子露荀意大利飯。

■ ADDRESS/地址
TEL.8803 6622
10F, Altira Hotel, Avenida de Kwong Tung, Taipa
氹仔廣東大馬路新濠鋒酒店10樓
www.altiramacau.com

■ OPENING HOURS, LAST ORDER
營業時間,最後點菜時間
Lunch/午膳 12:00-14:30 (L.O.)
Dinner/晚膳 18:00-22:30 (L.O.)

■ PRICE/價錢
Lunch/午膳   set/套餐   MOP188-228
              à la carte/點菜 MOP170-340
Dinner/晚膳 set/套餐   MOP680-980
              à la carte/點菜 MOP280-700

Aux Beaux Arts
寶雅座

This elegant Parisian-style brasserie has a true Belle Epoque feel with classic 1930s bubble-glass chandeliers, and original French paintings from that period, loaned from a Shanghai museum. There's a beautiful glass-enclosed cellar for private parties, the Russian room for caviar, and the Ice bar for champagne. Authentic French classics include 'les cocottes': casserole specialities.

這家巴黎風格的餐廳配置著三十年代的經典氣泡玻璃吊燈, 與從上海博物館借回來的法國原畫, 交織成美麗時期(Belle Epoque)的優雅品味和純正氣質。漂亮的玻璃牆地適合舉辦私人派對。魚子屋供應魚子醬, 香檳庫則提供香檳, 美饌佳釀各適其適。經典法國菜式原汁原味, 包括公認為砂鍋美食的各種烤肉(les cocottes)。

■ ADDRESS/地址
TEL.8802 3888
GF, MGM Grand Hotel, Avenida Dr
Sun Yat Sen , Nape
外港新填海區孫逸仙大馬路美高梅金殿地下
www.mgmgrandmacau.com

■ OPENING HOURS, LAST ORDER
營業時間, 最後點菜時間
Dinner/晚膳 18:30-22:30 (L.O.)

■ PRICE/價錢
Dinner/晚膳   set/套餐   MOP590-980
               à la carte/點菜 MOP360-700

Banza
百姓

Banza is the owner's nickname in Portuguese and he likes to visit the local markets each morning to decide on the chef's frequently-changing daily specials. The restaurant is in Taipa, on the much quieter side of Macau, and is on the ground floor of a huge apartment complex. Inside comes in tones of green and white, with large paintings. The cosy mezzanine seats about six. Banza can also give you advice on his selection of Portuguese wines.

「百姓」原是店主的葡萄牙文別名,他熱愛每天早上前往本地市場,為經常變出新煮意的每日精選作出決定。餐廳座落於氹仔,在澳門較寧靜的一區,位於一幢大型住宅大樓的地下。內部裝潢以白、綠為主色,掛有大型圖畫。洋溢溫暖氣氛的閣樓座位約有六個。百姓(店主)更會為你提供他精選的葡萄牙美酒名單。

■ ADDRESS/地址
TEL.2882 1519
Avenida de Kwong Tung, n°s 154A e 154B, Edf. Nam San Garden, Bl. 5, r/c "G" e "H", Taipa
氹仔廣東大馬路154A及154B號南新花園第5座地下G,H座

■ ANNUAL AND WEEKLY CLOSING
休息日期
Closed Monday
週一休息

■ OPENING HOURS, LAST ORDER
營業時間,最後點菜時間
Lunch/午膳 12:00-15:30 (L.O.)
Dinner/晚膳 18:30-23:00 (L.O.)

■ PRICE/價錢
Lunch/午膳 à la carte/點菜 MOP200-400
Dinner/晚膳 à la carte/點菜 MOP200-400

Belcanção
鳴詩

Belcanção is a casual-dining restaurant offering a buffet and so is ideal for those who can't decide on what to eat. The warm, natural colours of brown and beige decorate the room, while chefs from different countries man the open kitchens. There are stations offering mainly Portuguese, International, Chinese and Indian cuisines and a wide variety of mostly French pastries is also available. Brunch at weekends is from 9:00am -12:30pm.

鳴詩是一家提供自助餐的餐廳，氣氛輕鬆，最適合為選菜而苦惱的人。房間以溫暖、自然的棕色和米白色裝飾，來自不同國家的廚師則掌管各個開放式廚房。不同站點提供葡萄牙，國際，中國及印度美食，更有一系列著名法國糕點。周末早午併餐時間為早上九時至中午十二時三十分。

■ ADDRESS/地址
TEL.2881 8888
GF, Four Seasons Hotel, Estrada da Baia de N. Senhora de Esperanca, s/n, The Cotai Strip, Taipa
氹仔路氹金光大道 - 望德聖母灣大馬路四季酒店地下
www.fourseasons.com/macau/

■ OPENING HOURS, LAST ORDER
營業時間，最後點菜時間
Lunch/午膳 12:00-14:30 (L.O.)
Dinner/晚膳 18:00-22:30 (L.O.)

■ PRICE/價錢
Lunch/午膳 set/套餐   MOP268
Dinner/晚膳 set/套餐   MOP368

Canton
喜粵

Located in a corner of the world's biggest indoor gaming floor, Canton is a smart restaurant with a chic smoked glass façade and elegant walkway that has a glass floor and classic English Georgian-style plaster ceiling! The dining room is a deep sensual red in colour, and very modern in design. A Kouan-Chiau (gastronomic) version of Cantonese cooking prevails, though Shanghai steamed dumplings have their own section.

座落於世上最大室內娛樂場的一角，喜粵擁有時尚的煙灰玻璃外觀，配備玻璃地板的高貴走廊，以及英國喬治風格的經典灰泥天花板，設計別出心裁！餐室呈誘人的深紅色，設計甚具現代感。喜粵的菜單以廣州粵菜為主，亦有提供一系列的餃子。

■ ADDRESS/地址
TEL.8118 9930
Shop 1018, Casino level, The Venetian Resort, Estrada da Baia de N. Senhora de Esperanca, s/n, The Cotai Strip, Taipa

氹仔路氹金光大道-望德聖母灣大馬路威尼斯人酒店娛樂場地下1018號舖
www.venetianmacao.com

■ OPENING HOURS, LAST ORDER
營業時間，最後點菜時間
Lunch/午膳 11:00-14:45 (L.O.)
Dinner/晚膳 18:00-22:45 (L.O.)

■ PRICE/價錢
Lunch/午膳　à la carte/點菜 MOP260-700
Dinner/晚膳　à la carte/點菜 MOP260-700

Clube Militar de Macau
澳門陸軍俱樂部

This classic piece of 19th century Portuguese architecture used to be an army mess hall – unfortunately its lovely bar and lounge is only available to club members. Dining – for the public – takes place in a large room with echoing wood floors, potted palms at netted windows, and Colonial ambience. The Portuguese cooking is straightforward, hearty and tasty. Typical dishes are bacalhau (dried cod) and 'Bairrada' style suckling pig.

陸軍俱樂部始建於十九世紀，氣派典雅，原興建以供葡軍的食堂。雖然酒吧及休息室都是會員專用，不過餐廳對外開放，讓食客可盡情大快朵頤。餐廳地方寬敞，採用木地板，窗前擺放棕櫚盆栽，襯托著整幢建築的殖民地色彩。這裡的葡國菜既簡單又充滿心思，味道濃郁，香味十足。經典菜式包括馬介休(鹽醃製深海鱈魚)及葡式烤乳豬。

■ ADDRESS/地址

TEL.2871 4000

975 Avenida da Praia Grande

南灣大馬路975號

http//home.macau.ctm.net/~cmm

■ OPENING HOURS, LAST ORDER

營業時間，最後點菜時間

Lunch/午膳 12:00-15:00 L.O. 14:45

Dinner/晚膳 19:00-23:00 L.O. 22:45

■ PRICE/價錢

Lunch/午膳   set/套餐   MOP118

            à la carte/點菜 MOP290-400

Dinner/晚膳   set/套餐   MOP118

            à la carte/點菜 MOP290-400

Don Alfonso
當奧豐素

XXXX

  ♿ ☞♪ 🅿 🍽10 🕐🍴 🐝

This opulent dining room features dozens of red Murano chandeliers and a huge fresco of the Italian coast divided into five parts. The somewhat dated feel and bright lights can detract from the experience, but the Italian cuisine uses well selected ingredients, and flavours are clean and sharp. Service can be almost overly attentive. If you're lucky, you'll be here during one of the owner's quarterly trips when he prepares his tasting menu.

豪華的餐室設有許多紅色的穆拉諾穆玻璃吊燈，以及一幅把意大利海岸分為五部分的巨型壁畫，盡顯其獨特之處。古老的風格和明亮的燈光可能令人分心，不過這裡的意大利菜式選材不俗，清新味美，服務更幾乎是太過周到。如果你運氣不錯，還有機會一試店主每年一季的特備餐單。

■ ADDRESS/地址

TEL.8803 7722

3F, Grand Lisboa Hotel, Avenida de Lisboa
葡京路新葡京酒店3樓
www.grandlisboa.com

■ OPENING HOURS, LAST ORDER
　　營業時間，最後點菜時間
Lunch/午膳 12:00-14:30 (L.O.)
Dinner/晚膳 18:30-22:30 (L.O.)

■ PRICE/價錢
Lunch/午膳　set/套餐　　　MOP280-480
　　　　　　à la carte/點菜 MOP410-2,240
Dinner/晚膳 set/套餐　　　MOP1,590
　　　　　　à la carte/點菜 MOP410-2,240

Italian/意式

Il Teatro
帝雅廷

To recommend a restaurant for something other than its food may seem odd, but at Il Teatro it appears most diners turn up primarily to watch the stunning fountains; these are in a lake and are musically choreographed to change colour and appearance every few minutes. Book a table with a good view! And don't wear sneakers, or you won't get in. The cuisine? Straightforward Italian fare, such as seafood risotto or pasta, served with style and élan.

推薦一家餐廳的菜餚以外的物品聽上來有點奇怪，不過大部分到帝雅廷的食客似乎主要是為了觀賞噴泉美景。餐廳七成以上的座位是面向表演湖噴池，每數分鐘音樂水柱交替、激光穿梭的震撼，在帝雅廷可盡收眼簾。記得預訂面向噴泉的座位！不過要記住穿著波鞋是不准進入的。至於菜餚方面，餐廳提供簡單的意大利菜，例如海鮮意大利飯或意大利粉，菜式風格獨特，服務殷勤周到。

■ ADDRESS/地址
TEL.8986 3663
GF, Wynn Hotel, Rua Cidade de Sintra, Nape
外港填海區仙德麗街永利酒店地下
www.wynnmacau.com

■ ANNUAL AND WEEKLY CLOSING
休息日期
Closed Monday
週一休息

■ OPENING HOURS, LAST ORDER
營業時間，最後點菜時間
Dinner/晚膳 17:30-23:30 (L.O.)

■ PRICE/價錢
Dinner/晚膳 à la carte/點菜 MOP380-650

Imperial Court
金殿堂

This is an elegant and contemporary restaurant that is on the same floor as the VIP lobby. A recent addition, the Grand Imperial Court has been opened upstairs which has a more classical and comfortable setting. The main point of interest of the main room is its massive marble pillar with carved dragon. Celebrity chef Chow Chong supervises Cantonese cuisine that seeks to make the refined preparations which is served by attentive staff.

金殿堂集優雅與當代氣息於一身,與貴賓室同層。最近更在上層新開設金殿貴賓廳,提供更典雅舒適的環境。雕龍大雲石柱是大廳的最大特色。廣東菜由星級名廚周忠師傅主理,精心準備,服務周到。

■ ADDRESS/地址

TEL.8802 3888

GF, MGM Grand Hotel, Avenida Dr. Sun Yat Sen, Nape

外港新填海區孫逸仙大馬路美高梅金殿酒店地下

www.mgmgrandmacau.com

■ OPENING HOURS, LAST ORDER
營業時間,最後點菜時間
Lunch/午膳 12:00-14:30 L.O. 14:00
Dinner/晚膳 18:00-23:00 L.O. 22:30

■ PRICE/價錢
Lunch/午膳 à la carte/點菜 MOP300-1,000
Dinner/晚膳 à la carte/點菜 MOP500-1,000

Inagiku
稻菊

Gamblers, fashionistas and foodies make this a destination of choice in Macau. A serious and well-run Japanese restaurant, Inagiku has a laid-back, relaxing aura, which balances contemporary style, Japanese culture and clubby vibes. You can select a table, or sit at the sushi bar, tempura area or teppanyaki counter. The set lunches and the teppanyaki set are always a favourite at Inagiku.

稻菊是一家成功的日本餐廳，營運認真，娛樂場玩家、追捧潮流者和食家紛紛到此朝聖。這裡的輕鬆悠閒氣氛，與現代風格、日本文化及夜店感覺相映成趣。食客可以選擇在餐桌、壽司吧、天婦羅區或鐵板燒檯用餐。稻菊的午市套餐及鐵板燒套餐最受歡迎。

■ ADDRESS/地址
TEL.8290 8668
5F, StarWorld Hotel, Avenida da Amizade
友誼大馬路星際酒店5樓
www.starworldmacau.com

■ OPENING HOURS, LAST ORDER
營業時間，最後點菜時間
Lunch/午膳 12:00-14:30 (L.O.)
Dinner/晚膳 18:00-22:30 (L.O.)

■ PRICE/價錢
Lunch/午膳	set/套餐	MOP88-198
	à la carte/點菜	MOP300-600
Dinner/晚膳	set/套餐	MOP168-2,000
	à la carte/點菜	MOP300-600

Jade Garden
蘇浙匯

Its location at the heart of the peninsula makes it a suitable place for a business lunch or for high-rollers wanting a quick bite. There are private rooms at the entrance and within the restaurant and booth seating along one side. It's part of a popular group from Shanghai, offering fine Shanghainese dining with a blend of the traditional and the modern. Specialities include sautéed river shrimps and Jade Garden tea-smoked duck.

蘇浙匯位於半島的中心地帶，非常適合商務午餐或想趕快隨意進食的賭場高手。入口及整間餐廳內都設有貴賓房，其中一邊設有卡位雅座。餐廳屬於著名上海集團旗下，提供精緻上海菜，融和傳統與現代。著名菜式包括清炒河蝦仁及蘇浙樟茶鴨。

■ ADDRESS/地址

TEL.8290 8638
6F, StarWorld Hotel, Avenida da Amizade
友誼大馬路星際酒店6樓
www.starworldmacau.com

■ OPENING HOURS, LAST ORDER
營業時間，最後點菜時間
Lunch/午膳 11:30-15:00 (L.O.)
Dinner/晚膳 17:30-23:00 (L.O.)

■ PRICE/價錢
Lunch/午膳 à la carte/點菜 MOP150-400
Dinner/晚膳 à la carte/點菜 MOP150-400

Kwun Hoi Heen
觀海軒

The restaurant name translates as 'with a nice sea view', and it can't be contradicted on that score, as its large picture windows overlook Hac Sa Bay. It's a popular weekend spot for locals escaping Macau city, though the vibe is more corporate on weekdays. Appealing menus feature a great lunchtime selection of fresh and tasty dim sum; in the evenings there's a good seasonally changing Cantonese choice of dumpling, rice, noodles and dessert.

觀海軒名副其實，坐擁怡人的黑沙灣海景。澳門人喜愛在週末到訪，遠離城市的煩囂，而週日則較多商務客人光顧。餐廳的菜餚令人食指大動，包括午膳時間供應的點心，既新鮮又味美；而傍晚時分供應的粵菜，四季風味不同，更有多種選擇，涵蓋各種餃子、飯類、麵食及甜品。

■ ADDRESS/地址
TEL.8899 1320
3F, The Westin Resort, 1918 Estrata de Hac Sa, Coloane
路環黑沙馬路1918號威斯汀度假酒店3號
www.westin.com/macau

■ OPENING HOURS, LAST ORDER
營業時間，最後點菜時間
Lunch/午膳 11:00-15:00 L.O. 14:30
Dinner/晚膳 18:30-23:00 L.O. 22:30

■ PRICE/價錢
Lunch/午膳   à la carte/點菜 MOP200-1,000
Dinner/晚膳   à la carte/點菜 MOP250-1,000

La Paloma
芭朗瑪

Secluded like hidden treasure from the rest of the city, La Paloma is a very appealing restaurant and bar, enhanced by a charming terrace, floor-to-ceiling glass, and stone walls, which are part of the original 17th century fortress foundations. A bold nouveau riche style of furniture lends it a casual chic; it's wonderfully intimate and romantic at nights. The refined Spanish cuisine offers a great assortment of tapas and exquisite paellas.

芭朗瑪餐廳及酒吧，位於一座十七世紀舊城堡改建而成的酒店，遠離城市的煩囂。迷人的露台、落地玻璃和古堡原來的石牆，構成芭朗瑪的獨特風采。傢具陳設高尚優雅，氣派舒適時尚，晚上更是浪漫醉人。餐廳的西班牙菜精緻優雅，涵蓋多種西班牙前菜(tapas)及精美的西班牙海鮮飯(paella)。

■ ADDRESS/地址
TEL.2837 8111
2F, Pousada de São Tiago Hotel,
Avenida da República, Fortaleza
de São Tiago da Barra
西灣民國大馬路聖地牙哥古堡酒店2樓
www.saotiago.com.ma

■ OPENING HOURS, LAST ORDER
營業時間，最後點菜時間
Lunch/午膳 12:00-14:30 (L.O.)
Dinner/晚膳 18:30-22:30 (L.O.)

■ PRICE/價錢
Lunch/午膳   set/套餐   MOP1,600
               à la carte/點菜 MOP500-900
Dinner/晚膳   set/套餐   MOP1,600
               à la carte/點菜 MOP500-900

Laurel
丹桂軒

Part of a famous restaurant chain from Shenzhen and popular because of its reasonable prices. The chef serves authentic Cantonese food, delicious dim sum and a variety of soups. Some of the locals' favourites include roast pigeon, pan-fried beef fillet with sweetened pineapple and deep-fried steamed bean curd. The setting is elegant yet simple, mixing east and west and using whites and greens. There is also a large glass-enclosed wine cellar.

丹桂軒乃深圳著名連鎖餐廳集團的一員，因價格合理而廣受歡迎。大廚炮製正宗廣東菜，美味點心和一系列湯羹。部份本地人最愛菜式包括脆皮燒乳鴿、蜜餞鳳梨牛柳以及煎琵琶豆腐。餐廳佈置高雅簡約，混合了中西色彩，以白、綠為主色。餐廳內更有大型玻璃餐酒庫。

■ ADDRESS/地址
TEL.8290 8628
2F, Starworld Hotel, Avenida da Amizade
友誼大馬路星際酒店2樓
www.starworldmacau.com

■ OPENING HOURS, LAST ORDER
營業時間，最後點菜時間
11:00-23:00(L.O.)

■ PRICE/價錢
Lunch/午膳　à la carte/點菜 MOP250-500
Dinner/晚膳　à la carte/點菜 MOP250-500

Lei Garden
利苑酒家

Smart restaurant set amongst the canals of this vast hotel's third floor! Arrive on a gondola if you wish...Venetian guests predominate here; gamblers mostly give it a miss as it's too far from the gaming tables. Walls of marble provide the backdrop to a comprehensive range of traditional Cantonese dishes served at breakneck speed by an efficient team of waiters. The best place to be seated is in one of the cosy booths just inside the front door.

餐廳設於三樓，佔據此巨型酒店的運河旁位置，雄據地利。有興趣不妨乘坐貢朵拉前往餐廳。這裡的顧客以酒店住客為主；因為離博彩桌太遠，娛樂場玩家通常會選擇其他餐廳。大理石的牆壁與清一色的傳統廣東菜配合得天衣無縫。侍應生服務速度簡直快如閃電，極有效率！這裡最好的座位是靠近前門的舒適卡位。

■ ADDRESS/地址
TEL.2882 8689
Shop 2130, 3F Grand Canal Shoppes, The Venetian Resort, Estrada da Baia de N. Senhora de Esperança, Taipa
氹仔路氹望德聖母灣大馬路威尼斯人酒店大運河購物中心3樓2130號舖
www.venetianmacao.com

■ OPENING HOURS, LAST ORDER
營業時間，最後點菜時間
Lunch/午膳 11:30-15:00 L.O. 14:30
Dinner/晚膳 18:00-23:00 L.O. 22:15

■ PRICE/價錢
Lunch/午膳　à la carte/點菜 MOP130-350
Dinner/晚膳　à la carte/點菜 MOP250-350

Litoral
海灣餐廳

The neat and tidy façade of Litoral compensates for the charmless street in which it's located. The small exterior is deceiving: the interior goes over two floors and 250 diners can be accommodated — though this can prove a bit of a challenge to the waiting staff! The rustic atmosphere is courtesy of Portuguese nuance, which also influences the menus, along with local dishes. Try the curry shrimp with crabmeat and baked Portuguese chicken.

雖然餐廳所處的街道稍欠魅力，但整潔的正門令人留下好印象。看似狹窄的外觀頗有誤導成份：內裡共分為兩層，可以容納約250位顧客一不過這對餐廳員工來說可能是個挑戰！樸素的氣氛極具葡萄牙特色，這亦反映在餐廳菜式及本地菜式中。特別推介咖喱蟹肉蝦及焗葡國雞。

■ ADDRESS/地址
TEL.2896 7878
261A Rua do Almirante Sérgio
河邊新街261A舖
http://restaurante-litoral.com

■ OPENING HOURS, LAST ORDER
　營業時間，最後點菜時間
Lunch/午膳 12:00-15:00 (L.O.)
Dinner/晚膳 17:30-22:30 (L.O.)

■ PRICE/價錢
Lunch/午膳　à la carte/點菜 MOP250-450
Dinner/晚膳　à la carte/點菜 MOP250-450

Lung Wah Tea House
龍華茶樓

Little has changed from when this old-style Cantonese tea house, up a flight of stairs, opened in the 1960s: the large clock still works, the boss still uses an abacus to add the bill and you still have to refill your own pot of tea at the boiler. The owner buys fresh produce, including their popular chicken dish, from the market across the road. Their stir-fried noodles with beef is another speciality. Get here early for the fresh dim sum.

這家有一列樓梯的傳統廣東茶樓自一九六零年代開業以來,變化不大——古老大鐘依然不停擺動,老闆依然用算盤算帳單,你依然要自行到熱水器沖茶。店主從對面街市選購新鮮食材,包括茶樓名菜油雞。此外,此處的干炒牛河亦是一絕。建議預早前來享用新鮮點心。

■ ADDRESS/地址

TEL.2857 4456

3 Rua Norte do Mercado Aim-Lacerda
提督市北街3號

■ ANNUAL AND WEEKLY CLOSING
　休息日期

Closed 4 days Lunar New Year, May and October

農曆新年、五月及十月各休息4天

■ OPENING HOURS, LAST ORDER
　營業時間,最後點菜時間

07:00-14:00 (L.O.)

■ PRICE/價錢

Lunch/午膳　à la carte/點菜 MOP25-80

Morton's of Chicago

Big, butch and boasting a masculine-friendly ambience of dark wood, tuxedo-attired Maitre D' and swinging Rat Pack music, Morton's serves up a hearty steakhouse experience. There's even a bar serving all kinds of Martinis! The prices are certainly higher than they would have been fifty years ago, but casually elegant clientele create a lively atmosphere as they attack the hash browns, cream spinach and, of course, platefuls of prime cut beef.

地方寬敞、深色木材裝潢、身穿禮服的侍應總管，加上Rat Pack背景音樂，揉合成Morton's 餐廳的男士格調，為你帶來貼心的扒房用餐體驗。這家扒房餐廳的酒吧更提供各式各樣的Martini！餐飲價格當然比五十年前高，不過客人無拘無束，自然令餐廳氣氛輕鬆。經典美式佳餚包括馬鈴薯煎餅、忌廉菠菜，更少不了的當然是豐富的頂級牛扒。

■ ADDRESS/地址
TEL.8117 5000
Shop 1016, Casino Level, The Venetian Resort, Estrada da Baia de N. Senhora de Esperanca, s/n, The Cotai Strip, Taipa
氹仔路氹金光大道-望德聖母灣大馬路威尼斯人酒店娛樂場地下1016號舖
www.mortons.com

■ OPENING HOURS, LAST ORDER
營業時間，最後點菜時間
Dinner/晚膳 18:00-24:00 L.O. 23:30
Sunday/週日 17:00-22:00

■ PRICE/價錢
Dinner/晚膳   à la carte/點菜 MOP400-700

Naam
藍

An elegant and serene restaurant that's spot-on for décor
and location: there's the tranquil presence of a fountain in
the middle of the room and views on to a pool and luxurious
tropical garden outside. The restaurant, bathed in natural
light, focuses entirely on Thai cuisine, with recipes from all
regions of the country. Best way to start is to sample the
range of appetisers. Then follow symbols for vegetarian,
spicy or chef's signature dishes.

藍泰國餐廳優雅寧靜，地點和裝潢均恰到好處。餐廳中心設有寧靜的噴泉，
外面是泳池和茂密的熱帶花園，景致優美，天然陽光更滲透餐廳裡頭。菜餚全
都是泰國菜，包含不同地區的特色美食。建議先從前菜入手，然後從素食、
辛辣或廚師推介的云云菜式中挑選。

■ ADDRESS/地址

TEL.8793 4818

Grand Lapa Hotel , 956-1110 Avenida
da Amizade

友誼大馬路金麗華酒店956-1110號

■ OPENING HOURS, LAST ORDER
　營業時間，最後點菜時間

Lunch/午膳 12:00-14:30 (L.O.)

Dinner/晚膳 18:30-22:30 (L.O.)

■ PRICE/價錢

Lunch/午膳 　à la carte/點菜 MOP220-600

Dinner/晚膳 　à la carte/點菜 MOP220-600

New Furusato
新故鄉

Called 'New' Furusato because of a recent total refurbishment, this chic restaurant boasts quite tasteful décor which combines Japanese style with modern art and swish fabrics...though the walk-in wine cellar at the entrance, with a choice of 60 sake, may grab your attention first! There's the customary sushi bar, teppanyaki and tempura counters. The professional service is a bonus.

由於餐廳最近進行了全面裝修，顧名思義，這裡便命名為 'New' Furusato。餐廳風格時尚，設計品味獨特，揉合日本風格和現代藝術，並採用型格布料。不過，入口處擁有60種燒酒的酒櫃，可能已搶先吸引了你的注意力！餐廳設有壽司吧、鐵板燒和天婦羅檯。此外，專業的服務態度更令人賓至如歸。

■ ADDRESS/地址
TEL.2888 3888
2F, Hotel Lisboa, East Wing, 2-4
Avenida de Lisboa
葡京路2-4號葡京酒店東翼2樓
www.hotelisboa.com

■ OPENING HOURS, LAST ORDER
    營業時間，最後點菜時間
Lunch/午膳 12:00-14:30 (L.O.)
Dinner/晚膳 18:30-22:30 (L.O.)

■ PRICE/價錢

Lunch/午膳	set/套餐	MOP160-380
	à la carte/點菜	MOP160-900
Dinner/晚膳	set/套餐	MOP400-900
	à la carte/點菜	MOP160-900

Noodle & Congee Corner
粥麵莊

This simple, good value eatery is located – incongruously – on a gallery that opens onto the casino. It's really a cafeteria, or even 'tea-eria', as one wall is full of teapots. What's special for diners is the view they have of chefs from different parts of the country preparing a noodle speciality from their home region using fresh, tasty produce. These can be combined with various soups and ingredients: the menus, handily, include photos.

這家簡樸的餐廳提供價錢合宜的美食，位於娛樂場上層樓上，彼此風格迥然不同。粥麵莊的確是一家餐館，而其中一道牆更放滿茶壺，洋溢著「茶 檔」的感覺。特別的是食客更可在晚餐時觀賞來自五湖四海的廚師，採用新鮮味美的食材，分別炮製出家鄉的特色麵食的烹飪過程！餐廳亦提供不同款式的湯類和其他菜式；菜單附有圖片，便於瀏覽。

■ ADDRESS/地址
TEL.2828 3838
1F, Grand Lisboa Hotel, Avenida de Lisboa
葡京路新葡京酒店1樓
www.grandlisboa.com

■ OPENING HOURS, LAST ORDER
營業時間，最後點菜時間
Open 24 hours
24小時營業

■ PRICE/價錢
Lunch/午膳　à la carte/點菜 MOP50-200
Dinner/晚膳　à la carte/點菜 MOP50-200

Oja Sopa De Fita Cheong Kei
祥記

Although handily placed on Rua da Felicidade, you'll need to weave round shoppers and stalls to get to Cheong Kei. A family business since the '70s, this tiny noodle shop sticks to its roots and their thin, fine noodles are pressed by bamboo shoots in their own little factory nearby. Their soup uses dried prawns and bonito and is cooked for 8 hours. The wontons with noodles are clearly a must but also try the dried prawn roe with stewed noodles.

雖然祥記位於福隆新街，選址便利，但還是得花一番功夫繞過購物的人潮及攤販。這家小麵店是七十年代開業的家族生意，鄰近自設小型廠房製造幼細竹昇面。麵湯以蝦乾和柴魚熬製八小時，雲吞麵當然不能缺少，煆籽撈麵亦不容錯過。

■ ADDRESS/地址
TEL.2857 4310
68 Rua de Felicidade
福隆新街68號

■ ANNUAL AND WEEKLY CLOSING
　休息日期
Closed 3 days each month
每月休息3天

■ OPENING HOURS, LAST ORDER
　營業時間，最後點菜時間
12:00-01:00 (L.O.)

■ PRICE/價錢
Lunch/午膳　à la carte/點菜 MOP16-30
Dinner/晚膳　à la carte/點菜 MOP16-30

Okada
岡田

𝕏𝕏

☞ 📷20 🛒

Situated alongside the casino, there are no prizes for guessing the clientele of this attractive restaurant whose pale, dry-stone walls are its most appealing feature, its garden views obscured by a wall of bamboo. Apart from the main room, there's a sushi counter and grill bar. The menu delivers a large Japanese menu – sushi, sashimi, tempura, teppanyaki, grilled fish – but authenticity can be sacrificed in the desire to 'refuel' gamblers.

這間日式料理毗鄰娛樂場，不用猜想都知食客固然也是娛樂場的顧客。餐廳的淺色石牆魅力獨特，十分迷人；而竹林的排列則使園林景致若隱若現。餐廳設有主餐室、壽司吧和燒烤吧。菜單涵蓋大量日本菜式，包括壽司、天婦羅、鐵板燒、烤魚等等。味道可能不夠正宗，不過可以為食客「充 電」，然後繼續到娛樂場大展身手。

■ ADDRESS/地址

TEL.8986 3663
GF, Wynn Hotel, Rua Cidade de Sintra, Nape
外港新填海區仙德麗街永利酒店地下
www.wynnmacau.com

■ ANNUAL AND WEEKLY CLOSING
　休息日期
Closed Tuesday
週二休息

■ OPENING HOURS, LAST ORDER
　營業時間，最後點菜時間
Dinner/晚膳 17:30-23:30 (L.O.)

■ PRICE/價錢
Dinner/晚膳　à la carte/點菜 MOP250-600

Red 8
紅8

If you enjoy a buzzing atmosphere full of gamblers, then this is the place to eat. Mind you, if you like to gaze at the world outside, then give Red 8 a wide berth, as it's located in the hotel's casino room and there are no windows. You either face the chefs preparing food behind large glass windows, or stare at the players. Cheap, unpretentious cuisine features the signature Beijing duck, and an array of noodle dishes from across Asia.

假如你喜愛在滿佈娛樂場玩家的熱鬧的環境下用餐，這裡不失為一家好餐廳。假如你喜歡觀賞戶外景色，紅8在這方面則略嫌不足-餐廳位處酒店的娛樂場裡，沒有窗戶；你可面向玻璃窗後的廚師，或轉向娛樂場內的玩家。菜式簡單正宗，價錢便宜。招牌菜包括北京填鴨，以及多款亞洲各地風味的麵食。

■ ADDRESS/地址
TEL.2888 9966
GF, Wynn Hotel, Rua Cidade de Sintra, Nape
外港新填海區仙德麗街永利酒店地下
www.wynnmacau.com

■ OPENING HOURS, LAST ORDER
營業時間，最後點菜時間
Open 24 hours
24小時營業

■ PRICE/價錢
Lunch/午膳　à la carte/點菜 MOP80-300
Dinner/晚膳　à la carte/點菜 MOP80-300

Robuchon a Galera
法國餐廳

🏵 🏵 🏵   ✕✕✕✕

World famous Joël Robuchon's chic offering in Macau offers a suitably stylish location to dine. The restaurant's early 19th century ambience has a warm, soft, and cosy feel, accentuated by elegant and expensive fabrics. Excellent fresh ingredients underpin contemporary Gallic cuisine; the dessert trolley, with its large choice of wonderful home-made pastries, is of note. Make sure you leave room for the classical pastries like the vanilla millefeuille, religieuses (french puff pastry), rum baba and coffee tart. The wine list, too, is superb, with over 3,400 wines from around the world.

蜚聲國際的名廚羅布松(Joël Robuchon)於澳門營運時尚的Robuchon a Galera，餐廳洋溢著十九世紀初的氣氛，採用昂貴而高雅的布料，感覺溫暖舒適。優質新鮮的材料造就當代風格法國菜，謹記留肚試甜品車上的經典美點。此外，餐廳亦供應超過3,400種來自世界各地的上等美酒。

■ ADDRESS/地址

TEL.2888 3888

3F, Hotel Lisboa, 2-4 Avenida de Lisboa

葡京路2-4號葡京酒店3樓

www.hotelisboa.com

■ OPENING HOURS, LAST ORDER
營業時間，最後點菜時間
Lunch/午膳 12:00-14:30 (L.O.)
Dinner/晚膳 18:30-22:30 (L.O.)

■ PRICE/價錢
Lunch/午膳	set/套餐	MOP398-638
	à la carte/點菜	MOP398-638
Dinner/晚膳	set/套餐	MOP1,488-2,100
	à la carte/點菜	MOP1,160-2,500

Rossio
盛事

There's a minimalist Zen calm here: natural elements such as waterfalls and Japanese granite stones merge seamlessly into an elegant terrace. Chefs in the open kitchen conjure up a vibrant contrast as they produce a plethora of delicious international dishes on grill, steamer and wok. Pre-eminence is Mediterranean cuisine, particularly Portuguese, although sushi and steak are well represented, too. Ingredients and preparations are top-notch.

高雅的陽台採用了天然元素，包括瀑布和日本花崗石，交織成極簡抽象派藝術氣息及禪的寧靜感。開放式廚房呈獻豐富的美饌，菜式風味林林總總，包括來自不同國家的烤、 蒸、炒菜式，令人目不暇給。著名菜色包括地中海菜，特別是葡國菜，而壽司及牛排亦非常出眾。食材及烹調方式堪稱一流。

■ ADDRESS/地址
TEL.8802 3888
GF, MGM Grand Hotel, Avenida Dr. Sun Yat Sen, Nape
外港新填海區孫逸仙大馬路美高梅金殿酒店地下
www.mgmgrandmacau.com

■ OPENING HOURS, LAST ORDER
營業時間，最後點菜時間
07:00-23:00

■ PRICE/價錢
Lunch/午膳　à la carte/點菜 MOP200-700
Dinner/晚膳　à la carte/點菜 MOP200-700

Square Eight
食・八方

Square Eight is a large, informal, western-styled eatery that never closes its doors. It's vibrant and busy, and its cuisine covers large swathes of Asia, from China to Thailand to Korea. You're given a large sheet of paper with all the dishes, and you just tick the ones you'd like. Service is fast and furious, but staff are engaging and attentive. A long, open-plan kitchen adds to the hustle and bustle of the place.

食・八方二十四小時開放，地方寬敞，環境輕鬆時尚。餐廳人氣旺盛，生氣勃勃，美食超越中西界限，涵蓋中菜、泰國菜、韓國菜等。點菜單上羅列出全部菜式，食客可以自行打剔點選。環境時而喧鬧，不過服務快捷周到。長形的開放式廚房為餐廳更添一份忙碌氣氛。

■ ADDRESS/地址

TEL.8802 3888

GF, MGM Grand Hotel, Avenida Dr. Sun Yat Sen, Nape

外港新填海區孫逸仙大馬路美高梅金殿酒店地下

www.mgmgrandmacau.com

■ OPENING HOURS, LAST ORDER
營業時間，最後點菜時間

Open 24 hours
24小時營業

■ PRICE/價錢

Lunch/午膳　à la carte/點菜 MOP60-250

Dinner/晚膳　à la carte/點菜 MOP60-250

Tenmasa
天政

An utterly charming restaurant named after the original Tenmasa, which opened in Tokyo in 1937 and is still going strong. Taipa's version boasts sushi bar, tatami floor, decked walkways leading across golden pebble ponds to private rooms, and a tempura counter. Here you can sit and watch the chef at work, admiring his precise light frying of superb ingredients and wonderfully well-balanced dishes. Attentive waitresses wear smart kimonos.

譽滿東京的天政早於1937年開業，至今仍廣受歡迎，更把料理帶到澳門皇冠。澳門的天政設有壽司吧、榻榻米地板、鋪板走廊、金石水池、私人餐室，以及天婦羅檯。食客可安坐在天婦羅檯，觀看廚師大顯身手，將優質食材炮製成美味菜式。服務員穿著整潔的和服，服務周到。

■ ADDRESS/地址
TEL.8803 6611
11F, Altira Hotel, Avenida de Kwong Tung, Taipa
氹仔廣東大馬路新濠鋒酒店11樓
www.altiramacau.com

■ OPENING HOURS, LAST ORDER
營業時間，最後點菜時間
Lunch/午膳 12:00-14:30 (L.O.)
Dinner/晚膳 18:00-22:30 (L.O.)

■ PRICE/價錢
Lunch/午膳	set/套餐	MOP270-900
	à la carte/點菜	MOP400-1,200
Dinner/晚膳	set/套餐	MOP380-1,600
	à la carte/點菜	MOP400-1,200

The Eight
8餐廳

The Eight's stylish appearance can't fail to impress: water cascades down walls, images are projected onto the floor… and that's just the entrance corridor! Even the goldfish on the walls inside the restaurant are hand-sewn! The menu includes some very innovative Cantonese dishes which includes dim sum like deep-fried abalone puff stuffed with black mushroom and asparagus and the baked tartelette with crabmeat in curry sauce.

8餐廳的時尚設計令人印象深刻：流水沿著牆壁潺潺而下，地板上更投射著粼粼影像…這只是入口走廊而已！餐廳牆上的金魚也都是人手繡成的!餐牌包括部分非常創新的廣東菜，點心類如特式鮑魚酥及葡香焗蟹撻。

■ ADDRESS/地址
TEL.2828 3838
2F, Grand Lisboa Hotel,
Avenida de Lisboa
葡京路新葡京酒店2樓
www.grandlisboa.com

■ OPENING HOURS, LAST ORDER
營業時間，最後點菜時間
Lunch/午膳 12:00-14:30 (L.O.)
Dinner/晚膳 18:30-22:30 (L.O.)

■ PRICE/價錢
Lunch/午膳 à la carte/點菜 MOP160-800
Dinner/晚膳 à la carte/點菜 MOP300-1,000

The Kitchen
大厨

You can tell this is somewhere slightly different when you enter via a beautiful wooden screen and gain access to a bar in the shape of a golden cow. The restaurant itself is intimate and stylish, with shiny metal rods suspended from the ceiling and a wall of water behind the sushi counter. Cuisine is mix of Western steakhouse and Japanese dishes. There's also live fish from the tank and a superb wine list. For the gentlemen, don't forget to check out the floating money in the Men's bathroom.

踏進餐廳，經過美麗的木製屏風，看到金牛形的酒吧，你便會意識到這裡的非凡之處。餐廳時尚愜意，天花板懸掛著閃閃生輝的金屬棒，壽司吧後方更設有一道水牆。菜式揉合西式扒房風格和日本菜餚而成。餐廳亦設有游水魚魚缸，並提供優質美酒。男士們，不要忘記一睹男廁內的飄浮紙幣！

■ ADDRESS/地址
TEL.8803 7777
3F, Grand Lisboa Hotel,
Avenida de Lisboa
葡京路新葡京酒店3樓
www.grandlisboa.com

■ OPENING HOURS, LAST ORDER
營業時間，最後點菜時間
Lunch/午膳 12:00-14:30 (L.O.)
Dinner/晚膳 18:30-22:30 (L.O.)

■ PRICE/價錢
Lunch/午膳   set/套餐   MOP208-398
            à la carte/點菜 MOP430-2,200
Dinner/晚膳 à la carte/點菜 MOP430-2,200

Tim's Kitchen
桃花源小廚

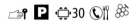

One for the connoisseurs – Hong Kong foodies make special pilgrimages here. This restaurant is filled with opera photos and costumes. The Cantonese dishes may look simple, but they are well prepared. These may include the steamed pork slices with eggplant & preserved vegetables and the sweet & sour pork ribs. Don't forget to try the crystal prawn while in winter there is always the snake ragout. A true joy for the taste buds!

桃花源是行家的必然之選，　香港食家也少不免到此朝聖。餐廳放滿歌劇照片和戲服裝飾。粵菜餐牌看似簡單，其實經過精心炮製。菜式包括梅菜肉片蒸茄瓜及京都骨。萬勿錯過玻璃蝦球，冬天的重頭戲則離不開蛇羹。實在能「感動味蕾」！

■ ADDRESS/地址
TEL.8803 3682
Shop F25, GF, Hotel Lisboa, East Wing, 2-4 Avenida de Lisboa
葡京路2-4號葡京酒店東翼地下F25號鋪
www.hotelisboa.com

■ OPENING HOURS, LAST ORDER
營業時間，最後點菜時間
Lunch/午膳 12:00-15:00 L.O. 14:30
Dinner/晚膳 18:30-23:00 L.O. 22:00

■ PRICE/價錢
Lunch/午膳　à la carte/點菜 MOP170-500
Dinner/晚膳　à la carte/點菜 MOP350-1,200

Tou Tou Koi
陶陶居

⭐24 📞🍴

As Tou Tou Koi is simply always packed it's vital to make a reservation; you can then also pre-order the eight treasure duck. It's dim sum during the day and Cantonese cuisine at night. The roast barbeque corner is next to the entrance; the seafood is found at the front of the shop in large tanks. Service is extremely swift to accommodate the non-stop flow of customers. Other favourites include deep-fried crab and shark fin and chicken soup.

陶陶居總是賓客如雲，必須訂座，你亦可順道預訂八寶鴨。日間以點心為主，晚上則提供粵菜。燒味櫃面位於入口附近，店面前方的大水缸放滿海鮮。服務非常具效率，以應付絡繹不絕的人流。其它著名菜式包括金錢蟹盒和古法雞煲翅。

■ ADDRESS/地址

TEL.2857 2629
6-8 Travessa do Mastro
爐石塘巷6-8號

■ OPENING HOURS, LAST ORDER
   營業時間，最後點菜時間
Lunch/午膳 08:00-15:00 (L.O.)
Dinner/晚膳 17:00-24:00 L.O. 23:30

■ PRICE/價錢
Lunch/午膳 à la carte/點菜 MOP60-150
Dinner/晚膳 à la carte/點菜 MOP200-400

Tung Yee Heen
東怡軒

Seriously run Cantonese restaurant that exudes comfort, its decor finding a nice balance between Chinese influences and contemporary flair. This is somewhere for a special occasion. There's a big choice of traditional dishes; specialities are shark's fin soup, deep-fried prawns with garlic in chilli sauce, or abalone - with options for all appetites. The well-regarded cuisine is prepared with unerringly fresh ingredients and cooked with talent.

這家舒適的粵菜餐廳營運認真，裝潢設計方面，中式和現代元素混合得宜，適合舉辦特別飲宴。餐廳提供多款傳統菜式，招牌菜包括魚翅、香辣蒜蝦或鮑魚，以及各種各樣的選擇，適合任何食客的胃口。這裡的菜餚享負盛名，採用了新鮮食材，貫徹始終，廚藝亦十分精湛。

■ ADDRESS/地址
TEL.8793 3821
2F, Grand Lapa Hotel, 956-1110
Avenida da Amizade
友誼大馬路956-1110號金麗華酒樓2樓

■ OPENING HOURS, LAST ORDER
　營業時間，最後點菜時間
Lunch/午膳 11:00-14:30 (L.O.)
Dinner/晚膳 18:00-23:00 (L.O.)

■ PRICE/價錢
Lunch/午膳　set/套餐　　MOP428-1,788
　　　　　　à la carte/點菜 MOP200-1,000
Dinner/晚膳　set/套餐　　MOP428-1,788
　　　　　　à la carte/點菜 MOP200-1,000

Wing Lei
永利軒

An opulent restaurant in vibrant red, characterised by vast lanterns at the entrance, and a superb three-dimensional dragon made of ninety thousand pieces of crystal. The comfy red dining chairs add to a feeling of well-being. The décor may be excellent, but the service can occasionally be somewhat lacklustre. Gamblers and a large number of families create a noisy ambience as they tuck in to a big menu of classical Cantonese dishes.

這家紅當當的餐廳入口掛著一些大型燈籠，襯托一條以九千片水晶製成的立體龍，盡展豪華氣派；而舒適的紅色座椅讓人更添好感。餐廳的裝潢實屬一流，不過相比之下，服務態度有時略嫌失色。食客多是一家大小或娛樂場玩家，環境熱鬧非常。餐廳供應傳統粵菜，菜式選擇良多。

■ ADDRESS/地址
TEL.8986 3663
GF, Wynn Hotel, Rua Cidade de Sintra, Nape
外港新填海區仙德麗街永利酒店地下
www.wynnmacau.com

■ OPENING HOURS, LAST ORDER
　營業時間, 最後點菜時間
Lunch/午膳 11:30-15:00 (L.O.)
Dinner/晚膳 18:00-23:00 (L.O.)

■ PRICE/價錢
Lunch/午膳　à la carte/點菜 MOP150-300
Dinner/晚膳　à la carte/點菜 MOP200-920

Ying
帝影樓

This is a terrific restaurant with breathtaking views looking north to Macau. The beautifully styled interior has been designed with real taste and quality; even the beaded curtains – featuring gold cranes and crystal trees – are fantastic. The Cantonese dishes on offer are prepared with contemporary twists and great flair, and are served by charmingly professional staff. The place to come for some of the best Cantonese cooking in the region.

帝影樓坐擁澳門北部的壯麗景致，扣人心弦。餐廳內部設計品味獨特，風格絢麗；甚至珠簾亦配有金鶴和水晶樹，使裝潢更添神采。餐廳的粵菜融入了當代元素，烹調技藝精湛。服務專業，態度令人賓至如歸。這裡的一些粵菜菜式可謂冠絕全城。

■ ADDRESS/地址

TEL.8803 6600

11F, Altira Hotel, Avenida de Kwong Tung, Taipa
氹仔廣東大馬路新濠鋒酒店11樓
www.altiramacau.com

■ OPENING HOURS, LAST ORDER
  營業時間，最後點菜時間

Lunch/午膳 11:00-14:30 (L.O.)
Dinner/晚膳 18:00-22:30 (L.O.)

■ PRICE/價錢

Lunch/午膳   set/套餐   MOP420-700
            à la carte/點菜 MOP200-800
Dinner/晚膳 set/套餐   MOP550-1,280
            à la carte/點菜 MOP200-800

Zi Yat Heen
紫逸軒

12

Conveniently located on the 1st floor of the Four Seasons Hotel Macao, Zi Yat Heen is an elegant and spacious restaurant, with a large glass-encased wine cellar at its centre. Chef Mak has created a traditional Cantonese menu but with a lighter, fresher taste by using premium ingredients and minimal seasonings. Interesting creations include the baked lamb chops with coffee sauce, while a more authentic choice would be the pigeon with Yunnan ham.

紫逸軒位於澳門四季酒店一樓，格調高雅，地方寬敞，正中位置更有大型玻璃櫃餐酒庫。大廚麥先生烹製傳統粵菜時採用最新鮮的食材與最少的調味料，帶來更鮮味清新的粵菜。有趣創作菜式包括咖啡汁焗羊排，而更傳統的選擇有酥香雲腿伴鴿脯。

■ ADDRESS/地址

TEL.2881 8888

GF, Four Seasons Hotel, Estrada da Baia de N. Senhora de Esperanca, s/n, The Cotai Strip, Taipa

氹仔路氹金光大道-望德聖母灣大馬路四季酒店地下

www.fourseasons.com/macau

■ OPENING HOURS, LAST ORDER

營業時間，最後點菜時間

Lunch/午膳 12:00-14:30 (L.O.)

Dinner/晚膳 18:30-22:30 (L.O.)

■ PRICE/價錢

Lunch/午膳	set/套餐	MOP1,288
	à la carte/點菜	MOP180-700
Dinner/晚膳	set/套餐	MOP1,288
	à la carte/點菜	MOP250-700

HOTELS
酒店

HOTELS BY ORDER OF COMFORT
酒店 — 以舒適程度分類

Pousada de São Tiago 聖地牙哥古堡 418 MAP/地圖 31/A-2

Lisboa 葡京 412 MAP/地圖 31/B-3

Rocks 萊斯 420 MAP/地圖 32/D-1

Pousada de Mong-Há 望廈賓館 416 MAP/地圖 30/C-2

Altira
新濠鋒

High quality design, a serene atmosphere and wondrous peninsula views produce something jaw-droppingly spectacular here. Guests arrive at the stylish lobby on the 38th floor; the luxury penthouse feel is enhanced by a superb lounge and terrace on the same level. Rooms, all on a lower floor, face the sea and merge tranquil tones with sheer contemporary style. As if this weren't enough, there's also a sumptuous spa boasting a pool-with-a-view.

RESTAURANTS/ 餐廳

Recommended/推薦			Also/其他
Aurora/奧羅拉	✿	✗✗✗	Kira/吉良
Tenmasa/天政		✗✗	
Ying/帝影樓		✗✗✗	

新濠鋒酒店設計獨特，舒適典雅，位處優越地段，讓澳門半島的環迴美景盡入
眼簾，令人讚嘆不已。時尚尊貴的大堂位於38樓，同層的「天宮」酒廊備有室
內酒廊及露天陽台高雅舒適，散發著豪華瑰麗的味道。客房位於其他較低樓層，
海景一望無際，寧靜感覺和現代設計相互交織，氣派超凡。此外，酒店設有豪
華的水療設施，享用服務的同時更可飽覽美景。

■ ADDRESS/地址
TEL. 2886 8888
FAX. 2886 6666
Avenida de Kwong Tung, Taipa
氹仔廣東大馬路
www.altiramacau.com

■ ROOMS AND SUITES/客房及套房
Rooms/客房 ＝184
Suites/套房 ＝32

■ PRICE/價錢

🧍	MOP5,380
🧍🧍	MOP5,380
Suites/套房	MOP8,880-12,800
☕	MOP125

Four Seasons
四季

Opened in the summer of 2008, the Four Seasons fuses East and West by blending together Colonial Portuguese and Chinese traditions. The lobby functions like a living room, with its fireplace, Portuguese lanterns and Chinese lacquer screens. The hotel also has a luxury shopping mall and connects to The Venetian and gaming at the Plaza Casino. If you want respite from the buzz and the glitz, then escape to the spa or lounge by one of five pools.

RESTAURANTS/ 餐廳

Recommended/推薦		Also/其他
Belcanção/鳴詩	✖✖	Splash/撲滿
Zi Yat Heen/紫逸軒	✿✿ ✖✖✖	Windows

2008年夏季開幕的四季融合了東方和西方元素，將殖民地時代葡萄牙與中國傳統元素融為一體。大堂有如客廳，設有壁爐、葡國燈籠和中國雕漆屏風。酒店亦設有豪華購物商場，直通威尼斯人酒店及百利沙娛樂場。如果你想從五光十色中喘息一下，可享用水療設備和五個泳池的池畔酒吧。

■ ADDRESS/地址
TEL. 2881 8888
FAX. 2881 8899
Estrada da Baia de N. Senhora de Esperanca, s/n, The Cotai Strip, Taipa
氹仔路氹金光大道-望德聖母灣大馬路
www.fourseasons.com/macau

■ ROOMS AND SUITES/客房及套房
Rooms/客房 =276
Suites/套房 =84

■ PRICE/價錢
🧍	MOP2,700-4,600
🧍🧍	MOP2,700-4,600
Suites/套房	MOP5,100-40,000
☕	MOP198

Grand Lapa
金麗華

One of the high points of this 25 year-old hotel is its staff, full of smiles and attentive to your every whim. Check in, and after a couple of hours the peaceful atmosphere induces a distinctly relaxing effect on even the most jaded guest. Rooms, of a good size and with a Portuguese slant, offer either a city or seaside and garden view, while the adjacent private resort is a hidden treasure, with a pool, Jacuzzi, tropical gardens and spa area.

RESTAURANTS/ 餐廳

Recommended/推薦		Also/其他
Naam/藍	✗✗	Café Bela Vista
Tung Yee Heen/東怡軒	✿ ✗✗✗	

酒店投入服務已有25年，過人之處首推其員工，不但笑容可掬，而且服務周到。寧靜舒適的氣氛四處洋溢，辦理登記手續後，客人很快便會感到輕鬆閒適，就算最疲倦的客人亦會頓時疲勞盡消。客房地方寬敞，設計偏重葡式，可遠眺城市美景，或欣賞園林景致及海景。至於毗鄰的私人度假中心，實在是隱秘的寶藏，設施包括泳池、水力按摩浴池、熱帶園林及水療區。

■ ADDRESS/地址
TEL. 2856 7888
FAX. 2859 4589
956-1110 Avenida da Amizade
友誼大馬路956-1110號
http://mandarinoriental.com/grandlapa/

■ ROOMS AND SUITES/客房及套房
Rooms/客房 ＝388
Suites/套房 ＝28

■ PRICE/價錢

👤	MOP2,000-3,900
👥	MOP2,000-3,900
Suites/套房	MOP5,300-28,000
☕	MOP188

Grand Lisboa
新葡京

Impossible to miss, the Grand Lisboa, opened in December 2008, can be seen from miles away with its eye-popping, brightly-lit lotus design atop a shining diamond! Opulent soundproofed bedrooms typically feature brown walls, red armchairs and Asian paintings, and offer grand sea or city vistas. If you have a corner room or a suite, you'll get the added bonus of a sauna. If you have neither corner room nor suite, you can make use of a sumptuous spa.

RESTAURANTS/ 餐廳

Recommended/推薦		Also/其他

Don Alfonso/當奧豐素	✕✕✕✕
Noodle & Congee Corner/	
粥麵莊	🍜 🥢
The Eight/8餐廳	✿ ✕✕✕
The Kitchen/大廚	✕✕

2008年12月開幕的新葡京外形像一片耀目的黃蓮葉，座落於一顆閃爍的鑽石之上，遠處可見，實在不容錯過！客房非常隔音，擁有典型的棕色牆壁、紅色扶手椅和亞洲油畫，並坐擁豪華海景或澳門的秀麗風光。角位客房及套房更設有桑拿設施，其他客房亦可享用豪華的水療設施。

■ ADDRESS/地址
TEL.2828 3838
FAX. 8803 3310
Avenida de Lisboa
葡京路
www.grandlisboa.com

■ ROOMS AND SUITES/客房及套房
Rooms/客房 ＝381
Suites/套房 ＝50

■ PRICE/價錢

🧍	MOP3,800-5,700
🧍🧍	MOP3,800-5,700
Suites/套房	MOP7,800-48,000
☕	MOP150

Lisboa
葡京

The Lisboa is one of the city's more 'traditional' hotels with its 1970s style façade providing a stark contrast to the brand new Grand Lisboa. There are 10 types of guestroom: ask for a Tower room, as these are more luxurious and larger in size than rooms in the east wing. You won't find a swimming pool, but, rather handily, you can nip over to the Grand Lisboa and use theirs.

RESTAURANTS/ 餐廳

Recommended/推薦			Also/其他
New Furusato/新故鄉		✕✕	Portas do Sol/葡京日麗
Robuchon a Galera/			
法國餐廳	❀❀❀	✕✕✕✕	
Tim's Kitchen/桃花源小廚	❀	✕✕	

葡京酒店是澳門的「傳統」酒店之一，保留著七十年代的外觀，與新落成的新葡京相映成趣。酒店共有十種客房，尊尚客房比東翼的客房更大更豪華，物有所值。雖然葡京沒有泳池，不過走到新葡京那邊使用泳池，亦十分方便快捷。

■ ADDRESS/地址

TEL.2888 3888
FAX. 2888 3838
2-4 Avenida de Lisboa
葡京路2-4號
www.hotelisboa.com

■ ROOMS AND SUITES/客房及套房
Rooms/客房 ＝876
Suites/套房 ＝50

■ PRICE/價錢

👤	MOP1,850-3,400
👥	MOP1,850-3,400
Suites/套房	MOP4,400-18,000
☕	MOP78

MGM Grand
美高梅金殿

This is one of the jewels of Macau. It's a stunning glass sky-scraper with Taipa views. The 35 floors have three distinct horizontal layers designed in chic curves – bronze, silver and gold – gold signifying the best rooms, although all are luxurious, built in a well-judged modern style with very fine materials, the huge windows proffering wow-factor views. A Chihuly glass display dominates the vast lobby; the superb spa boasts infinity pool.

RESTAURANTS/餐廳

Recommended/推薦		
Aux Beaux Arts/寶雅座		XX
Imperial Court/金殿堂		XXX
Rossio/盛事		XX
Square Eight/食 · 八方		X

Also/其他

美高梅金殿是澳門的一顆璀璨明珠。這幢摩天大樓擁有玻璃外牆，坐擁氹仔景色。樓高35層的酒店設計獨特，以波浪曲線由三種不同顏色(黃金色、白金色及玫瑰金色)的玻璃舖設外牆。黃金色部分標示著最佳的客房，但事實上所有客房都極盡奢華，以精細的物料塑造悅目的時尚風格。透過寬闊的窗戶，更將動人美景盡收眼底，令人讚嘆不已。宏偉的大堂展示著國際玻璃藝術大師Dale Chihuly的作品，星級的水療設施包括無邊際泳池。

■ ADDRESS/地址

TEL.8802 8888

FAX. 8802 1333

Avenida Dr. Sun Yat Sen, Nape

外港新填海區孫逸仙大馬路

www.mgmgrandmacau.com

■ ROOMS AND SUITES/客房及套房

Rooms/客房 =468

Suites/套房 =130

■ PRICE/價錢

👤	MOP3,200-3,800
👤👤	MOP3,200-3,800
Suites/套房	MOP7,800-9,800
☕	MOP150

Pousada de Mong-Há
望廈賓館

A very good value hotel with a distinct difference...it's run by the Institute for Tourism Studies, with a guaranteed peaceful environment away from the casinos. It's surrounded by a lovely garden, while inside, students learning their trade welcome you at the reception desk. Bedrooms are not big (especially singles), but they're quiet and feature some nice Asian touches. There's a restaurant offering a good opportunity to enjoy Macanese cuisine.

RESTAURANTS/ 餐廳

Recommended/推薦

Also/其他

IFT Educational Restaurant/
旅遊學院教學餐廳

這家超值的賓館由旅遊學院營運,位處寧靜的望廈山半山腰,遠離娛樂場的煩囂,確是與眾不同。賓館被一個可愛的花園環繞著,而接待處的學院學生則隨時為你服務。客房地方不大,尤其是單人房,不過環境寧靜,並擁有亞洲設計風格。賓館的餐廳是體驗澳門菜的好去處。

■ ADDRESS/地址
TEL.2851 5222
FAX. 2855 6925
Colina de Mong-Há, Rampe do Forte
de Mong-Há
望廈山
www.iftedu.mo

■ ROOMS AND SUITES/客房及套房
Rooms/客房 ＝16
Suites/套房 ＝4

■ PRICE/價錢

🧍	MOP500-600
🧍🧍	MOP600-800
Suites/套房	MOP1,000-1,200

Pousada de São Tiago
聖地牙哥古堡

Exquisite boutique hotel, built into the hillside on the foundations of a 17th century fort alongside traditional Portuguese villas. Atmospheric old steps lead from the entrance up to reception. By contrast, the interior is modern, chic and very stylish, with subdued taste the key. Guestrooms boast cool marble floors and rich colours and fabrics; all look onto the Straits of Macau. Discover the pool amongst charming little hillside terraces.

RESTAURANTS/ 餐廳

Recommended/推薦	Also/其他

La Paloma/芭朗瑪　　　　　　　XX

這家座落於山腰的精品酒店，精緻優雅。由一座十七世紀的舊城堡改建而成，
毗鄰傳統的葡式住宅。古樸的石階別具風情，拾級而上便可由入口到達接待處。
酒店內部與外觀形成鮮明的對比，設計十分現代時尚，獨樹一格，卻不浮誇造作。
客房採用大理石地板、鮮明的顏色和布質材料，品味非凡；所有客房都坐擁澳
門內港的醉人景色。迷人的山腰陽台設有一個戶外泳池。

■ ADDRESS/地址
TEL.2837 8111
FAX. 2855 2170
Avenida da República, Fortaleza de São
Tiago da Barra
西灣民國大馬路聖地牙哥大炮台
www.saotiago.com

■ ROOMS AND SUITES/客房及套房
Suites/套房 ＝12
■ PRICE/價錢
Suites/套房　　MOP3,200-3,500
　☕　　　　　MOP120

Rocks
萊斯

Being part of the Fisherman's Wharf, this interesting seaside hotel's ambience is inspired by the Victorian era and has a lobby full of Victorian-style décor and furnishings including fireplace, paintings, and large white marble staircase. A cosy terrace overlooks the bay, while relaxing bedrooms have a balcony and sea view. Of particular note...unlike most hotels, there's no casino here. Just right for those who prefer a quieter side of Macau.

RESTAURANTS/ 餐廳

Recommended/推薦	Also/其他
	Vic's Café/怡景

萊斯酒店座落於澳門漁人碼頭，海邊的醉人環境靈感來自維多利亞時期。酒店大堂佈滿富維多利亞風格的裝飾及傢俱，包括火爐、掛畫及大型白色雲石樓梯。舒適怡人的花園可盡收海灣醉人景致，設有海景露臺的臥室可讓你盡情放鬆身心。注意，和大部分酒店不同，這裡不設賭場，專為嚮往澳門寧靜一面的人士而設。

■ ADDRESS/地址
TEL.2878 2782
FAX. 2870 8800
Macau Fisherman's Wharf
澳門漁人碼頭
www.rockshotel.com.mo

■ ROOMS AND SUITES/客房及套房
Rooms/客房 ＝66
Suites/套房 ＝6

■ PRICE/價錢

👤	MOP1,880-2,880
👥	MOP1,880-2,880
Suites/套房	MOP4,080-6,660
☕	MOP123

Sands
金沙

This huge, bright gold building has a vast 'Sands' logo – prime Las Vegas real estate relocated in Asia. The hotel, with its own entrance and areas, is separate from the casino, though dining on the mezzanine, overlooking three vast gaming areas, resembles peering down onto a stock exchange trading floor! The spacious lobby is of western style, as are the bedrooms, which are all large and luxurious suites; each has a sea or city view.

RESTAURANTS/ 餐廳

Recommended/推薦	Also/其他
	Copa/高雅
	Golden Court/金沙閣
	Perola/金帆船

這家龐大的金沙酒店，金色外牆閃閃發亮，並擁有巨型的「金沙」霓虹燈招牌，是拉斯維加斯博彩業鉅頭於亞洲營運的娛樂場酒店。酒店與娛樂場分開，設有獨立的入口和範圍，不過在夾樓用餐時，卻可俯瞰三個大型博彩廳，恰似觀看股交所會場一般！寬敞的大堂和客房均以西式設計，所有客房都是寬闊的豪華套房，更坐擁海景或城市美景。

■ ADDRESS/地址

TEL.2888 3388
FAX. 2888 3377
203 Largo de Monte Carlo
蒙地卡羅前地203號
www.sands.com.mo

■ ROOMS AND SUITES/客房及套房
Rooms/客房 = 198
Suites/套房 = 36

■ PRICE/價錢

👤	MOP2,088-2,788
👥	MOP2,088-2,788
Suites/套房	MOP3,588-4,588
☕	MOP200

Sofitel at Ponte 16
十六浦索菲特

Swish new boutique hotel in an enviable location on the harbour front, with views reflecting the fine setting. Sofitel has a gracious feel, the rooms well appointed with a blend of brown and beige creating an atmosphere of restful chic. The good taste unites French style with soft Portuguese nuance. And for those with the ability to really splash out, there are 19 super luxury suites in a beautiful mansion next door to the main building.

RESTAURANTS/ 餐廳

Recommended/推薦	Also/其他
	Mistral

新開幕的索菲特大酒店，是時尚的精品酒店。酒店地理位置優越，海景與酒店外形相映成趣。索菲特氣派優雅，棕色和杏色的融合，為客房營造時尚悠閒之感。酒店結合了法國和葡萄牙風格，演繹高雅品味。主建築旁的漂亮大樓，設有19間貴賓豪華套房，適合高消費的客人。

■ ADDRESS/地址

TEL.8861 0016
FAX. 8861 0018
Rua do Visconde Paço de Arcos
內港巴素打爾古街
www.sofitel.com.cn

■ ROOMS AND SUITES/客房及套房

Rooms/客房 =346
Suites/套房 =44

■ PRICE/價錢

🚹	MOP1,420-2,920
🚹🚹	MOP1,420-2,920
Suites/套房	MOP3,990-4,220
☕	MOP150

StarWorld
星際

You will be impressed with the hotel's attractive glass façade, and glittery night lighting. Those who stick with Starworld will find supremely luxurious rooms, full of every mod con. They're named after the view – City, Sea or Lake – with Lake View rooms offering the best vista while the Starworld suite provides all you can imagine. The hotel also has a good selection of restaurants with Asian cuisines.

RESTAURANTS/ 餐廳

Recommended/推薦			Also/其他
Inagiku/稻菊		✗✗	Temptations/品味坊
Jade Garden/蘇浙匯	✿	✗✗	
Laurel/丹桂軒	☺	✗✗	

你會被酒店極為吸引的玻璃正門和閃爍晚間燈飾迷倒。留宿星際的貴客可享用美輪美奐的豪華套房，配備所有現代生活所需。套房根據所享景色命名——都會景、海景或湖景，提供最佳景致。星際將你的無限想像變成可能。酒店內設有一系列精選餐廳，提供亞洲名菜。

■ ADDRESS/地址
TEL.2838 3838
FAX. 2838 3888
Avenida da Amizade
友誼大馬路
www.starworldmacau.com

■ ROOMS AND SUITES/客房及套房
Rooms/客房 ＝465
Suites/套房 ＝42
■ PRICE/價錢
👤 MOP2,300-2,800
👥 MOP2,300-2,800
Suites/套房 MOP4,600-38,000

The Venetian
威尼斯人

You need a map to around the largest integrated resort in Asia! The concept is based on Venice: third floor canals feature singing gondoliers! Identikit luxury is assured in a towering bedroom skyscraper that has 3,000 capacious rooms. Opulent fakes are everywhere: frescoes, colonnades, sculptures. It's impossible to stay here without being swept along by hoards of gamblers. The Cirque de Soleil show, ZAIA, will be sure to take your breath away.

RESTAURANTS/ 餐廳

Recommended/推薦		Also/其他
Canton/喜粵	XXX	Cecconi's
Lei Garden/利苑酒家	✿ XX	Roka
Morton's of Chicago	XXX	

你需要一張地圖才能環遊全亞洲最大型的綜合度假酒店！概念源自威尼斯，三
樓運河上的貢多拉船夫更會一邊掌船一邊唱歌！高聳而立的摩天大樓擁有三千
間寬敞客房，同樣極盡奢華。壁畫、列柱、雕塑等均依照原物而製，展露豪華
氣派。置身於威尼斯人難免會到娛樂場一展身手。Cirque du Soleil®(太陽劇團
™)ZAiA™肯定會讓你屏息。

■ ADDRESS/地址

TEL. 2882 8888

FAX. 2882 8889

Estrada da Baia de N. Senhora de
Esperanca, s/n, The Cotai Strip, Taipa
氹仔路氹金光大道-望德聖母灣大馬路
www.venetianmacao.com

■ ROOMS AND SUITES/客房及套房
Rooms/客房 ＝2900
Suites/套房 ＝100

■ PRICE/價錢

👤	MOP1,400-2,000
👫	MOP1,400-2,000
Suites/套房	MOP2,500-3,500
☕	MOP200

The Westin Resort
威斯汀度假酒店

A rather stark cream pyramid in a hilly oasis a long way from the nearest casino! Its best feature is the superb vista it offers over the beach and sea to outlying islands. It also boasts a beautiful garden with attractive roofed terrace, pool and bar. A decent leisure facility and indoor pool livens up the spacious, somewhat unremarkable interior. Each bedroom has a large terrace with views, fitting compensation for the rather ordinary décor.

RESTAURANTS/ 餐廳

Recommended/推薦		Also/其他
Kwun Hoi Heen/觀海軒	✗✗✗	Café Panorama

威斯汀度假村座落於路環島，米色金字塔形的外觀頗為突出。酒店離最近的娛樂場也有一段距離，實在是城市中的綠洲！威斯汀坐擁黑沙海灘及離島的怡人海景，景致堪稱一絕。酒店亦設有漂亮的花園、迷人的有蓋露台、游泳池及酒吧。酒店內部寬敞但較不起眼，不過優良的消閒設施及室內泳池使其生色不少。所有客房均設有寬廣的美景露台，補足較為普通的裝潢設計。

■ ADDRESS/地址
TEL.2887 1111
FAX. 2887 1122
1918 Estrada de Hac Sa, Coloane
路環黑沙馬路1918號
www.westin.com/macau

■ ROOMS AND SUITES/客房及套房
Rooms/客房 =202
Suites/套房 =6

■ PRICE/價錢

♂	MOP2,200-2,700
♂♀	MOP2,300-2,700
Suites/套房	MOP5,500-25,000
☕	MOP180

Wynn
永利

The Wynn's easy-on-the-eye curving glass façade is enhanced with a lake and dancing fountains, while the classically luxurious interior includes Murano glass chandeliers, plush carpets and ubiquitous marble. An attractively landscaped oasis pool forms the centrepiece to corridors lined with the top retail names. Bedrooms – classical but contemporary - display a considerable degree of taste. The Prosperity tree, meanwhile, is not easily forgotten...

RESTAURANTS/ 餐廳

Recommended/推薦

Il Teatro/帝雅廷	✕✕✕
Okada/岡田	✕✕
Red 8/紅8	✕
Wing Lei/永利軒	✿ ✕✕✕

Also/其他

Café Esplanada/咖啡苑

永利的弧形玻璃外觀十分奪目,更設有表演湖及噴池。至於酒店內部則散發著
經典的豪華氣息:穆拉諾穆玻璃吊燈、豪華的地毯,且觸目所及皆是大理石。
走廊中心設有一個造形迷人的綠洲池,而兩旁則置滿名店。客房融合了經典和
當代的風格設計,盡顯優越品味。此外,永利的吉祥樹更會令你印象深刻。

■ ADDRESS/地址
TEL.2888 9966
FAX. 2832 9966
Rua Cidade de Sintra, Nape
外港新填海區仙德麗街
www.wynnmacau.com

■ ROOMS AND SUITES/客房及套房
Rooms/客房 ＝460
Suites/套房 ＝140

■ PRICE/價錢

👤	MOP3,300-3,700
👥	MOP3,300-3,700
Suites/套房	MOP7,800-35,000
☕	MOP168

MAPS
地圖

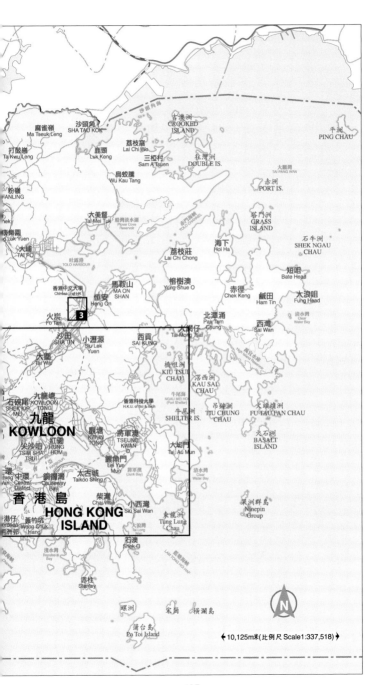

庵雀嶺 Ma Tseuk Leng
沙頭角 SHA TAU KOK
吉澳洲 CROOKED ISLAND
平洲 PING CHAU

打鼓嶺 Ta Kwu Ling
荔枝窩 Lai Chi Wo
鹿頸 Luk Keng

三椏村 Sam A Tsuen
往灣洲 DOUBLE IS.

烏蛟騰 Wu Kau Tang
粉嶺 FANLING

大龍灣 TAI PANG WAN

赤洲 PORT IS.

精樂園 o Lok Yuen

大埔 TAI PO

大美督 Tai Mei Tuk
船灣淡水湖 Plover Cove Reservoir

塔門洲 GRASS ISLAND

石牛洲 SHEK NGAU CHAU

吐露港 TOLO HARBOUR
荔枝莊 Lai Chi Chong
海下 Hoi Ha

短咀 Bate Head

香港中文大學 Chinese Uni.of HK
馬鞍山 MA ON SHAN
榕樹澳 Yung Shue O
赤徑 Chek Keng
鹹田 Ham Tin
大浪咀 Fung Head

恒安 Heng On
恒安 Heng On

北潭涌 Pak Tam Chung
西灣 Sai Wan
清水灣 Clear Water Bay

火炭 Fo Tan
3
大網仔 Tai Mong Tsai

沙田 SHA TIN
小瀝源 Siu Lek Yuen
西貢 SAI KUNG

大圍 Tai Wai
橋咀洲 KIU TSUI CHAU
滘西洲 KAU SAI CHAU

九龍塘 KOWLOON TONG
香港科技大學 H.K.U. of Sci & Tech
牛尾海 NGAU MEI HOI (Port Shelter)

石硤尾 SHEK KIP MEI
牛尾洲 SHELTER IS.
吊鐘洲 TIU CHUNG CHAU
火燒磡洲 FU TAU FAN CHAU

九龍 KOWLOON
觀塘 KWUN TONG
將軍澳 TSEUNG KWAN O

尖沙咀 TSIM SHA TSUI
紅磡 HUNG HOM
火石洲 BASALT ISLAND

大坳門 Tai Au Mun

鯉魚門 Lei Yue Mun
佛堂門 (Junk Bay)
清水灣 Clear Water Bay

中環 Central District
銅鑼灣 Causeway Bay
太古城 Taikoo Shing

香港島 HONG KONG ISLAND
柴灣 Chai Wan
小西灣 Siu Sai Wan
東龍洲 Tung Lung Chau

果洲群島 Ninepin Group

港仔 黃竹坑 Wong Chuk Hang
大潭篤
鹿頸灣 Tai Long

石澳 Shek O

淺水灣 Repulse Bay

赤柱 Stanley
LAU TONG HOI HAP

螺洲 宋崗 橫瀾島

蒲台島 Po Toi Island

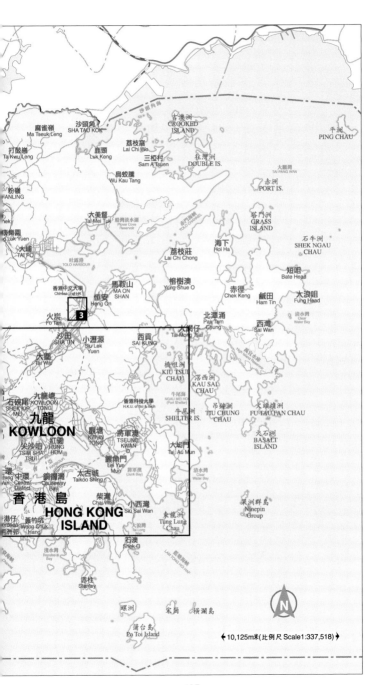 ←10,125m米(比例尺 Scale1:337,518)→ N

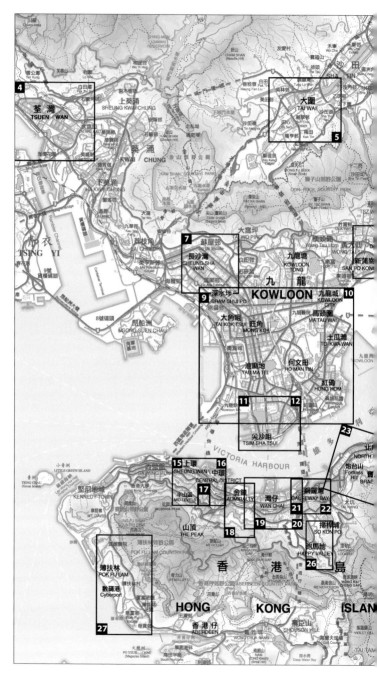

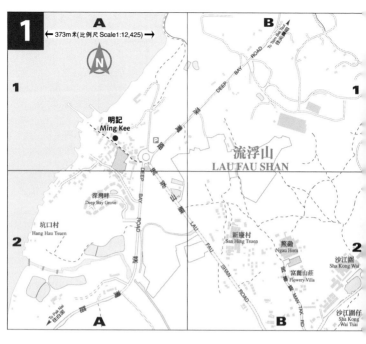

A ← 373m米(比例尺 Scale 1:12,425) →

B

DEEP BAY ROAD

To Tsim Bei Tsui
往尖鼻咀

明記
Ming Kee

流浮山
LAU FAU SHAN

深灣畔
Deep Bay Grove

DEEP BAY ROAD

坑口村
Hang Hau Tsuen

新慶村
San Hing Tsuen

牛磡
Ngau Hom

LAU FAU SHAN ROAD

NAM TAK RD

沙江園
Sha Kong Wai

富麗山莊
Flowery Villa

沙江園仔
Sha Kong Wai Tsai

To Pak Nai
往白泥

A

B

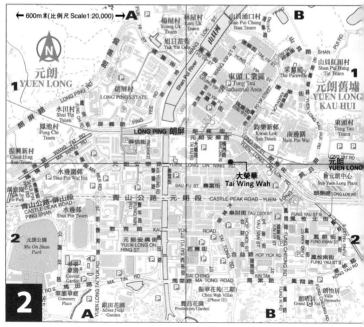

← 600m米(比例尺 Scale 1:20,000) → **A**

B

元朗
YUEN LONG

楊屋村
Yeung Uk Tsuen

林屋村
Lam Uk Tsuen

山貝涌口村
Shan Pui Chung Hau Tsuen

旭日花苑
Yuk Yat Gdn

東頭工業園
Tung Tau
Industrial Area

山貝紅田村
Shan Pui Hung
The Parkville

元朗舊墟
YUEN LONG
KAU HUI

朗屏邨
LONG PING ESTATE

Shan Pui River 山貝河

東頭村
Tung Tau
Tsuen

LONG PING ROAD

水田村
Shui Tin
Tsuen

鳳池村
Fung Chi
Tsuen

鈞樂新邨
Kwan Lok
San Tsuen

南邊圍
Nam Pin Wai

LONG PING 朗屏

振興新村
Chun Hing
San Tsuen

WANG YAT RD
MA WONG RD

LONG ON NING RD

元朗
YUEN LONG

水邊圍邨
Shui Pin Wai Est

大榮華
Tai Wing Wah

新元朗中心
Sub Yuen Long Plaza

CASTLE PEAK ROAD - YUEN

朗樂路 LONG LOK RD

青山公路-屏山段
CASTLE PEAK ROAD -
PING SHAN

水邊邨
Shui Pin Tsuen

鳳群街 FUNG KWAN ST

FUNG YAU ST N

元朗公園
Ma On Shan
Park

YUEN LONG
ON HING ST

YUK
ROAD

元朗安興街

FAU TSOI ST

HOP CHOI ST

HOP YICK RD

鳳琴街
FUNG KWAN ST

鳳攸南街
FUNG YAU S ST

MA TIN RD

西菁街
SAI CHING ST

MA TONG ROAD

鳳群花園
Chun Wah Gdn
(Phase III)

鳳翔花苑
Prettiocity Garden

翠怡花園
Covent
Garden

綠怡華庭
Greenery
Place

銀田花園
Silver Field
Garden

鳳群街
Grand Del Sol

朗明苑
Fung Ming
Villa

KIN TAK

FUNG KI RD

KONG KONG RD

A

B

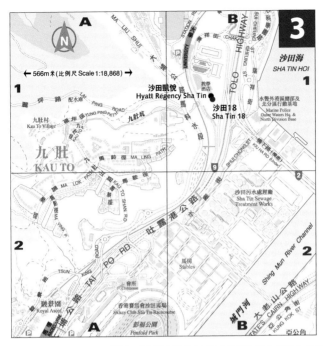

441

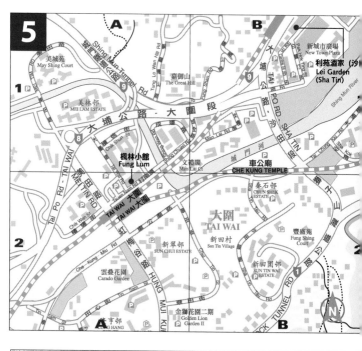

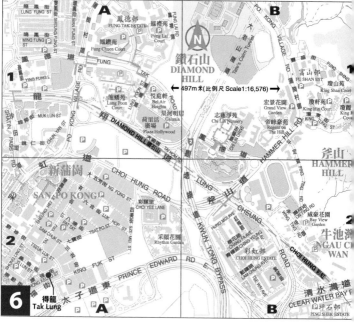

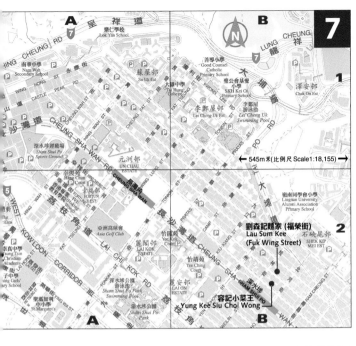

呈祥道
CHEUNG RD
樂仁學校
Lok Yan School

菁莪小學
Good Counsel Catholic Primary School
瓊公會基賢小學
SKH Kei Oi Primary School

LUNG 龍祥
CHEUNG

深安邨
Chak On Est

HING CHEUNG RD
南華中學
Nam Wah Secondary School

蘇屋邨
So Uk Est

大磡中學
Tai Hang College

大埔道
PO

李鄭屋邨
Lei Cheng Uk Est

李鄭屋游泳池
Lei Cheng Uk Swimming Pool

沙灣道 CASTLE PEAK RD

CHEUNG SHA WAN RD

深水埗運動場
Sham Shui Po Sports Ground

元洲邨
UN CHAU ESTATE

← 545m 米(比例尺 Scale1:18,155) →

CHEUNG SHA WAN RD

WEST KOWLOON CORRIDOR

興華街 HING WAH

幸俊苑
Hang Chun Court

富昌邨
FORTUN

怡閣苑
Yee Kok Court

亞洲高球會
Asia Golf Club

麗閣邨
LAI KOK ESTATE

荔枝角道 LAI CHI KOK RD

深水埗公園游泳池
Sham Shui Po Park Swimming Pool

深水埗公園
Sham Shui Po Park

怡靖苑
Yee Ching Court

麗安邨
LAI ON ESTATE

大埔道 PO

嶺南同學會小學
Lingnan University Alumni Association Primary School

石硤尾邨
SHEK KIP MEI EST

劉森記麵家 (福榮街)
Lau Sum Kee (Fuk Wing Street)

深水埗 SHAM SHUI PO

容記小菜王
Yung Kee Siu Choi Wong

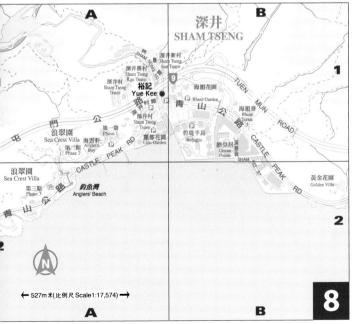

深井
SHAM TSENG

深井新村
Sham Tseng San Tsuen

深井舊村
Sham Tseng Kau Tsuen

海韻花園
Rhine Garden

TUEN MUN ROAD

屯門公路

裕記
Yue Kee

深井村
Sham Tseng Tsuen

青山公路

海韻軒
Rhine Terrace

海雲軒
Anglers' Bay

深井村
Sham Tseng Tsuen

浪翠園
Sea Crest Villa

第一期
Phase 1

第二期
Phase 2

鳳鄰花園
Lido Garden

碧堤半島
Bellagio

劉皇發
Ocean Pointe

CASTLE PEAK RD

浪翠園
Sea Crest Villa

第三期
Phase 3

釣魚灣
Anglers' Beach

青山公路

SHAM TSENG

CASTLE PEAK RD

黃金花園
Golden Villa

← 527m 米(比例尺 Scale1:17,574) →

443

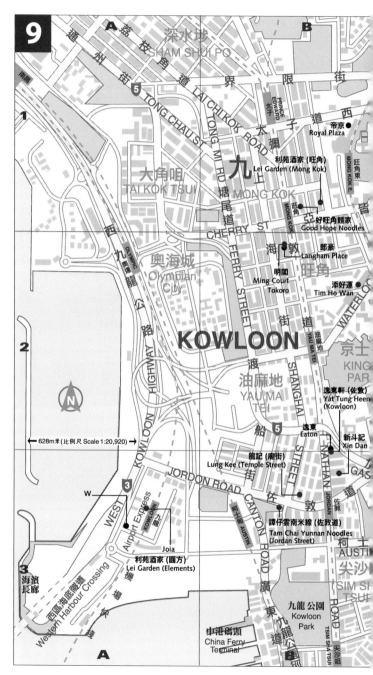

9

荔枝角道 LAI CHI KOK RD

深水埗 SHAM SHUI PO

界限街 PRINCE EDWARD 太子

通州街 TONG CHAU ST

太子道西 MONG KOK E.

帝京 Royal Plaza

九 大角咀 TAI KOK TSUI

塘尾道

旺角 MONG KOK

利苑酒家 (旺角) Lei Garden (Mong Kok)

CHERRY ST 櫻桃街

FERRY STREET 渡船街

好旺角麵家 Good Hope Noodles

海庭敦 Langham Place 朗豪

奧海城 Olympian City

OLYMPIC 奧運

九龍公路 KOWLOON HIGHWAY

明閣 Ming Court Tokoro

添好運 Tim Ho Wan

WATERLOO

KOWLOON

油麻地 YAU MA TEI

SHANGHAI STREET 上海街

京士 KING PAR

逸東軒 (佐敦) Yat Tung Heen (Kowloon)

逸東 Eaton

新斗記 Xin Dan

628米 (比例尺 Scale 1:20,920)

龍記 (廟街) Lung Kee (Temple Street)

船街

NATHAN 彌

JORDAN 佐敦

JORDON ROAD 佐敦道

WEST 西

Airport Express

KOWLOON 九龍

W

Joia

利苑酒家 (圓方) Lei Garden (Elements)

CANTON ROAD 廣東道

佐敦道 敦

譚仔雲南米線 (佐敦道) Tam Chai Yunnan Noodles (Jordan Street)

柯士甸 AUSTIN

柯士 AUSTIN

尖沙 TSIM SH TSUI

海濱長廊

西區海底隧道 Western Harbour Crossing

機場快線

申港碼頭 China Ferry Terminal

九龍公園 Kowloon Park

廣東九 道龍 TSIM SHA TSUI

BOUNDARY STREET

PRINCE EDWARD ROAD WEST

窩打

九龍醫院

馬頭圍
MA TAU WAI 道

ARGYLE STREET

龍

佛

光

街

老

道

公

街

5 1

九

龍

城

道

土瓜灣
TO KWA WAN

MA TAU WAI RD

KOWLOON CITY RD

TO KWA WAN RD

PRINCESS

FAT KWONG STREET

何文田
HO MAN TIN

5

馬

頭

圍

道

2

MARGARET

沙伯
醫院
losp

ROAD

NE ROAD

居

道

5

紅磡
HUNG HOM

香港
理工大學
Hong Kong
Polytechnic
University

都會海逸
Harbour Plaza
Metropolis

千鶴
Senzuru

香港體育館
Hong Kong Coliseum

正斗粥麵專家 (紅磡)
Tasty (Hung Hom)

黃埔花園
Whampoa
Garden

海逸
Harbour Plaza Kowloon

Harbour Grill

海逸軒
Hoi Yat Heen

HUNG HOM
紅磡

香港科學館
Hong Kong
Science Museum

CHATHAM ROAD

AD

SALISBURY RD

C 1

維多利亞港
VICTORIA HARBOUR

3

D

11

A   B

柯士甸 CANTON

AUSTIN RD W 柯士甸道西

避風塘興記
Hing Kee

港景峯
The Victoria
Towers

香港童軍
中心
HK Scout Ctr

尖沙咀警署
Tsim Sha Tsui
Police Station

1

太湖海鮮城 (尖沙咀)
Tai Woo (Tsim Sha Tsui)

室內體育館
Sports Centre

九龍公園
游泳池
Swimming Pool

聖安
St.A

標誌
Landmark
Centre -
Piece

廣東道 CANTON ROAD

中港城 China HK City

皇家太平洋
The Royal Pacific

九龍公園

栢麗購物大道
Park Lane Shopper's Boulevard

金

China Ferry Terminal
中國客運碼頭

港威大廈
Gateway

香港文物探知館
HK Heritage
Discovery Ctr

九龍公園

執加

2

翡翠拉麵小籠包 (尖沙咀)
Crystal Jade La Mian
Xiao Long Bao (TST)

林柏軒
La Brasserie

KOWLOON PARK

清真寺
Jamia Masjid
Mamie Centre

尖沙咀

海港城
HARBOUR CITY

海港 CANTON ROAD

北京道 港
World Phase I
Centre
(南段)

九龍太平洋會

鼎泰豐
Din Tai Fung

世界商業中心
World Comm Ctr

HAIPHONG RD 海防道

九龍公園
ASHLEY

清真寺

唐閣
T'ang Court

朗廷
The Langham

新港中心
Silvercord

新港中心 漢口實太陽廣場
New T&T Centre Lippo Sun Plaza

宜昌街

漢口

國際
廣場
iSquare

NATHAN ROAD

尖沙咀 TSIM SHA TSUI

HARBOUR
BOULEVARD

海洋中心
Ocean
Centre

PEKING RD 北京道

北京道1號
1 Peking Rd

漢口
中心
Hankow
Ctr

八月居
House of Jasmine

Spasso

胡同
Hutong

3

馬哥孛羅
Marco Polo

海運大樓
Ocean Terminal

Cucina

BLT Steak

夜上海 (九龍)
Yè Shanghai (Kowloon)

星光行
Star House

王子飯店
Prince

北京樓 (九龍)
Peking Garden
(Kowloon)

香港文化中心
HK Cultural Centre

半島
The Peninsula

瑞樵閣
Chesa

吉地士
Gaddi's

嘉麟樓
Spring Moon

香港太空館
HK Space Museum

香港藝術館
HK Museum of

旅客諮詢中心
Visitor Info Centre

往中環
To Central

天星碼頭
Star Ferry Pier

往灣仔
To Wan Chai

鐘樓 Clock Tower

九龍公眾碼頭
Kowloon Public Pier

尖沙咀
TSIM SHA TSUI

← 250m米 (比例尺 Scale 1:8,333) →

A   B

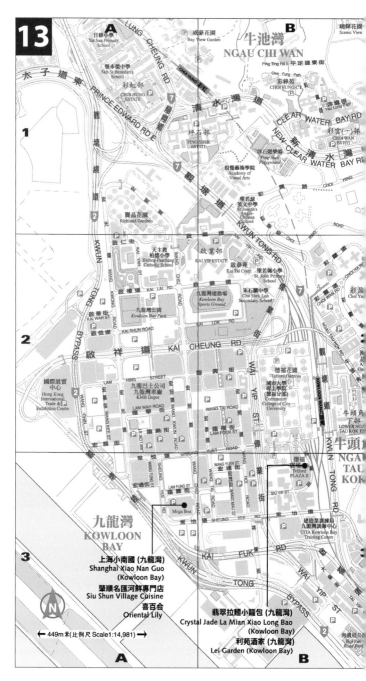

日修小學
Yat Sau Primary School

威豪花園
Bay View Garden

A

B

曉景花園
Scenic View

牛池灣
NGAU CHI WAN

聖本篤中學
Skh St Benedict's School

Ping Ting Rd E 平定道東街

彩霞道E

彩絲苑
CHOI FUNG CT.

太子道東
PRINCE EDWARD RD E

彩虹邨
CHOI HUNG ESTATE

清水灣道

CLEAR WATER BAY RD

滿田 Wan Fung Wai
滿福
滿福

坪石邨
PING SHEK ESTATE

新清水灣道
NEW CLEAR WATER BAY RD

1

彩雲(一)邨
CHOI WAN EST(1)

觀塘道

P
坪石遊樂場
Ping Shek Playground

彩虹
CHOI HUNG

麗晶花園
Richland Gardens

視覺藝術學院
Academy of Visual Arts

聖若瑟
英文中學
St Joseph's Anglo-Chinese School

啟仁街

2

啟德大
KWUN TONG

天主教
柏德小學
Bishop Paschang Catholic School

啟業邨
KAI YIP ESTATE

啟泰苑
Kai Tai Court

聖若翰小學
St John Primary School

朱石麟中學
Chu Shek Lun Secondary School

7

彩盈
Choi Ying

九龍灣運動場
Kowloon Bay Sports Ground

BYPASS

啟禮街 KAI LAI RD

啟業街 KAI WAH ST

九龍灣公園
Kowloon Bay Park

P

P

啟信街 KAI SHUN ROAD

啟樂街 KAI LOK ST

啟祥道 KAI CHEUNG RD

偉業街 WAI YIP ST

觀塘道

德福花園
Telford Gardens

P

城市大學
專上學院
(德福分部)
Community College of City University

牛頭角
LOWER NGAU TAU KOK EST

2

國際展貿
中心
Hong Kong International Trade & Exhibition Centre

宏光道 WANG KWONG RD

宏泰道 WANG TAI ROAD

宏照道 WANG CHIU RD

宏開道 WANG HOI RD

臨興街 LAM HING STREET

九龍巴士公司
九龍灣車廠
KMB Depot

臨華街 LAM WAH ROAD

臨樂街 LAM KWUN ROAD

宏泰道 WANG TAI ROAD

臨福街 LAM FOOK ST

臨豐街

臨澤街

偉業街 WAI YIP ST

觀塘道 KWUN TONG BYPASS

牛頭角
NGAU TAU KOK

2

德福
廣場II
Telford PLAZA II

宏遠街

宏基街 WANG KEE ST

宏通街

宏遠街 WANG YUEN ST

臨豐街 LAM FUNG ST

宏泰道 WANG TAI RD

常怡街 SHEUNG YEE ST

小業街 SIU YIP ST

建造業訓練局
九龍灣訓練中心
CITA Kowloon Bay Training Centre

九龍灣
KOWLOON BAY

P

Mega Box

常悅道 SHEUNG YUET RD

上海小南國 (九龍灣)
Shanghai Xiao Nan Guo
(Kowloon Bay)

3

肇順名匯河鮮專門店
Siu Shun Village Cuisine

喜百合
Oriental Lily

觀塘
KWUN

啟福道 KAI FUK RD

常怡道 SHEUNG YEE RD

常悅道

常和道

觀塘道 KWUN TONG BYPASS

海濱道公園
Hoi Bun Road Park

2

← 449m米(比例尺 Scale1:14,981) →

翡翠拉麵小籠包 (九龍灣)
Crystal Jade La Mian Xiao Long Bao
(Kowloon Bay)

利苑酒家 (九龍灣)
Lei Garden (Kowloon Bay)

A

B

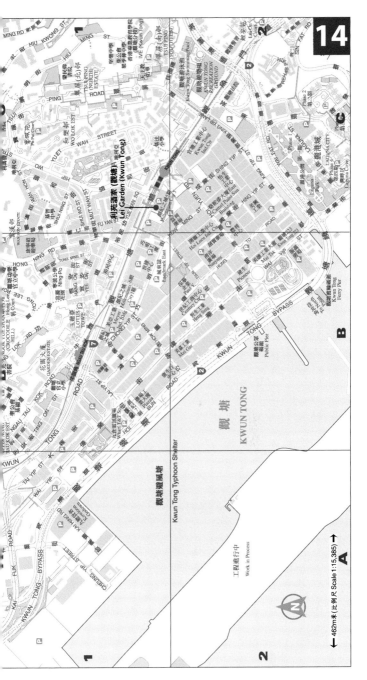

利庄亞家 (觀塘)
Lei Garden (Kwun Tong)

觀塘 KWUN TONG

觀塘避風塘
Kwun Tong Typhoon Shelter

工程進行中
Work in Process

←462m米 (比例尺 Scale 1:15,385)→

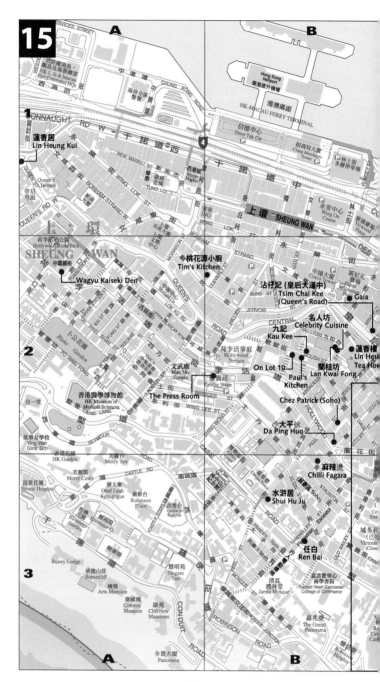

SERVICES STREET

消防機構總部
艦隊及海務總部
HK. I. s & Marine
Fire Command HQ.

中港道
CHUNG KONG ROAD

海務分區署
西消防

Hong Kong
Helliport
香港直升機場

港澳碼頭
HK-MACAU FERRY TERMINAL

1

CONNAUGHT RD W — 干諾道西

蓮香居
Lin Heung Kui

信德中心
Shun Tak Ctr

China Merchants
Tower

林士街
多層停車場

Queen's
Terrace
帝后
樓

NEW-MARKET ST 新街市街

西港城
Western
Market

WING LOK ST

BONHAM STRAND W

永
樂
街

永安中心
Wing On
Centre

WING LOK
永樂

上 環

干諾道中

上環 SHEUNG WAN

QUEEN'S RD W

WING
NAM

永安中心
Wing On
Centre

DES

SHEUNG WAN

荷李活道公園
Hollywood Road Park

桃花源小廚
Tim's Kitchen

STRAND

承

樂
街

中遠大廈
Cosco Tower

新紀元廣場
Grand
Millennium

Wagyu Kaiseki Den

QUEEN'S

JERVOIS

ROAD

沽仔記 (皇后大道中)
Tsim Chai Kee
(Queen's Road)

CENTRAL

Gaia

九記
Kau Kee

名人坊
Celebrity Cuisine

蓮香樓
Lin Heu
Tea Ho

Blake
Garden

荷李活華庭
Hollywood
Terrace

2

文武廟
Man Mo
Temple

On Lot 10

蘭桂坊
Lan Kwai Fong

Paul's
Kitchen

Centre Stage

The Press Room

Chez Patrick (Soho)

香港醫學博物館
HK Museum of
Medical Sciences

大平伙
Da Ping Huo

英華女學校
Ying Wah
Girls' Sch

SEYMOUR

CAINE

麻辣燙
Chilli Fagara

香港花園
HK Garden

美麗閣
Merry Terr

雅麗台
Merry Court

CASTLE RD

衛城道

水滸居
Shui Hu Ju

富景花園
Scenic Heights

Obel Leah
Synagogue

雅景台
Robinson
Place

景台
Goldwin
Heights

ROBINSON

任白
Ren Bai

逸廬
Excelsior Ct

慧雅苑
Elegant
Terr

3

Buxey Lodge

承德山莊
Scenecliff

清真寺拜堂
Jamia Mosque

嘉諾撒聖心
商學書院
Sacred Heart Canossian
College of Commerce

康威園
Conway
Mansion

Arts Mansion

康苑
Cliffview
Mansions

CONDUIT

全景大廈
Panorama

ROBINSON

The Grand
Panorama

ROAD

A

B

中環（中區）
CENTRAL DISTRICT

The Lounge
Caprice
稻菊 (國際金融中心)
Inagiku (IFC)
龍景軒
Lung King Heen

1號碼頭 Pier 1

2號碼頭 Pier 2

3號碼頭 Pier 3

4號碼頭 Pier 4

5號碼頭 Pier 5

6號碼頭 Pier 6

7號碼頭 Pier 7

往珀麗灣 To Park Island

往愉景灣 To Discovery Bay

往榕樹灣 To Yung Shue Wan

往索罟灣 To So Kwu Wan

往長洲 To Cheung Chau

往坪洲 To Ping Chau

往梅窩 To Mui Wo

往尖沙咀 To Tsim Sha Tsui

國金軒
Cuisine Cuisine
Harlan's
H One
Isola
利苑酒家 (國際金融中心)
Lei Garden (IFC)
正斗粥麵專家 (國際金融中心)
Tasty (IFC)

天星碼頭
Star Ferry Pier

四季
Four Seasons

麥奀記（忠記）麵家（永吉街）
Mak An Kee Noodle
(Wing Kut Street)

Watermark

國際金融中心商場
IFC Mall

國際金融中心
一期
Intern'l Finance
Centre

國際金融中心二期
Two International
Finance
Centre

HONG KONG

Agnès b. Le Pain Grillé (Central)

中環中心
The Center

Gusto

洞庭樓 (中環)
Hunan Garden
(Central)

交易廣場
Exchange
Square

翠玉軒
The Square

文華扒房＋酒吧
Mandarin Grill + Bar

文華廳
Man Wah

Pierre

文華東方
Mandarin Oriental

CENTRAL
中環

Harvey Nichols
Zuma

北京樓 (中環)
Peking Garden (Central)

L'Atelier de
Joël Robuchon

Dot Cod

Amber

港島廳
Island Tang

置地文華東方
The Landmark
Mandarin Oriental

451

沾仔記 (威靈頓街)
Tsim Chai Kee (Wellington St)

麥奕雲吞麵世家
Mak's Noodle

蛇王芬
Ser Wong Fun

黃色門廚房
Yellow Door Kitchen

Café Siam

Tandoor

陸羽茶室
Luk Yu Tea House

なお膳
Naozen

Goccia

DiVino

鏞記 (中環)
Yung Kee (Central)

客家爺爺
Hakka Yé Yé

Union J

壽司喰
Sushi Kuu

Va Bene

Tuscany by H

蘭桂坊
LKF

雲府
Yun Fu

環貿
Universal Trade

會督府

HKC Hospital

Church Guest Hse

天主教總堂
Rome Catholic Cathedral

聖母無原罪堂

明愛大廈
Caritas House

宏基國際賓館

Central Police Station (Closed)
中區警署 (已停用)

域多利監獄 (已停用)
Victoria Prison (Closed)

中央廣場
The Centrium

Man Yee Building

POTTINGER ST
QUEEN'S RD C
STANLEY ST
WELLINGTON ST
LYNDHURST TERR
GAGE ST
GRAHAM ST
GUTZLAFF ST
COCHRANE ST
Pedestrian Escalator
HOLLYWOOD RD
OLD BAILEY ST
CHANCERY L
WYNDHAM ST
D'AGUILAR ST
LAN KWAI FONG
ARBUTHNOT RD
CAINE RD
GLENEALY
UPPER ALBERT RD
LOWER ALBERT RD
ALBANY RD

← 98m 米 (比例尺 Scale 1:3,250)

← 250m米 (比例尺 Scale 1:8,333) →

A　施工中 中環填海計劃第三期 Central Reclamation Phase 3 In Progress

B

N

EDINBURGH PLACE

LUNG WUI RD. 龍匯道

大會堂 CITY HALL

中國軍部 Central Barracks

中環軍部

1

分域碼頭 Fenwick Pier

干諾道中

夏慤道

CHATER RD.

和記大廈 Hutchison House

紫玉蘭 Shanghai Garden

美國銀行中心 Bank of America Tower

LAMBETH WALK

車昌道 Fairmont House

中信大廈 Citic Tower

紅十字會總部 HK Red Cross Headquarters

FENWICK PIER ST.

ARSENAL ST.

MURRAY RD.

HARCOURT 夏慤道 ROAD

金鐘道

力寶大廈II Lippo Tw II

力寶中心 Lippo Centre

ADMIRALTY

海富中心 Admiralty Centre

金鐘

金鐘廊 Queensway Plaza

夏慤花園 Harcourt Garden

堅偉樓 Caine House

警察大樓 Arsenal House

警察總部 Police Headquarters

警政大樓東翼 Police HQ East Wing

中銀大廈 Bank of China Tower

TREE DRIVE

銀行廣場 Bank Plaza

茶具文物館 Museum of Tea Ware

力寶軒 Lippo Chiuchow

力寶大廈I Lippo Tw I

統一中心 United Ctr

太古廣場 PACIFIC PLACE

QUEENSWAY

COTTON

羅桂祥茶藝館 KC Lo Gallery

高等法院 High Court

夜上海 (金鐘) Yè Shanghai (Admiralty)

QUEEN'S ROAD EAST

皇后大道東

2

香港公園 HONG KONG PARK

Park Plaza

政府合署 Queensway Govt Offices

Domani

萬豪殿 Man Ho

北京樓 (金鐘) Peking Garden (Admiralty)

2

中國會 China Club

KENNEDY RD.

SUPREME COURT RD.

港島香格里拉大 Island Shangri-La

港麗 Conrad

Roka

采蝶軒 Zen

STAR ST.

MONMOUTH TERRACE

龍蝦吧 Lobster Bar and Grill

JUSTICE DRIVE

萬豪 JW Marriott

Thai Basil

珀翠 Petrus

夏宮 Summer Palace

英國文化協會 British Council

英國總領事館 British Consulate

金葉庭 Golden Leaf

意寧谷 Nicholini's

BOWEN ROAD

KENNEDY ROAD

FOREST

ROBBETT ROAD

BOWEN ROAD

實雲道遊樂場

BOWEN ROAD

港燈中心 HK Electric Ctr

BOWEN DRIVE

港島學校 Island School

3

Island Club

3

Magazine Gap Towers

馬己仙 Magazine Heights

MAGAZINE GAP ROAD

甘道花園

PEAK ROAD

A

B

A

B

↑ N

← 236米(比例尺 Scale 1:7,851) →

1

博覽海濱花園
Expo Promenade

金紫
Golden Bauhi

博　覽　道

香港會議展覽中心
新翼
HKCEC New Wing

香港貿易
發展局
HK Trade
Development
Council

EXPO. DRIVE. CENT

博　覽　中

滿福樓 (灣)
Dynasty (Wan Ch

EXPO. DRIVE

Grissini
港灣壹號
One Harbour Road

君悅
Grand Hyatt

CONVENTION

分域碼頭
Fenwick Pier

LUNG KING ST.

會　議　道

香港會議展覽中心
HK Convention &
Exhibition Centre

十八溪
Eighteen Brook

中信大廈
Citic Tower

紅十字會
總部
HK Red Cross
Headquarters

FENWICK PIER ST.

分域碼頭街

香港演藝學院
HK Academy
for Performing Arts

香港
藝術中心
HK
Art Centre

瑞安中心
Shui On Centre

灣仔政府大樓
Wanchai
Tower

港灣消防局

入境事
務大樓
Immigration
Tower

中環廣
Central Pl

夏愨道

電訊大廈
Telecom House

稅務大樓
Revenue
Tower

留園雅敍
Liu Yuan Pavilion

華氏粵菜軒
Che's

告士打道

GLOU

2

夏愨花園
Harcourt Garden

堅偉樓
Caine House

警察大樓
Arsenal House

警察總部
Police Headquarters

警政大樓東翼
Arsenal House
East Wing

美國萬通大廈
Mass Mutual Tower

夏愨大廈
Harcourt House

東亞銀行
港灣中心
Bank of
East Asia

祥記飯店
Cheung Kee

大新金
Dah Sing
Finan

照記
Asian

分域街

溫莎公
Windsor
House

押永華雲吞麵家
Wing Wah

生記道
Sang Kee

布

QUEENSWAY

軒尼詩道

Uno Más

灣　仔　道

WAN CHAI

中環海外

灣仔 WAN CHAI

正　義　道

囍宴 甜·藝
Xi Yan Sweets

Cépage

Cinecitta

1/5 Nuevo

Chez Patrick
(Wan Chai)

STAR ST.

東美中心

SUN ST.

LUN FAT ST.

GRESSON ST.

福臨門 (灣仔)
Fook Lam Moon (Wan Chai)

帝后殿
Queen's Palace

LUARD

譚魚頭火鍋 (灣仔)
Tanyoto Hotpot
(Wan Chai)

South
Southern
Centre

THOMSON RD.

SHIP ST.

SWATOW ST.

一碗麵 (聖佛蘭士街)
Olala (St. Francis Street)

洪聖廟

Bo Innovation

GLOUCESTER RD.

JAFFE RD.

LOCKHART RD.

HENNESSY RD.

CROSS ST.

AMOY ST.

LEE TUNG ST.

祇月
Ovologue
The Pawn

灣仔街
Da

KENNEDY

寶雲道
兒童遊樂場

ROAD

聖佛蘭士
Canossian
聖諾瑟書院灣仔各分部

St. Francis
Canossian

BOWEN ROAD

QUEEN'S

合和中心
Hopewell Ctr

胡忠大廈
Wu Chung Hse

WU CHUNG FONG TERR

香港
華仁書院

3

寶雲道
網球場

BOWEN DRIVE

道

A

B

灣仔渡輪碼頭
Wan Chai Ferry Pier

灣仔海濱長廊
Wan Chai Waterfront Promenade

逸東軒 (灣仔)
Yat Tung Heen (Wan Chai)

中心
Eagle
Centre

海港中心
Harbour Centre

HARBOUR

ROAD

香港
展覽
中心
HK
Exhibition
Centre

港灣道花園

華潤大廈
China Resources
Building

新鴻基
中心
Sun Hung
Kai Centre

灣仔運動場
WAN CHAI
SPORTS GROUND

GLOUCESTER

富發
Fu Sing

利苑酒家 (灣仔)
Lei Garden (Wan Chai)

HARBOUR DRIVE

ROAD

灣仔警署
Wanchai
Police Station

諾富特世紀
Novotel Century

楊記麵家
Yeung's Noodle

HENNESSY ROAD

翡翠拉麵小籠包 (灣仔)
Crystal Jade La Mian Xiao
Long Bao (Wan Chai)

杭州酒家
Hang Zhou

律敦治醫院
Ruttonjee Hospital

灣仔公園
Wan Chai Park

WAN CHAI

摩利臣山游泳池
Morrison Hill
Swimming Pool

摩理臣山
MORRISON HILL

SKH Tang Shiu Kin

伊利沙伯
體育館
QE Stadium

悅悅
Cosmo

麗都
Cosmopolitan

育馬博物館
Racing Museum

香港足球會球場
HKFC Soccer/Rugby Field

馬會總部
HKJC
Headquarters

EAST

循道衛理
Methodist
Church

香港華仁書院
Wah Yan Coll, HK

AIA
友邦大廈

高主教書院
回教墳場
MUSLIM CEMETERY

A

B

海底隧道

N

← 161m米 (比例尺 Scale 1:5,376) →

1

奇力島
KELLETT ISLAND

臨時直升機坪

香港遊艇會
Royal
HK Yacht Club

At Corner
功德林 (銅鑼灣)
Kung Tak Lam (Causeway B.

警官俱樂部
Police
Officers Club

上海綠楊邨
Shanghai Lu Yang Cu

灣仔海濱長廊

Waterfront Promenade

HUNG HING RD

Wan Chai

CROSS HARBOUR TUNNEL

WAN SHING ST

R

CANNON ST

MARSH RD

告

士

翠園 (駱克道)
Jade Garden (Lockhart Road)

信和廣場
Sino

鵬利中心

ROAD

富臨
Forum

壽司翔太
Sushi Shota

ROAD

銅鑼灣

2

GLOUCESTER

ROAD

伊利莎伯大廈
Elizabeth House

JAFFE

銅鑼灣廣場

LOCKHART

PERCIVAL STREET

蛇王二
Se Wong Yee

D17

太湖海鮮城 (銅鑼灣)
Tai Woo (Causeway Bay)

道

克

西

東

道

波

TANG LUNG ST

太平館 (銅鑼灣)
Tai Ping Koon (Causeway Ba

RUSSELL ST

KAI

池記
Chee Kei

LEE

道

尼

軒

詩

駱

洞庭樓 (銅鑼灣)
Hunan Garden (Causeway Bay)

WEST

EAST

金滿庭 (銅鑼灣)
Modern China (Causeway Bay)

何洪記
Ho Hung Kee

3

MORRISON HILL

灣仔道

TIN LOK LN

渣甸坊

堅拿道

山葵
Wasabisabi

SHARP

湘江 (銅鑼灣)
Wu Kong Shanghai (Causeway Bay)

EAST

禮頓中心
Leighton Cr

伊斯蘭中心

觀群商業大廈
Guardian
House

BOWRINGTON

CANAL

SHARP ST W

CANAL

渣甸東街

羅素街

渣甸坊

YIU WA ST

MATHESON

渣華道

LEIGHTON

ROAD

禮頓山
LEIGHTON

A

B

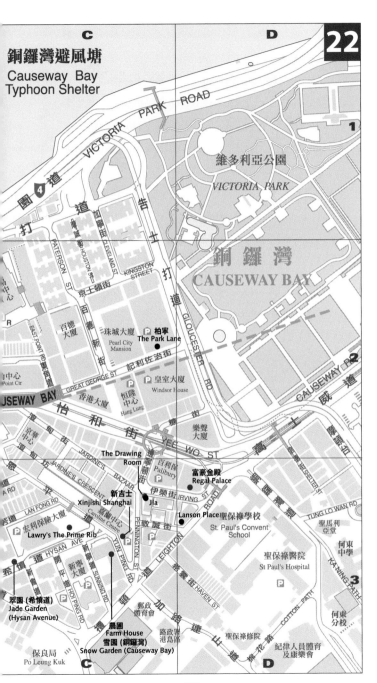

銅鑼灣避風塘
Causeway Bay
Typhoon Shelter

VICTORIA PARK ROAD

維多利亞公園
VICTORIA PARK

園 4 道

打 士

告 告 士 打 道

PATERSON ST

加路連山道 CLEVELAND ST

傳諾衛 HOUSTON 頓街

KINGSTON STREET

京士頓街

GLOUCESTER RD

銅 鑼 灣
CAUSEWAY BAY

EAST POINT RD 東角道

R

百德
大廈
Pearl City
Mansion

珠城大廈
新街

百德新街

記利佐治街

P 柏寧
The Park Lane

CAUSEWAY RD 威道

USEWAY BAY

中心
Point Ctr

P 皇室大廈
Windsor House

GREAT GEORGE ST

香港大廈

恒隆
中心
Hang Lung

怡 和 街

YEE WO ST

樂聲
大廈

渣甸坊 JARDINE'S BAZAAR

記利佐治街

高士威道 SHELTER

TUNG LO WAN RD

The Drawing
Room

百利保
Palibury

富豪金殿
Regal Palace

松街 JARDINE'S CRESCENT

渣甸坊

寶靈頓道

新吉士
Xinjishi Shanghai

嘉蘭中心
Caroline Centre

伊榮街 IRVING ST

Jia

LAN FONG RD

宏利保險大廈

敬誠街

Lanson Place 聖保祿學校
St. Paul's Convent
School

聖馬利
亞堂

Lawry's The Prime Rib

P

KA NING PATH

何東
中學

HYSAN AVE 道

新寧
大廈

SUNNING RD

YUN PING RD

LEIGHTON 道

聖保祿醫院
St Paul's Hospital

P

何東
分校

翠園 (希慎道)
Jade Garden
(Hysan Avenue)

P

HOI PING RD

禮頓道

禮頓道

加路連山道

HAVEN ST

COTTON PATH

農圃
Farm House
雪園 (銅鑼灣)
Snow Garden (Causeway Bay)

郵政
體育會

路政署
港島區

聖保祿修院

保良局
Po Leung Kuk

紀律人員體育
及康樂會

C D

23

北角
NORTH POINT

北角渡輪碼頭
North Point Ferry Pier

1

← 313m米 (比例尺 Scale 1:10,417) →

維多利亞港
VICTORIA HARBOUR

WEST EMBANKMENT

HARBOUR
PARADE

阿鴻小吃
Hung's Delicacies

加藤壽司
Sushi Kato

利苑酒家 (北角)
Lei Garden (North Point)

城市花園
City Garden

電燈中心
The Electric
Centre

2

摩天大廈
Sky Scraper

珊瑚閣
Coral Court

富澤園
Beverly
Height

峰景大廈
Hilltop

海峰園
Harbour Heights

弘利保險中心
Manulife
Tower

海峰大廈
Manulife
Tower

香港城市大學
Shue Yan
University

雅景台
Braemar
Heights

海景閣
Seaview
Garden

雲景台
Evelyn
Towers

Victoria Cntr

2

WATSON RD

Belilios
Pub Sch

東院李鄭田
Lee Ching Dea
Mem Col

星悅 (天后)
Empire (Tin Hau)

北角官立
(雲景路)

北角協同
Concordia
Lutheran Sch

留家廚房
Kin's Kitchen

3

維多利亞公園游泳池
Victoria Park
Swimming Pool

柏景臺
Park Tower

維多利亞公園
VICTORIA PARK

金鑾大廈
Dragon
Court

銅鑼灣維景 (銅鑼灣)
Metropark (Causeway Bay)

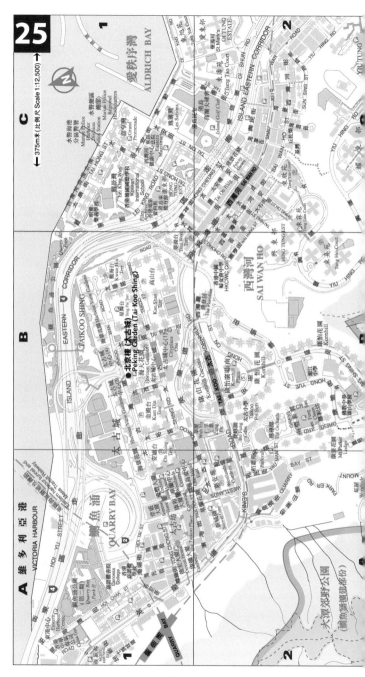

禮頓山
Leighton Hill

加路連山
CAROLINE HILL

掃桿埔
SO KON
RECREATION GROUND

LEIGHTON HILL RD

連道

CAROLINE HILL ROAD

加路連山道

WONG NAI CHUNG RD

黃泥涌道

BROADWOOD RD
樂活道

HAPPY VIEW TERRACE

聖瑪加利教堂
St Margaret's

南華體育會
南華體育會運動場
SOUTH CHINA ATHLETIC
ASSN STADIUM

印度遊樂會

東院道

EASTERN HOSPITAL ROAD

1

比華利山
Beverly Hill

臺山村道

聖保祿天主教

Winfield Bldg

孔聖堂
Confucius Hall

奧運大樓
Olympic House

樂翠台
Villa Rocha

跑馬場遊樂場
HAPPY VALLEY
RECREATION GROUND

聖保祿中學
St.Paul's
Sec Sch

香港三育中學

雲地利台
Villa Lotto

樂陶苑
Villa Lotto

掃桿埔
SO KON PO

← 234米(比例尺 Scale 1:7,463) →

跑馬地
HAPPY VALLEY

VENTRIS ROAD

源公廟

BROADWOOD ROAD

N

2

養和醫院
K.Sanatorium
& Hospital

正斗粥麵專家 (跑馬地)
Tasty (Happy Valley)

YIK YAM ST
奕蔭街

KING KWONG ST
景光街

成和道

YUK SAU ST
毓秀街

HIP WO LANE

SING WOO ROAD

駿業台

Valley
View
Terr

皇駿景
e Emperor

山村道

景光街

TSUI MAN ST
聚文街

SHAN KWONG RD
山光道

譽滿坊
Dim Sum

SING WOO

藍塘道

BLUE POOL ROAD

3

駿景軒
Golden Valley

WANG TAK ST

VILLAGE TERR

山光苑
Shan Kwong
Towers

東蓮覺苑

KWAI FONG ST

跑馬地警署

SING WOO ROAD

永光坊

STUBBS

ROAD

司徒拔道

ROAD

SHAN KWONG ROAD

猶太墳場
JEWISH
CEMETERY

HAWTHORN RD

賽馬會體育綜合大樓

藍塘別墅

冬青道 HOLLY RD

賽馬會會所
Jockey Club
Clubhouse

寶璧坊
GREEN LANE

玫瑰新邨
Villa Monte Rosa

A

B

461

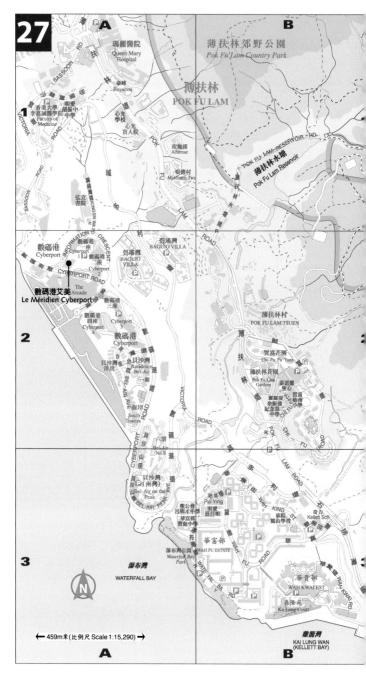

A

瑪麗醫院
Queen Mary Hospital

SASSOON RD

豪峰
Royalton

薄扶林郊野公園
Pok Fu Lam Country Park

B

薄扶林
POK FU LAM

香港大學
李嘉誠醫學院
Faculty of Medicine

明愛胡振中中學

心光學校
心光盲人院

POK FU LAM ROAD

VICTORIA ROAD

玫瑰邨
Alberose

POK FU LAM RESERVOIR RD.

薄扶林水塘
Pok Fu Lam Reservoir

KONGSIN WEST CRESCENT

弘立書院

明德村
Middleton Twr

1

數碼港
Cyberport

INFORMATION

數碼港二座
Cyberport

碧瑤灣
BAGUIO VILLA

薄扶林村
POK FU LAM TSUEN

CYBERPORT ROAD

數碼港艾美
Le Méridien Cyberport

The Arcade

數碼港一座
Cyberport

碧瑤灣
BAGUIO
VILLA

賈富花園
Chi Fu Fa Yuen

數碼港四座
Cyberport

數碼港三座
Cyberport

薄扶林花園
Pok Fu Lam Gardens

聖嘉勒
聖心
余振強
紀念第二中學
賈富南華中學

2

數碼港
Cyberport

貝沙灣洋房
Bel-Air

VICTORIA ROAD

POK FU LAM ROAD

CHI FU ROAD

貝沙灣三期
Residence Bel-Air

南岸
South Towers

CYBERPORT ROAD

BEL-AIR AVE

貝沙灣道

六期
Bel-Air No.8

WAH KING ST

培英
Pui Ying

奇力灣
Kellett Bay

Kellett Sch

貝沙灣（南灣）
山Bel-Air on the Peak

BEL-AIR PEAK AVE

聖公會
呂明才中學
明愛
莊月明中學
華富邨
寶血小學

WAH FU ROAD

東華三院
鶴山學校

WAH KWAI EAST

布廠道

瀑布灣公園
Waterfall Bay Park

華富邨
WAH FU ESTATE

華貴邨
WAH KWAI EST

3

瀑布灣
WATERFALL BAY

嘉隆苑
Ka Lung Court

WAH FU BA RD

WAH KWAI RD

N

← 459m米 (比例尺 Scale 1:15,290) →

雞籠灣
KAI LUNG WAN
(KELLETT BAY)

A

B

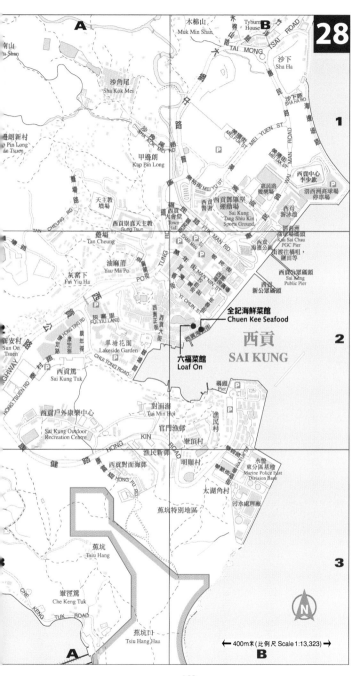

南山
a Shan

木棉山
Muk Min Shan

Tyburn
House

B

沙下
Sha Ha

沙角尾
Sha Kok Mei

TAI MONG TSAI ROAD

沙下海道場路

蠄蟛朗新村
p Pin Long
an Tsuen

甲蠄朗
Kap Pin Long

MEI YUEN ST

MEI YUEN ST

惠民路遊樂場

西貢中心李少欽

潛西洲高球場停車場

1

天主教墳場

西貢崇真天主教堂

西貢警署

西貢鄧肇堅運動場
Sai Kung
Tang Shiu Kin
Sports Ground

西貢游泳池

海球場碼頭
Kai Chau PGC Pier

西貢海濱公園

渡往糧船灣，鹽田等

TAN CHEUNG ROAD

疊場
~ Tan Cheung

油麻莆
Yau Ma Po

FUK MAN RD

POI TUNG ROAD

萬年街 MAN NIN ST

西貢大街

義民街

PUI MAN ST

YI CHUN ST

西貢公眾碼頭
Sai Kung
Public Pier

西貢公眾碼頭

灰窰下
Fui Yiu Ha

灰窰里
FUI YIU LANE

全記海鮮菜館
Chuen Kee Seafood

西貢 SAI KUNG

2

新安村
Sun On
Tsuen

SAI KUNG HONG TSUEN RD 崇正里

翠塘花園
Lakeside Garden

CHUI TONG ROAD

六福菜館
Loaf On

碼頭
Pier

西貢篤
Sai Kung Tuk

對面海
Tui Min Hoi

西貢戶外康樂中心
Sai Kung Outdoor
Recreation Centre

HONG KIN ROAD

官門漁邨

漁民村

水警東分區基地
Marine Police East
Division Base

HONG TSUEN HIGHWAY

西貢對面海邨

漁民新邨

墾頂村

明順村

太湖角村

污水處理廠

蕉坑特別地區

3

蕉坑
Tsiu Hang

CHE KENG TUK ROAD

崔徑篤
Che Keng Tuk

N

蕉坑叶
Tsiu Hang Hau

←400m米(比例尺 Scale 1:13,323)→

A

B

463

MACAU
澳門

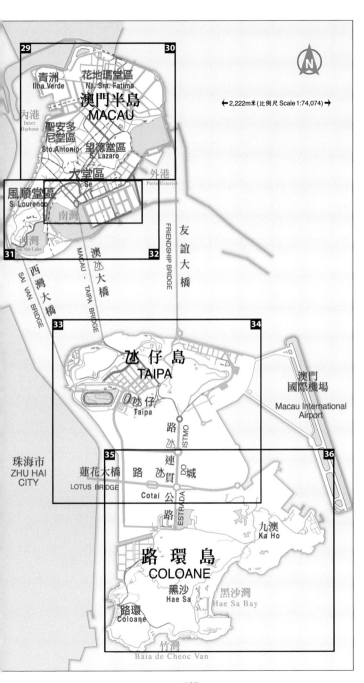

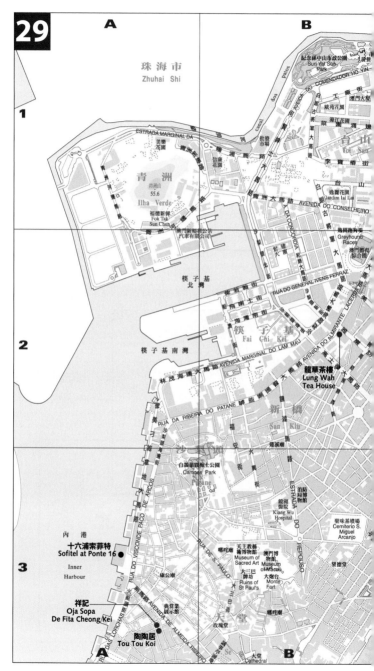

A   B

珠海市
Zhuhai Shi

紀念孫中山市政公園
Sun Yat Sen
Park

AVENIDA DO COMENDADOR HO YIN

工
人
體
育
場

澳門大酒店

威尼花園

樂江花園

1

ESTRADA MARGINAL DA

青洲新馬路

美樂
花園

批發
市場

馬
路

河
道
馬
路

青
洲
河
道
馬
路

東方貨城

筷子基北灣馬路

青洲
青洲山
55.6
Ilha Verde

福德新邨
Fok Tak
Sun Chun

台
山

李寶椿街

逸麗花園
Jardim Iat Lai

AVENIDA DO CONSELHEIRO

古
廟
街

逸園跑狗場
Greyhound
Races

澳門跑狗
綜合館

DA CONCORDIA

澳門新福利公共
汽車有限公司

林茂塘

青洲大馬路

台
山
新
街

筷子基
北灣

RUA DO GENERAL IVENS FERRAZ

飛
南
第
馬
路

河
邊
新
街

飛
喇

2

筷子基南灣

筷子基
Fai Chi Kei

AVENIDA MARGINAL DO LAM MAU

筷
子
基
大
馬
路

沙
梨
頭
海
邊
街

AVENIDA DO ALMIRANTE LACERDA

龍華茶樓
Lung Wah
Tea House

林茂海邊大馬路

青
洲
街

藍
田
街

福
隆
新
街

RUA DA RIBEIRA DO PATANE

新
橋
San
Kiu

連勝馬路

美
副
將
大
馬
路

沙梨頭
Patane

白鴿巢賈梅士公園
Camoes Park

ESTRADA DO

鏡湖醫院
Kiang Wu
Hospital

消防博物館
Museum of
Macau

聖味基墳場
Cemiterio S.
Miguel
Arcanjo

望德堂

REPOUSO

內 港
十六浦索菲特
Sofitel at Ponte 16

Inner
Harbour

RUA DO VISCONDE PACO DE ARCOS

天主教藝術博物館
Museum of
Sacred Art

澳門博物館
Museum
of Macau

大三巴
牌坊
Ruins of
St Paul's

大炮台
Monte
Fort

3

祥記
Oja Sopa
De Fita Cheong Kei

RUA DE S. PAULO

RUA DAS LORCHAS新馬路 AVENIDA DE ALMEIDA RIBEIRO

陶陶居
Tou Tou Koi

天堂

大堂
Cathedral

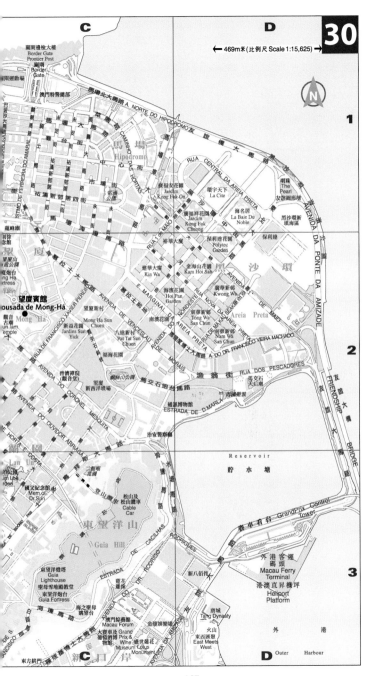

關閘通檢大樓
Border Gate
Frontier Post

關閘
Border
Gate

澳門特警總部

愚場北大馬路 A. NORTE DO HIPODROMO 友誼橋

馬場
Hipodromo

心
街

RUA CENTRAL DA AREIA PRETA

明珠
The
Pearl 友誼圓形地

廣福女花園
Jardim
Kong Fok On

環宇天下
La Cité

海名居
La Baie Du
Noble

黑沙環新
填海區

黑
沙
環

廣福祥花園
Jardim
Kong Fok
Cheong

保利達花園
Polytec
Garden

保利達

AVENIDA DA PONTE DA AMIZADE

裕華大廈
Yu Wa

金海山花園
Kam Hoi Sah

建華大廈
Kin Wa

海濱花園
Hoi Pan
Garden

RUA NOVA DA AREIA PRETA

廣華新邨
Kwong Wa

黑
沙
環

AVENIDA DA AMIZADE

望度賓館
ousada de Mong-Há

Mong
Há

AVENIDA DE FRANCISCO XAVIER PEREIRA

望廈新村
Mong Ha Sun
Chuen

新益花園
Jardins Sun
Yick

八達新邨
Pat Tat Sun
Chuen

福海花園

AVENIDA DE VENCESLAU

南澳大馬路 4 DE MORAIS

AVENIDA DA AREIA PRETA

廣華新邨
Tong Wa
San Chun

南華新邨
Nam Wa
San Chun

東華新邨
San Chun

RUA DO DR. FRANCISCO VIEIRA MACHADO

RUA DOS PESCADORES

渔翁街

媽祖石
天后廟

友
誼
大
橋

FRIENDSHIP BRIDGE

RUA DE FERREIRA DO AMARAL

ISTMO DE FERREIRA DO AMARAL

慕
古
廟

望廈山
望廈公園
炮台
ng Ha
Fortress

RUA DE FRANCISCO XAVIER PEREIRA

望廈山公園

螺絲山公園

馬交石炮台馬路

國父紀念館

自
念館

AVENIDA DO CORONEL MESQUITA

望廈墳場
新西洋墳場

三龍廟
花園

國際博物館
ESTRADA DE D.MARIA II

海揚艇

治安警察廳

AVENIDA DO OUVIDOR ARRIAGA

Reservoir
貯 水 塘

AVENIDA DE S. ANDR E F. COSTA

新
園
Lan
rden

三龍廟
花園

登山馬路

松山及
松山纜車
Cable
Car

東望洋山
Guia Hill

ESTRADA DE CACILHAS

ESTRADA DO DR. RODRIGUES

RODRIGUES

賽車看台 GrandPrix Control
Tower

外港客運
碼頭
Macau Ferry
Terminal

港澳直昇機坪
Heliport
Platform

東望洋燈塔
Guia
Lighthouse

望洋聖母小教堂

東望洋炮台
Guia Fortress

ESTRADA

葡花
連海

海之聖母
瞭望台

新八佰伴

唐城
Tang Dynasty

海環馬路

澳門綜藝館
Macau Forum

金龍娛樂場

火山
東西匯館
East Meets
West

外   港

AVENIDA DA AMIZADE

AVENIDA DE S.
ANDIOGO DA SILVA

東方拱門

大賽車及
葡萄酒博
物館
Macau Grand
Prix & Wine
Museum

蓮世蓮花
Lotus
Monument

金蓮娛樂場

2

3

D Outer   Harbour

新口岸

C

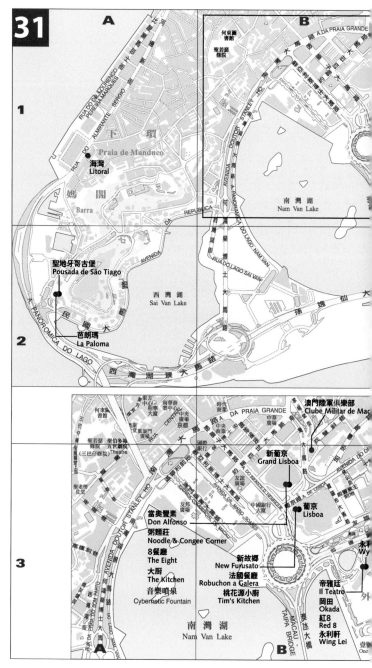

A·DA PRAIA GRANDE

A

B

何東圖書館
聖若瑟修院

1

Praia de Manduco

海灣
Litoral

媽閣
Barra

南灣湖
Nam Van Lake

聖地牙哥古堡
Pousada de São Tiago

芭朗瑪
La Paloma

2

西灣湖
Sai Van Lake

A·PANORÂMICA DO LAGO

何東圖書館

東方
拍賣行
中央
商場
南華廣場
中央廣場

時代
商場

DA PRAIA GRANDE

中華
廣場

澳門陸軍俱樂部
Clube Militar de Macau

聖若瑟
修院
聖伯多祿
五個銅鐘
(三巴仔修院)
Theatre

新葡京
Grand Lisboa

聖老楞
佐堂

3

當奧豐素
Don Alfonso

粥麵莊
Noodle & Congee Corner

8餐廳
The Eight

大廚
The Kitchen

音樂噴泉
Cybernetic Fountain

中國銀行
大廈

新故鄉
New Furusato

法國餐廳
Robuchon a Galera

桃花源小廚
Tim's Kitchen

葡京
Lisboa

永和
Wy

帝雅廷
Il Teatro

岡田
Okada

紅8
Red 8

永利軒
Wing Lei

南灣湖
Nam Van Lake

MACAU
TAIPA
BRIDGE

澳氹大橋

壹號

A

B

468

新口岸
Outer Harbour
Reclamation Area

外港
Outer Harbour

鑑賞嘉諾
Legend
Wharf

遠阿密館

文化中心
廣場

萊斯
Rocks

1

美高梅金殿
MGM Grand

壹號湖畔
One Central

參考下面
See below

寶雅座
Aux Beaux Arts

金殿堂
Imperial Court

盛事
Rossio

食·八方
Square Eight

2

←469m米(比例尺 Scale 1:15,625) →

中學

新 口 岸
Outer Harbour
Reclamation Area

金麗華
Grand Lapa

南方
大廈

漁人碼頭
Fisherman's
Wharf

灘
Naam

東怡軒
Tung Yee Heen

金沙
Sands

星際
StarWorld

澳門
回歸賀禮
陳列館
Macao
Handover
Pavilion

文化中心
廣場

稻菊
Inagiku

蘇浙匯
de Garden

丹桂軒
Laurel

澳門文化中心
Macao Cultural Centre

澳門藝術博物館
Museum of Art

港 新 填 海 區
N A P E

觀音像
Statue of
Kun Iam

3

←356m米(比例尺 Scale 1:11,856) →

D

← 627米(比例尺 Scale 1:20,909) →

A　　　　　　　　　B

澳氹大橋
Macau-Taipa Bridge

奧羅拉
Aurora

天政
Tenmasa

帝影樓
Ying

觀音岩　澳門大
University of

西灣大橋
Sai Van Bridge

史伯泰海軍馬路

海洋花園大馬路

花園大馬路

氹仔舊大橋

七潭公馬路
Est dos Sete Tanques

新濠鋒
Altira

將軍馬路

氹仔雕塑
Taipa
Monument
110.8

小潭山

菩提禪院
Pou Tai Un
Monastery

海洋花園
Nordeste de Tgo

Estrada

玫瑰山莊

氹仔炮台

廣　　　　若

Est Lou de Lim Lok

Avenida de Kwong Tung

百姓
Banza

柯維納馬路
Est Governador Albano Oliveira

四面佛
Four-Faces
Buddha

澳門賽馬會
Macau Jockey Club

賽馬場
Macau Jockey Club

Av do Estadio

澳門
運動場
Stadium &
Aquatic Centre

奧林匹克
游泳館
Stadium &
Aquatic Centre

葡國美食天地
A Petisqueira

安東尼奧
Antonio

Avenida dos Jogos da Asia Oriental

Taipa
Bridge

孫逸仙博士大馬路

埃斯珀蘭薩大馬路
Estrada da Baia de

西堤馬路
A MARGINAL FLOR DE LOTUS

珠 海 市
ZHU HAI CITY

Avenida de Cotai

路

人工濕地

通往珠海市，橫琴
To Zhu Hai City

蓮花大橋
Lotus Bridge

蓮

路邊橫
Borde

ESTRADA FLOR DE

A　　　　　　　　　B

友誼大橋
Friendship Bridge

北安大馬路
永富街
永寧街
Avenida Son On 信安馬路
Estrada de Pac On
東京街
東成街
東陸街
嘉樂街

澳門氹仔臨時客運碼頭
（北安碼頭）
Taipa Temporary Ferry Terminal

Estrada da Ponta da Cabrita

氹仔
Taipa

159.2
大潭山

天文台科館

偉龍馬路
Avenida Wai Long

客運大樓
Terminal Building

澳門國際機場
Macau International Airport

式館
pa
Museum

Avenida D. São

大潭山壹號

澳門
科技大學
Macau University of
Science &
Technology

Senhora da Esperança

路氹連貫公路
（金光大道）

喜粵
Canton
利苑酒家
Lei Garden
Morton's of Chicago

尼斯人
enetian

四季
Four Seasons
鳴詩
Belcanção
紫逸軒
Yat Heen

氹
城

十二生肖雕像

ESTRADA DO ISTMO

星麗門
Cotai

ng
US

澳門東亞運動會
體育館(澳門蛋)
Macau East
Asian
Games
Dome

蓮花路

Avenida de Cotai

路 氹 城 B

A

莲花海濱大馬路
西堤大馬路

人工濕地

路氹連貫公路

(金光大道)

星麗門
Cotai

澳門東亞運
體育館(澳門
Macau
Asia
Game
Dom

通花大橋
Lotus Bridge

蓮花大橋

ESTRADA FLOR DE LOTUS

花

路氹城
邊檢大樓
Border Crossing

海濱圓形地

A MARGINAL FLOR DE LOTUS

蓮花路

東方高爾夫毬場
Oriental Golf Club

ESTRADA DO ISTMO

蓮

石排灣
水塘
Reservoir

路環小型
賽車場
Coloane
Go-Carting Track

和諧圓形地

石排灣馬路

九澳高頂馬路 Estrada d

1

Rua das Contoreiras

Rua do Pagode

梅樹街
榕樹街
紅森樹街
石排灣街

金柯路
菩柯路
柏柯路
紫荊街

鳳鳥村

聯生工業村

路

138.1

路 環

Coloane

2

Rua da Concordia

Rua da da 濱海路

Estrada de Seac Pai Va

生海濱路

合歡街

荔枝灣
Lai Chi Van

石排灣
郊野公園

土地暨自然
博物館
Museum of Nature &
Agriculture

文化村
牌坊

高頂路

媽祖雕像
Statue of the
Goddess A-Ma
178.5

媽祖文化村
A-Ma Culture Village

Wa
Mac
BB

Estrada de Coloane

3

Estrada de Lai Chi Vun

古砲馬路

澳門監獄

竹

Estrada

de Cha

黑沙村

黑沙
公園

賈梅士馬路

海蘭花園

初

聖方濟
各教堂
S. Francisco
Xavier Chapel

天后古廟
Tin Hau Temple

疊石塘山
171

竹灣
燒烤公園
BBQ Park

黑沙海灘馬路

宇宙葡星
通訊公司
公

譚公廟
Tam Kung
Temple

路環墳場
Coloane Cemeteries

122.2

竹灣泳池
Cheoc Van
Swimming Pool

Estrada de Cheoc

竹灣馬路
竹灣豪園

漁村馬路

Estrada de Aledia

竹灣海灘
Cheoc Van Bay

B

A

1

九澳發電廠
Power Station

三聖廟
Sam Seng
Temple

九澳提壩
九澳水庫
郊野公園

九澳深水碼頭

九澳水庫
Ka-Ho Dam

九澳村

九澳
聖約瑟學校

水泥廠

ho de Ka-Ho

聖路濟亞
中心

九澳
老人院

九澳
燈塔

淡水站路

九澳坊眾

七苦
聖母小堂

大擔角

九澳高頂
燒烤公園

112.6
九澳山

Park

蝙蝠洞

鷹鷹洞

2

澳門哥爾夫球
鄉村俱樂部
Macau Golf and
Country Club

觀海軒
Kwun Hoi Heen

Beach

威斯汀度假酒店
The Westin Resort

沙海灣
ae Sa Bay

海酒路
島

N

3

PICTURE COPYRIGHT
圖片版權

Michelin, 22, 23, 24 - Agnès b. Le Pain Grillé (Central), 58 - Amber, 59 - Angelini, 60 - Aspasia, 61 - Michelin, 62 - BLT Steak, 63 - Michelin, 64 - Café Siam, 65 - Caprice, 66 - Michelin, 67 - Celestial Court, 68 - Cépage, 69 - Michelin, 70, 71 - Chesa, 72 - Michelin, 73 - Chez Patrick (Soho), 74 - Chez Patrick (Wanchai), 75 - Michelin, 76 - Chiu Chow Garden (Tsuen Wan), 77 - Michelin, 78 - Cinecittà, 79 - Crystal Jade La Mian Xiao Long Bao, 80 - Michelin, 81, 82 - Cucina, 83 - Cuisine Cuisine, 84 - Michelin, 85, 86 - Din Tai Fung, 87 - DiVino, 88 - Domani, 89 - Dong Lai Shun, 90 - Michelin, 91 - Dynasty, 93 - Michelin, 94, 95, 96, 97, 98, 99, 100, 101 - Gaddi's, 102 - Gaia, 103 - Michelin, 104, 105 - The Golden Leaf, 106 - Golden Valley, 107 - Michelin, 108 - Grissini, 109 - Gusto, 110 - Hakka Yé Yé, 111 - Michelin, 112 - Harbour Grill, 113 - Michelin, 114 - Harvey Nichols, 115 - Michelin, 116, 117 - Hoi Yat Heen, 118 - H One, 119 - Michelin, 120 - Hunan Garden (Causeway Bay), 121 - Hunan Garden (Central), 122 - Michelin, 123 - Hutong, 124 - Michelin, 125 - Inagiku (Kowloon), 126 - Island Tang, 127 - Isola, 128 - Maxims/Michelin, 129 - Jade Garden (Causeway Bay), 130 - Joia, 131 - Michelin, 132, 133, 134 - La Brasserie, 135 - L'Atelier de Joël Robuchon, 136 - Michelin, 137 - Lawry's The Prime Rib, 138 - Lei Garden (Elements), 139 - Lei Garden (IFC), 140 - Lei Garden (Kowloon Bay), 141 - Lei Garden (Kwun Tong), 142 - Lei Garden (Mong Kok), 143 - Lei Garden (North Point), 144 - Lei Garden (Sha Tin), 145 - Lei Garden (Tsim Sha Tsui), 146 - Lei Garden (Wanchai), 147 - Le Soleil, 148 - Michelin, 149, 150, 151, 152, 153 - Lobster Bar and Grill, 154 - Luk Yu Tea House, 155 - Michelin, 156 - Lung King Heen, 157 - Michelin, 158, 159 - Mandarin Grill + Bar, 160 - Man Wah, 162 - Ming Court, 163 - Michelin, 164, 165, 166 - Naozen, 167 - Nicholini's, 168 - Nobu, 169 - Olala (St. Francis Street), 170 - 1/5 Nuevo, 171 - One Harbour Road, 172 - Michelin, 173 - Oriental Lily, 174 - Ovologue, 175 - Oyster & Wine Bar, 176 - Paul's Kitchen, 177 - Peking Garden (Admiralty), 178 - Peking Garden (Central), 179 - Peking Garden (Kowloon), 180 - Peking Garden (Tai Koo Shing), 181 - Petrus, 182 - Pierre, 183 - Michelin, 184 - Queen's Palace, 185 - Regal Palace, 186 - Michelin, 187 - Roka, 188 - Sabatini, 189 - Michelin, 190 - Senzuru, 191 - Michelin, 192, 193 - Shanghai Garden, 194 - Michelin, 195 - Shanghai Xiao Nan Guo, 196, 197 - Shang Palace, 198 - Sha Tin 18, 199 - Shui Hu Ju, 200 - Michelin, 201, 202 - Spasso, 203 - Spoon by Alain Ducasse, 204 - Michelin, 205 - Spring Moon, 206 - Summer Palace, 207 - Michelin, 208, 209, 210, 211,

212 - Michelin, 213, 214 - Tak Lung, 215 - Michelin, 216, 217 - T'ang Court, 218 - Michelin, 219, 220, 221, 222 - Thai Basil, 223 - The Drawing Room, 224 - The Lounge, 225 - The Pawn, 226 - The Press Room, 227 - The Royal Garden, 228 - Michelin, 229 - The Steak House, 230 - Michelin, 231 - Tim's Kitchen, 232 - Tokoro, 233 - Michelin, 234, 235 - Tuscany by H, 236 - Union J, 237 - Unkai, 238 - Uno Más, 239 - Va Bene, 240 - Wagyu Kaiseki Den, 241 - Wasabisabi, 242 - Watermark, 243 - Michelin, 244 - Wu Kong Shanghai, 245 - Michelin, 246, 247 - Xi Yan Sweets, 248 - Yan Toh Heen, 249 - Yat Tung Heen, 250, 251 - Michelin, 252 - Yè Shanghai, 253, 254 - Michelin, 255, 256 - Yun Fu, 257 - Yung Kee, 258 - Michelin, 259, 260 , 261 - Zuma, 262 - Michelin, 264 - Conrad, 268, 269 - Cosmo , 270, 271 - Cosmopolitan, 272, 273 - Eaton, 274, 275 - Empire (Tin Hau), 276, 277 - Four Seasons, 278, 279 - Grand Hyatt, 280, 281 - Harbour Plaza Kowloon, 282, 283 - Harbour Plaza Metropolis, 284, 285 - Harbour Plaza North Point, 286, 287 - Hyatt Regency Sha Tin, 288, 289 - Intercontinental , 290, 291 - Intercontinental Grand Stanford, 292, 293 - Island Shangri-La, 294, 295 - JIA, 296, 297 - JW Marriott, 298, 299 - Kowloon Shangri-La, 300, 301 - Langham Place, 302, 303 - Lan Kwai Fong, 304, 305 - Lanson Place, 306, 307 - Le Méridien Cyberport, 308, 309 - LKF, 310, 311 - Mandarin Oriental/Michelin, 312, 313 - Marco Polo, 314, 315 - Metropark (Causeway Bay), 316, 317 - Nikko, 318, 319 - Novotel Century, 320, 321 - Panorama, 322, 323 - Renaissance Kowloon, 324, 325 - Royal Plaza, 326, 327 - Sheraton, 328, 329 - The Emperor, 330, 331 - The Landmark Mandarin Oriental, 332, 333 - The Langham, 334, 335 - The Luxe Manor, 336, 337 - The Park Lane, 338, 339 - The Peninsula, 340, 341 - The Royal Garden, 342, 343 - The Royal Pacific, 344, 345 - W, 346, 347 - Michelin, 348, 349, 350, 362, 363 - Aurora, 364 - MGM, 365 - Michelin, 366 - Four Seasons, 367 - Venetian, 368 - Michelin, 369 - Don Alfonso/Michelin, 370 - Wynn, 371 - Imperial Court/Michelin, 372 - Michelin, 373 - Starworld, 374 - Kwun Hoi Heen, 375 - La Paloma, 376 - Starworld, 377 - Michelin, 378 - Litoral, 379 - Michelin, 380 - Morton's of Chicago, 381 - Naam/Michelin, 382 - New Furusato/Michelin, 383 - Grand Lisboa, 384 - Michelin, 385 - Okada, 386 - Wynn, 387 - Robuchon a Galera, 388 - MGM, 389 - MGM, 390 - Tenmasa, 391 - The Eight, 392 - The Kitchen, 393 - Tim's Kitchen, 394 - Michelin, 395 - Tung Yee Heen/Michelin, 396 - Wing Lei, 397 - Ying, 398 - Four Seasons, 399 - Michelin, 400 - Altira, 404, 405 - Four Seasons, 406, 407 - Mandarin Oriental, 408, 409 - Michelin, 410, 411 - Lisboa/Michelin, 412, 413 - MGM Grand, 414, 415 - Pousada de Mong-Há, 416, 417 - Pousada de São Tiago/Michelin, 418 ,419 - Michelin, 420, 420 - Sands, 422, 423 - Sofitel at Ponte 16, 424, 425 - StarWorld/Michelin, 426, 427 - The Venetian, 428, 429 - The Westin Resort, 430, 431 - Michelin, 432, 433, 434, 435, 436

NOTES
備註

NOTES
備註

. . . .

. . . .

. . . .

. . . .

. . . .

. . . .

. . . .

. . . .

. . . .

. . . .

. . . .

. . . .

. . . .

. . . .

. . . .

. . . .

. . . .

. . . .

. . . .

. . . .

. . . .

. . . .

. . . .

. . . .

. . . .

. . . .

. . . .

. . . .

A better way forward

Manufacture française des pneumatiques Michelin
Société en commandite par actions au capital de 304 000 000 EUR
Place des Carmes-Déchaux – 63000 Clermont-Ferrand (France)
R.C.S. Clermont-Fd B 855 200 507

© Michelin et Cie, Propriétaires-éditeurs
Dépot légal Novembre 2009

Made in Japan

Published in 2009

Although the information in this guide was believed by the authors
and publisher to be accurate and current at the time of publication,
they cannot accept responsibility for any inconvenience, loss, or
injury sustained by any person relying on information or advice
contained in this guide. Things change over time and travellers
should take steps to verify and confirm information, especially time
sensitive information related to prices, hours of operation, and
availability.

Maps : (C) 2009 Cartographic data Universal Publications,
Ltd / Michelin
Design : Akita Design Kan Inc. Tokyo, Japan

E-mail : michelinguide.hongkong-macau@cn.michelin.com

Pre-Press: Nord Compo, Villeneuve-d'Ascq, (France)
Printing and Binding: Toppan, Tokyo (Japan)